NERD III
NEW EXPERIMENTAL RESEARCH
IN DESIGN

Board of International Research in Design
BIRD

Members:
Tom Bieling
Uta Brandes
Michelle Christensen
Sandra Groll
Wolfgang Jonas
Ralf Michel
Marc Pfaff

Advisory Board:
Alireza Ajdari
Lena Berglin
Elena Caratti
Dora El Aidi
Orit Halpern
Denisa Kera
Michael Wolf

Tom Bieling
Michelle Christensen
Florian Conradi
(Eds.)

# NERD III
# New Experimental Research in Design

*Positions and Perspectives*

Birkhäuser
Basel

# TABLE OF CONTENTS

Preface . . . . . . . . . . . . . . . . . . . . . . . . . . . . . . . . . . . . . . . 7
    Wolfgang Jonas

Introduction: Un/Designing, Per/Forming, Re/Becoming . . . . 9
    Michelle Christensen and Florian Conradi

Bioreceptive Textiles: An Experimental Inquiry
into the Bio-colonisation of Architectural Façades. . . . . . . . . 21
    Svenja Keune, Ariel Cheng Sin Lim, Delia Dumitrescu
    and Mette Ramsgaard Thomsen

First-Person Perspective as a Form of
Inquiry in Biodesign . . . . . . . . . . . . . . . . . . . . . . . . . . . . . . 47
    Barbara Pollini

Vitality of Salt: A Methodology for Exploring
Vibrant Materiality. . . . . . . . . . . . . . . . . . . . . . . . . . . . . . . 75
    Julia Ziener

Does the Tree Say No?
On Design, Consent, and Uncertainty . . . . . . . . . . . . . . . . 103
    Franca López Barbera

The Body I Live in is Melting:
Becoming in Times of Catastrophic Convergence . . . . . . . . 127
    Athena Grandis

Doing Participation in the Midst of
Algorithm Troubles. . . . . . . . . . . . . . . . . . . . . . . . . . . . . . 151
    Axel Meunier

Tunnel Visions: Exploring the
Emerging Intersections of Intimacy and AI . . . . . . . . . . . . 177
    Florian Porada

Design and Difference in a World of
Contradictory Instructions . . . . . . . . . . . . . . . . . . . . . . . . 203
     Dulmini Perera

Turning Up the Design Research Dial:
Commentary on Permission to Muck About . . . . . . . . . . . . . 223
   Joseph Lindley and David Philip Green

Re-placing the Earth. . . . . . . . . . . . . . . . . . . . . . . . . . . . 245
     Jozef Eduard Masarik

Incomprehensibility:
World-Chaos and Chaos-World. . . . . . . . . . . . . . . . . . . . . 271
     Torben Körschkes


Authors . . . . . . . . . . . . . . . . . . . . . . . . . . . . . . . . . . . . 300

# PREFACE

The Dadaist and Surrealist visual artist *Man Ray* (1890–1976) stated in 1948:

> *There is no progress in art, any more than there is progress in making love. There are simply different ways of doing it.*

Art and design should by no means be equated, but there are parallels with regard to the question of their respective foundations.

Skepticism and doubts about the epistemological validity of current design research are growing. Its alleged development into a science is at an *impasse* (Beckett 2021). An empirical analysis of 20 years of design debate concludes that consensus regarding basic concepts is not foreseeable (Blackler et al. 2021). The weird suggestion of the study's authors for a way out is that distinguished experts should end the fruitless discussion and set some "rigorous" theories and definitions. What nonsense. How can a field that claims to be scientific seriously come up with the idea of establishing its missing foundations through dogmatic setting?

The classic *Münchhausen Trilemma* (Albert 1968) shows up, depicting the inevitable choice between circular reasoning, infinite regress, or dogmatic setting. That of all things the third option is suggested as a remedy appears as simple self-deception, only consolidating the presumptuous design research bubble which claims to serve the good of mankind in a unique way. This confirms my long-held view that there are *no foundations* and *no progress*, but rather growing archives of theoretical perspectives, emerging from the ongoing co-evolution of design and its changing socio-cultural contexts. Substantial and sustainable answers to urgent social issues are missing.

The basic paradox seems to lie in the fact that design research is the object of its own study, i.e. that design discourse is an artefact in itself (Redström 2017). Design research models are designs, disguised as theories. We should be more modest; be happy with small, transient contributions to the ongoing process of *muddling through*. This would be a big relief for the community with its heavy, self-imposed moral burdens of saving the world (Jonas 2021).

One may conclude that irreducible complexity (the problem of control) and evolutionary uncertainty (the problem of prediction) can be handled neither scientifically nor in terms of design, but only by a new form of *research through design through research* (Jonas 2007), which can be characterized as the development towards a fuzzy and fragile "trans-domain of knowing" (Jonas 2024), where design and science collaborate and at times even converge.

The texts in this volume, based on the *NERD_for* (Hamburg 2021) and *NERD Take Five* (Berlin 2023) conferences – number 30 in the BIRD series – are intended to illustrate and incite this unique perspective. ↗

Wolfgang Jonas, May 2024

# Introduction:

Michelle Christensen and Florian Conradi

## Un/Designing, Per/Forming, Re/Becoming

Design cannot be detached from the values and assumptions on which it is assembled; the paradigm and culture that it emerges out of and is situated into. It is intervening as both a professional field and as a research practice – both produced and actively producing. Finding methods and approaches to situate oneself and one's research practice has become one of the most present debates in the field – experimenting with developing an epistemological and ontological starting point to incite design into a world that operates from a place of consideration and care – whether this be care for the environment, for the culture that it generates, or for the knowledge that it incites. The questions that are raised in the field are both ancient and speculative, critical and reassuring, wicked and applicable, condensed into the thick and sticky present – and thus, best case, "staying with the trouble" (Haraway 2016). Hidden in the mundanity of the everyday and relating to all the fields of disciplinary and tacit knowledge surrounding it, it calls for approaches that makes it present through curiosity and consideration. Based in a still rather recent history of experimentation and a postdisciplinary context – this makes it both an opportunity and a challenge to perform.

    In times of global polycrisis – from climate crisis and injustice, armed conflict and displacement, rapid-capitalism and neo-colonialism on new ubiquitous scales, and extensive political polarisation just to name a few, an international society of students and young researchers grapple with having an impact on a melting world, whilst finding a way to engage into futures without giving in to the power structures that these futures are so entangled in. In this context, experimental research in design means engaging in nonlinearity, blurred boundaries, continuous becoming, flaws and glitches – making space for other forms of knowledge and representation. Oftentimes, it is exactly the design project itself that will reveal its own findings – not as generalisable, scalable and transferable answers, as universal truths; rather, the experiment itself serves to reveal its own concealed contribution as it contributes. This is not to say that one does not need to meticulously formulate the experiment, form a methodology and a commensurable theoretical framework. It is rather the argument that when it comes to experimental research in design, the experiment will often reveal more than we could have anticipated, if we listen to it. Or, as French philosopher Maurice Merleau-Ponty has put it, "sometimes my own words take me by surprise and teach me what to think" (Merleau-Ponty in Derrida 1978: 11). Thus, each project is a contribution; it allows us to understand the epistemic quality of experimental practice-based design research, as well as its limitations. And when we tie the strings together between projects – then we can weave context, entangle crises, go deeper, and allow the hopefully greater contribution of our work to emerge.

The contributions in this book are exactly that – examples of specific projects, often entirely different from each other, which independently but especially in their collectivity contribute to both experiment, relevance and rigour. The authors in the following chapters in this book unravel underlying power structures in relation to nature, space, technology and methodology – composing theoretical and methodological experiments to unravel, decompose and reimagine other histories, presents and possible futures. With sensitivity, humility and braveness, they propose ways to begin to take responsibility for a broken paradigm manifested in perceptions, realities, codes and materialities. Between theory and practice, observation and insinuation, speculation and designed artifact – critiques, questions and proposals connect stories and discussions within and between the texts.

The first three articles delve deeply into the experiment of autoethnographic engagements within hybrid cospecies assemblages, engaging into the experiment of self-confrontation and taking responsibility at both a personal and planetary scale. In *Bioreceptive Textiles: An Experimental Inquiry into the Bio-colonisation of Architectural Façades*, Svenja Keune, Ariel Cheng Sin Lim, Delia Dumitrescu and Mette Ramsgaard Thomsen explore a sustainable material culture that mediates between humans, landscapes, and more-than-human cohabitants. Positioning their work within the current occupation of the deign field with designing for living organisms, they explore the design of façades that actively participate in their ecological context with a focus on what textile and soft multi-materiality can offer for otherwise rigid mono-material expressions in bioreceptive architecture. Through their experiments with biodegradable materials paired with textile and 3D-printed ceramics in interaction with environmental factors such as sun radiation, rain, frost, snow, wind, flora and fauna, they speculate about textile-based biohabitats, gathering information about the relationships and interactions that form with local ecosystems over time. Merging material craftsmanship and an auto-ethnographic observation, the authors challenge the Western tradition of an architectural design practice founded on ideas of permanence and stasis, to rather include concepts of decay, gentleness, and observing with humbleness – thereby cultivating an aesthetics of care, curiosity, and empathy.

In the following article, *First-Person Perspective as a Form of Inquiry in Biodesign,* Barbara Pollini continues to explore Biodesign as an approach entangling design and science, and the concept of using living organisms in the design process to create materials, structures, and artefacts. With a focus on the complex, relational and interactive practice-based form of Biodesign that she frames as "biotinkering", she engages autoethnographically into the considerations that come with considering living agents as they co-author the design process. She biotinkers with kombucha, silk, bioreceptive materials for lichens' and mosses' survival and spontaneous colonisation over time, and biofabricated edible electronics. Following her immersion into co-species co-design, Pollini reflects upon the unique knowledge generation on which this practice-based project relies, allowing for an intuitive approach to practice that can be advantageous for emerging and testing novel concepts in scientific domains and in biodesign.

In *Vitality of Salt: A Methodology for Exploring Vibrant Materiality,* Julia Ziener emerges into the practice of salt extraction as a performative act. Based on the handling of salt waste, she illustrates the dichotomy between "dull matter" and "vibrant life", employing a framework of New Materialism to challenge traditional understandings of matter as passive and unpolitical. As an experiment into materialising new materialism, her work provides practical approaches to abstract theoretical ontologies, as salt is actively involved in the design and production process of the ancient evaporation vessel of the briquetage (3100–2560 BC). As archaeological excavation meets 3D scanning and printing, time is stretched, and artifacts re-situated in performative and political (re)use. The briquetage becomes the object of research, extracting salt in ecologically threatened rivers, providing a research tool for exploring the vitality of salt as a phenomenon and insights into salt as an actor in cultural practice and environmental crisis. The object is no longer only stored in the inaccessible archaeological archive but is made globally available as an open-source object, not only embodying the connection between historical and contemporary technology, but also reflecting the concept of materiality for future technologies and future existential crises.

In line with the argument of vibrant matter, Franca López Barbera ventures with great sincerity and poetry into the conversation *Does the Tree Say No? On Design, Consent, and Uncertainty*. In this piece, the Quebracho Colorado tree – which is in danger of extinction at the level of materiality, agency, and voice, becomes our companion in the discussion of the gendered and colonial underpinnings of the prevailing modern conceptualisations of both nature and consent that underscore design's role in reproducing extractive approaches to nature. The concept of "more-than-human consent" is introduced as a framework for design capable of attending to the relational, plural, and uncertain dimensions and expressions of all life, emphasising the need to explore non-modern principles of relation, acknowledging onto-epistemologies that offer alternative frameworks for engaging with nature to the modern one that is destructive and violent. In order to answer the question posed in the title – or more decisively, to not answer it, the author argues for a more-than-human approach to consent that seeks to think outside modern grammar: that refuses to separate human agency from nature's agency, that thinks of consent as a transaction, that refuses to answer the questions altogether, but reformulates them into a grammar that stays with the onto-epistemological uncertainties and is nurtured by them.

Athena Grandis continues to stay with the trouble of the more-than-human and the deconstruction of dualisms in the text *The Body I live in is Melting: Becoming in times of catastrophic convergence*, where we turn our feminist gaze toward critical posthuman ecology, melting the boundaries of human, machine, and material. Taking her own body and a second skin in the form of experimental prosthetics as a core of the project, she explores the catastrophic convergence of crises as she interrogates power and environmental collapse. Materializing critical posthuman theory through hands-on experimentation, the author embraces open-source knowledge and prototyping techniques for assembling the prosthetics and a tattoo gun. Embodying the intricate ambiguity of human existence, power dynamics, and the search for self-determination through the performative act of body marking, the melting body installation embodies principles of relationality, embeddedness, embodiment, and accountability, emphasizing introspection and interconnectedness over mere technological augmentation. By embracing a state of ambiguity, of being an agent in the very system it is subjected to, it attempts to act as a tangible manifestation of a critical theory, bridging the gap between theory and practice in navigating the complexities of the posthuman condition in times of crises.

Remaining within the critical human-machine entanglement, the following two texts adopt a critical yet playful lens. In *Doing Participation in the Midst of Algorithm Troubles*, Axel Meunier explores glitches, failing and the unexpected – proposing establishing troubles as triggers for participation. Contextualized within the way in which AI systems based on Machine Learning models reproduce and amplify bias and discrimination against minorities and vulnerable communities, he draws attention to the potential of a more diverse decision-making process in the design of AI sociotechnical assemblages and a participatory turn in AI. Utilizing the moments of friction in the otherwise seamless interaction with systems, the author argues in favour of instability and the production of sociotechnical troubles as opposed to the persistence of technical error. From this perspective, doing participation in the midst of troubles refocuses attention on the present rather than on an imagined future where technical errors would be fixed and optimisation objectives safe. He suggests indexing participation in AI on the flow of stirred-up impurities that AI streams carry, making experimental collectives through upstream and downstream inquiry.

Florian Porada continues to unravel the threads of algorithmic trouble in the text *Tunnel Visions: Exploring the Emerging Intersections of Intimacy and AI*. As digital companions designed for forming emotional bonds are raising significant concerns about their potential to disrupt social dynamics, infringe on privacy, and create emotional dependencies, the author argues for the necessity of a critical examination of their deep-seated impacts. He emphasizes understanding how intimate conversational interactions with AI affects perception and handling of emotional and private information. A series of prototypes explore alternative relationships between AI and digital intimacy, entering into a dynamic process of transitioning from one to the next iteration, allowing fragments and findings to be taken into the subsequent prototypes. Playfully finding, discarding and combining miscellaneous parts, the subfields of AI, intimacy, and their medialization into AI companions are explored in the context of intimate communication, allowing participants to experience an intimate dialog with an AI companion.

Continuing in the context of locating approaches to opposing ethical precariousness, Dulmini Perera advocates the necessity to question whether methods of framing how difference operates within design processes that are marked by epistemic limitations of modernity and coloniality are capacious enough to escape from the problematic of framing change.

In the text *Design and Difference in a World of Contradictory Instructions,* the author argues how the concept of the double bind is particularly useful to reflect on forms of contradictions that arise in attempts to work with change. She reframes the double bind through Gayathri Spivak's politicised and refractive reading, connecting the concept to Antonio Gramsci and Jacques Derrida's concerns around difference, asymmetrical agency, and the question of transformative change. On this base, Perera argues "playful epistemological performance" as a necessity within design education, in order to overcome what is politically and ethically at stake. The double bind provides an approach to understanding the destructive relationships between design and economic, technological, social and environmental contexts, providing an approach to being better able to articulate asymmetries in the power relations in which designers are embedded, cultivating sensibilities to better understand such experiences.

In *Turning Up the Design Research Dial: Commentary on Permission to Muck About,* Joseph Lindley and David Philip Green remain in the meta discussion of design research and its challenges and potentials, introducing a project – and a film – as a base for debating what Design Research is, how it works, and why such an assemblage of attributes might be useful, alluring, and profound. Aspects discussed include how Design Research's uniquely flexible epistemological machinery, synthetic and future-oriented stances, and inherent interdisciplinarity lend it an unrivalled ability to engage with rapidly evolving and wickedly intractable challenges. How the world that it operates in is more complex, globalised, fast-paced, digital, unequal, and in need of vision and sense than it ever has been before – and how we need new ways to understand how to deal with its consequences. The film deals with metaphors, examples, diverse points of view and allegorical portrayals of what Design Research is and does, framing these elements in terms of practical challenges that hold back the Design Research movement, and discussing steps which might be taken to overcome them. In a final call to action, the authors propose that it is ultimately education that helps to fine-tune the dials in the imaginary control room to affect this change in the world.

Engaging further into the capacity of metaphor and allegory, Jozef Eduard Masarik enters into the duscussion of design's de-earthing of human and environment in the text *Re-placing the Earth*. Based on an astonishing historical, perhaps even design archaeological genealogy of the raising of the city of Chicago, the author demonstrates how the indigenous monster "earth" is systematically excluded, creating an emotional and physical detachment between the city and the earth. Raised sidewalks hover at various heights, fighting the terrors of the earth, floating in the air to form extra-terrestrial artificial landscapes that ignore the natural topographies as a step towards the otherworldly. The story displays how we inscribe our imaginaries into reality though built environments, and how the newly adjusted realities modify our imaginaries in an endless chain of reactions. And that, as this text shows, deeply forms the relations between the human and the Earth, as we now encircle the planet with layers of technocultural nets, posing an ever-greater threat to our own survival.

As a last contribution in the book, *Incomprehensibility: World-Chaos and Chaos-World*, Torben Körschkes remains with the entangled relations between the built and the abstracted. Un- and re-entangling on the one hand the diversification of the world, and on the other hand the dissolution of the concrete into a total abstraction, the author argues that both aspects can be seen as chaos in the sense that they both represent complexes that are no longer tangible for humans in terms of comprehension or predictability. Operating between philosopher Édouard Glissant's concept of chaos-world and the framing of the world-chaos, the notion of chaos is explored as something productive in re-conceiving our identities and our places in the world, a productivity that can assist in formulating approaches and challenges for the field of design. On this basis, the author raises questions regarding what the (spatial) requirements for doing so would be, how we might create coherence and preserve difference at the same time, and how one can think and design spaces that open up possibilities and at the same time are open to being transformed by these possibilities. He contemplates wobbly and restless spaces of searching, spaces that emphasise the complexity of the world and do not reduce it. However, it remains a question and a task of design, he argues, to make this tangible in a way that can be interpreted without breaking it down.

In times of *ontological crisis* therefore, where design is not merely political, but designers find themselves entangled in the midst of the muddy middle-ground of making and being made (Conradi & Christensen 2019), this book has been curated to display experiments into designing and undesigning, forming and performing, and not least becoming and rebecoming – as species, as cultures and as a field of research and practice.

REFERENCES

Christensen, M. and Conradi, F. (2020). *Politics of Things: A Critical Approach Through Design*. BIRD Series, Basel: Birkhäuser.

Derrida, J. (1969/1978). *Writing and Difference*. London/New York: Routledge.

Haraway, D. (2016). *Staying with the Trouble. Making Kin in the Chthulucene*. Durham, North Carolina: Duke University Press

# Bioreceptive Textiles:

Svenja Keune, Ariel Cheng Sin Lim, Delia Dumitrescu, Mette Ramsgaard Thomsen

## An Experimental Inquiry into the Bio-colonisation of Architectural Façades

Nowadays, a central question in the architectural field is the development of a sustainable material culture that integrates and mediates between humans, landscapes, and more-than-human cohabitants. Consequently, an increasing body of research work that introduces post-anthropocentric perspectives to our conventional ways of living becomes an emergent topic for the design development of sustainable built environments (Voyatzaki 2018; Franklin 2017; Heitlinger, Bryan-Kinns, and Comber 2018; Steele, Wiesel, and Maller 2019; Smith, Bardzell, and Bardzell 2017). In this context, the principle of cohabitation with nature, e.g. living organisms such as plants, animals, and microorganisms, opens new design opportunities for architectural design. In addition, the notion of regenerative design complements these approaches by introducing a systemic perspective toward architectural materiality to support, integrate, and regenerate the natural environment and its ecosystems. Grounded by the idea of resilience in ecosystems, regenerative design considers "nature as both model and context" (Lyle 1994; Pedersen Zari and Hecht 2019) and places the human being as an equal actor in the ecosystem among other natural elements (Alcamo et al. 2003, 26). Thus, these design principles suggest a regenerative and nature-inclusive approach toward the material culture in architecture that can expand from traditional construction methods with natural materials to cohabitation with nature. They echo earlier discourses of ecology – driven architects from the 1970s and 80s such as Hundertwasser. His visionary methods allowed landscapes and buildings to flow into one another and paid particular attention to a diversity of surface expressions, e.g. textures, colours, and materials (Restany 2022).

Similarly, current bio-digital architectural research (Beckett 2024; Cruz and Beckett 2016; Lewandowski et al. 2023; Pierre and Latour n.d.) is particularly concerned with the design and treatment of façades porosities as potential habitats for the living agents of local ecosystems. This emergent design field is being explored through the design of buildings and façades that actively participate in their ecological contexts, for instance by filtering water through the targeted inoculation of algae (Malik et al. 2020), bio-colonizing mosses and cryptograms (Cruz and Beckett 2016; Beckett 2018), or creating inclusive biomes for the coexistence of people, plants, and butterflies (Terreform ONE 2020 c).

These examples demonstrate that the principle of bio-receptivity in the context of architecture can be achieved by interlacing design, fabrication, and materiality and that it can lead to the creation of new ecological habitats within the built environment. Further examples ideate how larger organisms such as migrating birds (Super Galaxy: NYC Tropospheric Refuge by Jason Johnson and Nataly Gattegno in Gissen 2009), bees (Souza 2022) or bats (NEXT Architects 2015) can be addressed and integrated into the design as well.

The majority of the materials utilised for these bioreceptive architectural surfaces are concrete and ceramics, hard and permanent materials with conventional architectural qualities, behaviours and fabrication methods (Cruz and Beckett 2016). Soft materials and combinations of materials with varying degrees of temporality, porosity, and permeability have hitherto not been explored in the context of bioreceptive architecture.

This paper aims to discuss and exemplify what textile perspectives and soft multi materiality can offer for otherwise rigid mono-material expressions in bioreceptive architecture. Exploring the design possibilities of textile materiality, expressions, and interactions with local ecosystems through experimental research, this paper proposes material diversity and variety in expressions to support biodiversity. It therefore links diversity as a foundational principle in nature to the expressions and materiality of architectural façades.

As part of the research project "Designing and Living with Organisms" this paper presents a series of experimental and experiential design probes that instead of serving as objective, quantitative results that could give information about the materials' feasibility and applicability in a real-life architectural context, allow speculation, theorisation, and establishing design criteria (Thomsen and Tamke 2009).

The probes are used to speculate about textile-based bio-habitats and gather information about the relationships and interactions that form between the probes and the local ecosystem over time. By using and observing biodegradable materials paired with textile ceramics and 3D-printed ceramics in interaction with environmental factors such as sun radiation, rain, frost, snow, wind, flora and fauna, we gain knowledge about the potential of soft materials in bioreceptive architecture. The characteristics of the textiles, textile ceramics, and 3D-printed ceramics express variations in surface smoothness, surface roughness, porosity and permeability. By using a variety of materials, shapes, surface expressions and colours, we examine their varying potential for receptivity. In the context of this paper, we understand bioreceptivity as the potential for ecosystem entanglements, not only represented by microorganisms and plants, but also through insects, birds, and other cohabitants.

## Research Methods

The research combines two methods of exploring textile-based bio receptive perspectives to architecture: an open-ended research-by-design experimentation through which probes are made through material craftsmanship and an auto-ethnographic observation method to evaluate interactions with the local ecosystem over time.

Four types of probes were developed: freeform-crocheted textiles, ceramic textiles, textile joinery, and 3D-printed clay elements.

The project employs an arts- and design-led practice-based research methodology (Frayling 1993; Archer 1995; Cross 2006; 2007). Here, research experiments are of fundamental importance as they link design experiments, explorations, craftsmanship, and experiential knowledge to exemplify an alternative view of what architectural materiality could be. They serve as instruments for generating knowledge and advancing the design practice as "epistemological and methodological medi[a]" (Jonas 2015).

Additionally, multispecies auto-ethnography (Gillespie 2022) is employed as it is a relational methodology. The focus on the self is complemented by attending to others and considers the intimate entanglements that evolve through such relations. The combination of multispecies fieldwork and autoethnography allows "knowledge-making that comes from relationship-building" (Ibid.). In the context of design, this relational methodology is established as *design events*, a non-anthropocentric approach in participatory design in which the artefact and the more-than-human and human agents not only come together, but become together (Jönsson 2014, 116). As such, the artefacts have epistemic qualities (Ballestrem and Gasperoni, 2023) and serve not only as a representation of an idea but also as probes to test how the design idea manifests in practice, as an experiential substitute to investigate how it is to interact with the artefacts/design events, and as catalysts that are evoking new ideas. Therefore, the artefacts presented in this paper are design probes and a means of gaining knowledge and material evidence, allowing speculation, theorisation, and the establishing of design criteria (Thomsen and Tamke 2009). They don't serve as objective, quantitative results that could give information about the material's feasibility and applicability in a real-life architectural context.

As an initial experimental setup, this research explores at the material level the potential of textile-based receptive elements for façades that consist of a diverse set of surface textures and colours and combine materials with different levels of permanence, porosity (cf. Bedarf, 23, 4), and interactions with the local ecosystem, e.g., weather, seasons, plants, animals, and microorganisms. At the scale of architecture, a so-called Tiny House on Wheels (THoW) located in the rural outskirts of Hvalsø, Denmark, was used as a set up for the design events and their observation and documentation. Material transformations through seasons and weather and interactions with animals and microorganisms took place over two years and were documented and analysed via multispecies autoethnograohy by a researcher who inhabited the THoW.

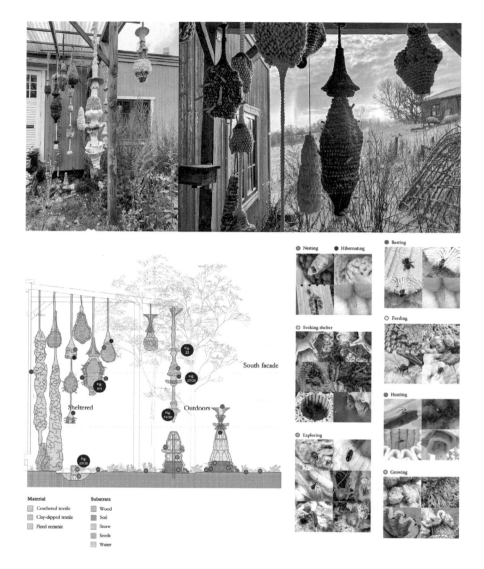

*Fig. 1.* Top left: Image of the Tiny House on Wheels on a sunny summer day. Its roofed entrance area served as a site for the design events. Top right: The picture shows the roofed entrance area with the design probes on a sunny winter morning in January 2024. Bottom: Graph illustrating the location of the experiments and their involvement in different types of multi-species interactions.

The examples are described through two categories: material craftsmanship and auto-ethnographic observation. In the sections about the material craftsmanship, we provide information about the materials, geometries, and techniques involved in the making of the probes. The probes examine the idea of porosity as a design notion and examine how surfaces that feature voids, pores, and temporal expressions can become meeting places and habitats for insects and plants, creating a shared osmotic membrane. Where existing works have mainly focused on exploring the bio-colonisation of façades through rigid architectural materials, e.g. concrete or ceramics: the approach in this research explores the design and use of textile-based materials and textile methodology as designed materials to negotiate space with living organisms. Moving from the materials craftmanship to how they can be experienced, a second research dimension is the observation of the local ecosystem interacting with the shape and materiality of the probes. Here, the use of biodegradable materials and their interaction with environmental factors is used as a deliberate way of orchestrating the probes' temporal performance and seasonal changes. As the shared membrane is occupied, it is changed by its occupants, such as microorganisms, plants, and animals.

*Fig. 2*: The graph shows the different levels of interaction ability of the material in relation to the textile technique and the mode of making.

The subsequent section presents the autoethnographic observation of living with the probes. As part of the multispecies ethnography approach, we present and examine the probes via a series of close-up photographs and written annotations that the author who cohabited with the installation narrated from memory. This personal and experiential perspective of the probes and their relationships with the local ecosystem is paired with contextual factual information, e.g. about the insects observed.

The four types of probes: freeform-crocheted textiles, ceramic textiles, textile joinery, and 3D-printed clay elements combine a variety of techniques, materials, qualities, and expressions as a representation of diversity. The crocheted artefacts represent emergence, multi materiality, colour, lightness, temporality, and resilience. 3D-printed ceramic elements represent parametric design, digital fabrication, monomateriality, heaviness, rigidity, permanence, and resilience. The ceramic textiles connect both spectrums and represent emergence, mono materiality, lightness, and fragility. The textile joinery is a physical connection between the 3D-printed elements and freeform crochet.

The probes exhibit various levels of surface textures that in the context of this chapter are categorised as surface smoothness, surface roughness, porosity, and permeability. We refer to surface smoothness as a closed surface with little texture and closed pores, such as the glossy-glazed clay 3D-prints, or the glossy-glazed ceramic textiles. Surface roughness describes a surface with texture and potential openings but primarily closed pores, such as a high-fired clay 3D-print. Porosity, in this chapter, is understood as a surface with texture, likely openings, and open pores that can be expressed through a brittle materiality and air-pockets in their substance, such as ceramic textiles. Permeability describes a materiality with a high absorption capacity and potential openings in the surface construction, such as the crocheted textiles crafted from cellulosic textiles.

# DESIGN PROBES

## Freeform-crocheted Textiles

Material craftsmanship: Freeform crocheting is a technique that involves hand craftsmanship and allows the generation of creative expressions and direct experimentation by the eschewing of traditional patterns and rules, and encourages the creation of unique, organic shapes and textures using a variety of stitches and materials.

The pieces were created using four application categories within the larger sculptures: cylindrical shapes, funnel-shaped forms, textile adapters, and connecting pieces.

Cylindrical shapes were crocheted using two material systems, a multi-strand cotton yarn for the base stitch and a woollen felted carpet yarn for increased size and stability of the shape. Woollen fibre strands and cellulose fibre strands have been used as secondary material systems to increase and loosen the surface area through loops. All shapes have openings so that they can be filled with a loose and dry substrate; e.g. dried grass or leaves for hibernating insects, e.g. lacewings, flies, and ladybugs in winter. The openings also allow small birds to enter.

Smaller funnel-shaped forms were crocheted to be turned into ceramic textiles. White multi-strand cotton yarn and cellulose fibres such as cotton have been used for their absorption of the stoneware slip and their inflammability, ensuring the stoneware slip penetrates through the textile material, replacing them as they burn away in the firing process.

Observations: Figure 3 shows a few of the cylindrical pieces that were filled with hay and suspended in the entrance of the THoW, where most of them were roofed but still exposed to the elements.

One of the suspended probes visible in Figure 1 was a cocoon-like shape crocheted with a red woollen yarn and a red carpet yarn. It was filled with hay and decorated with hand-shaped and fired clay tubes with a closed end and openings of around 3-5 mm.

*Fig. 3*: Colourful cotton yarns and woollen carpet yarns for the cylindrical shapes.

*Fig. 4*: The Hylaeus is hatching and ready to fly off. 1 August 2023 at 13:16:58 Hvalsø

*Fig. 5*: The common wasp is eating the coating off the fibres with its mandibles. The wasps are looking for sugary feasts as they become under-employed when the ratio of workers to larvae shifts at the end of the summer, and therefore change behaviour in search of food. 17 May 2023 at 15:52:40 Hvalsø, DK

On a sunny day in August 2023, two of the authors spotted the cellophane-like material that closed the opening of some of those ceramic tubes. This material is a waterproof and contaminant-proof substance. It is used by Hylaeus, also known as the yellow-faced bees or masked bees, who use it to line their nests. They use premade holes and fill the bottom part of the waterproof cells with food mass for their offspring.

*We found a tube in which the transparent film was opened and investigated it with a lamp and a magnifying glass. We observed a tiny black-bodied insect moving inside the tube. Researching about the transparent film led us to the Hyaleus, a large genus within the bee family Colletidae which are known for plastering the walls of their nest cells. We installed the tube into the crocheted object, and finally observed how the freshly hatched masked bee emerged from the tube, took off for a short flight investigation and then disappeared from our sight. After having observed this event, our awareness was accustomed to the size of the bee, and we observed others investigating the openings of the clay tubes in this and other suspended artefacts.*

This design event exemplifies the importance of auto-ethnographic observation and attunement to the size, speed, and timing of different living organisms. No wildlife camera would have been able to capture this specific moment, which is only feasible when the previous state is known and all angles and dimensions are under constant surveillance.

The human-made probe in this case made it possible for a non-expert in biology to spot the change, observe the moving Hylaeus inside the tube, and follow the hatchling and its first flight. This event/experience leaves an imprint in the observer and evokes an expanded sense of perception.

Observations: The probe in Figure 5 is a freeform crochet into which a cotton fibre strand has been integrated. The lower half of the object has then been dipped into bacterial cellulose that has been blended into a viscous mixture. The cellulose formed a thin, glossy, brownish, leather-like coating/film that covered the spaces inside the crochet loops and encapsulated the carded cotton fibres and the twisted cotton yarn.

> *The freeform crochet with kombucha coating was hanging outside since May and attracted a fly here and there. In August, however, it attracted so many wasps that I moved it a bit away from the house to prevent them from getting indoors. I could calmly observe how the wasps were eating the sugary bacterial cellulose and I felt good about them being busy and fed well at a close but good enough distance to my house. It was also in August that the activity around the 3 wasp nests I have in my storage and entrance significantly decreased.*

The behaviour of the common wasps drastically changes in late summer when they are no longer needed to take care of the larvae and cannot feed from their sugary juices anymore. As a result they look for food in other places and can therefore be found pollinating flowers, eating fruits, and enjoying human gatherings with sugary beverages.

This design event, similarly to the previous one, exemplifies the specific timing of events and seasonal changes in animal behaviour and how these can effect cohabiting with them. Through sharing a home with wasps, their behavioural changes became very evident. The mobile artefact provided the wasps with what they needed and therefore created a more relaxed co-habitation experience and less wasps inside the THoW.

## Ceramic Textiles

Material craftsmanship: The processing of crocheted pieces with stoneware slip is a complex and uncertain endeavour, as the example in Figure 6 illustrates. The fibres, the density of the stoneware slip, the time given for the absorption process, and the force and movement of wringing excess slip all determine the weight, stability, level of porosity, and surface roughness that the fired piece exhibits. Its shape also depends on the position in which it was left to dry. Even though the textiles burned away completely, the visual expression of the thin cotton thread and the carded cotton fibres are still intact (Figure 6, right). Some ceramic textiles broke and pulverised into small pieces as they were too fragile to be handled. In some cases, the slip just encapsulated the cotton thread, leaving out the core of the carded cotton band, which burned away and left a tunnel-like cavity inside the former crochet.

Observations: Another ceramic textile artefact was formed from a cylindrical crochet and suspended in combination with other elements as the final piece in the bottom of the artefact. Through the previously deep folds of the crochet, the object had some deeper cracks in which substrate and seeds could be collected and through which water could flow through.

*Initially I had the object inside the THoW. It was filled with barley grass seeds and was hanging above a plant so that the excess water from keeping the seeds moist would not drop onto the floor. Barley grass grew and withered over time, adding grown materials and expressions to the object. Finally, it was used as the bottom piece of a new arrangement and moved outdoors. The grass blew away, grew again, froze, melted, and withered. I feel like this artefact has had so many different lives already, and it will continue to transform again and again, finally dropping to the ground as the crocheted connections degrade from the ravages of time, sun, rain, wind, and frost. I hope it reaches its highest potential before it does.*

Reflections: This probe exemplifies the span of time over which a design event can occur. The author lived together with the textiles and ceramic textiles for months until she found a combination that pleased her aesthetically and expressed aspects of the previous design ideas. The high level of engagement through improvisation and cohabitation led to probes that evoked not only hours of making but also weeks of contemplation, temporary

*Fig. 6.* Left: A soft textile crocheted with a cotton thread and carded cotton fibres. Middle: The resulting ceramic textile with a finely detailed surface structure and high level of porosity. Right: A close-up of a detail of Figure 6 Middle. What looks like yarn holding together strings of fibers is the stoneware that is left after the textile materials burned away during the firing process.

*Fig. 7.* Left: A textile adapter connecting to a ceramic 3D-print. Centre: A textile adapter almost indistinctly connecting to a ceramic textile. Right: Crocheted sculpture carries a ring from ceramic textile. The surfaces are covered with snow crystals. 05 January 2024, 13:34 Hvalsø, DK

frustration, not knowing, sudden inspiration, and adaptation. In addition to the time spent letting the probe emerge, a lot of time went by observing the object in its different stages indoors and outdoors. The search for its potential is still ongoing, keeping the researcher's mind alert and searching.

## Textile Joinery

Material Craftsmanship: In order to join the different pieces together, freeform crochet has been utilised in the form of textile adapters and connecting pieces (Figure 8). Textile adapters have been directly crocheted onto the ceramic 3Dprints and the ceramic textiles. Therefore, all of the 3D-printed elements and ceramic textiles have an opening in the centre and many of them were provided with holes or channels through which the threads could be pulled and a crochet-work developed. Textile adapters were crocheted onto some of the 3D-printed elements and the ceramic textiles in order to be able to connect them into a sculptural artefact.

Connecting pieces, mostly tubes, were crocheted to thread together up the 3D-printed elements and the ceramic textiles in order to connect them into a sculptural artefact. This allowed the prototyping of diverse element constellations. Once a combination was decided, the textiles were permanently joined using textile joinery.

Observations: Figure 7 (right) shows a white-brown textile crochet onto which a ceramic textile has been threaded. The organic aesthetic is composed by the regular cell-like loops and their irregularities that are present in both the flexible textiles and the rigid ceramic textile elements. The hybrid aesthetics are also supported by the interaction of the artefact with water, which is represented by snow crystals on the ceramic textile collar and on one side of the crocheted textile, providing wind directionality.

*When I look at the objects I am just astonished how well they integrate into the landscape. They look like mushrooms with their pores and lamellae, and they have this dynamic and very poetic expression that one could wonder about and observe for hours.*

While the crocheted textiles in their original form are flexible and serve as connections, the ceramic textiles are rigid and potentially brittle. The organic and dynamic aesthetics however are still present in their form and texture. The elements not only express different levels of temporality in regard to the speed of biodegradation but also different aesthetics.

Reflections: This artefact exemplifies the potentials of crochet-based elements and artefacts. The aesthetic potential, the possibilities of improvisation, and the flexibility regarding the choice of materials are simply endless. The resulting expressions suggest an alternative aesthetic to the prevailing aesthetics of architectural façades and materiality.

### 3D-printed Clay Elements

Material craftsmanship: A separate parametric model was developed for the heavier ground pieces, which were designed to create porous spaces with internal compartments. These pieces were envisioned as extensions of the earth, speculate to accumulate rich micro-biomes and build connections with ground-dwelling species. The model is composed of two different logics: a light outer layer and an inner structure for support. A hollow core provides space for a textile channel for connecting the stackable pieces, while also reducing the amount of material use and weight of the artefacts.

The outer layer was a prototyped experiment with a range of porosities through a thread-like pattern that complements the textile counterpart. With the toolpath alternating between connecting to the structure and a free-hanging thread, loose strands of clay allow gravity to pull them downwards, creating a softer, thread-like appearance and forming openings. These

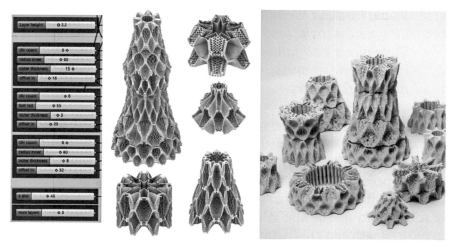

*Fig. 8*: Variation of parameters for producing different forms and porosity levels and comparison of digital model and physical print.

*Fig. 9*: Left: Suspended element with a bird taking off from the platform filled with seeds. Right: 3D-printed platform combined with crocheted textiles and ceramic textiles. The platform contains seeds to feed local birds, e.g. blackbirds, robins, and blue tits in winter.

strands carry a parallel to drop-stitches or floatings in textile terms.

Through a continuous iterative process, an understanding of the printer as a tool was gained in order to control the extent of hanging and looseness of the threads. The limits of the toolpath were tested as we varied different parameters, some of which failed to hold its structure. Glazing was also applied to strategic points for creating pools of water for the organisms. Platform elements were intended to be installed in hanging modules, which can hold substrate and water and provide a landing, resting, drinking area for flying organisms and / or a place for plant growth.

Observations:

Thought of as water points in summer, feeding stations in winter, and flat containers for growing sprouts indoors, the platforms proved most suitable for feeding birds in winter. Their size allowed only smaller birds such as blue tits and robins to sit on the rim and they are out of reach for cats. The platforms themselves were easily combined with the crocheted elements, complement the organic aesthetics and harmoniously combine textiles, ceramic textiles, and clay 3Dprints.

*I love observing birds interacting with the artefacts and the vegetation outside the THoW. In spring I noticed birds pulling out fibres from objects to build their nests, and on frozen and sunny winter days I can follow them flying around the objects searching for food. I stopped cleaning my garden of so-called weeds because I observed how sought-after they are. In summer and autumn they are full of caterpillars, beetles, butterflies, bees, and wasps; in winter the birds come to pick their seeds when everything else is frozen and covered by snow. I also stopped cleaning my windows to decrease the number of birds hurting themselves by bumping into them and spotted some bird-poo in one of the objects with an opening in the bottom. Even though birds are so much easier to trace than insects or microorganisms, and can be observed from a distance, there is so much going on that I am not yet noticing!*

Reflections: This artefact exemplifies the multilayered complexity of observation that is necessary to evaluate it and its emerging relationships with the local ecosystem. Sensitivity to the scale and expressions of other species is needed for the art of noticing (Tsing 2021). Some observations can be done from a distance, with liminal intimacy; some observations need physical closeness.

The needs of individual species depend on their lifecycle, seasons, and the diversity of the local ecosystem they are part of. Therefore, these observations demand a lot of time and awareness. Snippets of short observations for a day, a week, a month, a year, several years, deepen the understanding and curiosity for the species and their context, and can lead to behavioural changes such as those described in the journal text above.

The so-called ground pieces – the heavier 3D-printed clay elements – were stacked in different places on the ground, where they started to change colour within just a week. Figure 10 shows the tip of an artefact that was placed into a small pond next to the THoW. Groups of Armadillidium vulgare, the common pill woodlouse, gathered on the triangular shaped edges that were sticking out of the water and covered with a yellow-ochre biofilm.

*I am used to spotting woodlice under fallen leaves, in soil full of plant matter, or dark and moist basements. Witnessing them on this 3D-printed piece in the middle of the pond was quite a surprise. How did they get there? What are they doing? Where does the yellow colour suddenly come from? Most likely, they grazed the biofilm that had developed on the 3D-printed element between July and August 2023. Why did this biofilm develop within just a month? After learning about woodlice and biofilms I don't necessarily have more answers, but my curiosity and sense of wonder and respect drastically increased and I am excited for more discoveries.*

*Fig. 10*: Woodlice gathering on a yellow/greenish biofilm that developed on a 3D-printed piece that rested in a small pond.

This artefact exemplifies the power of human-made artefacts when it comes to becoming aware and curious about other species. Witnessing them outside of the context from which we usually know them allows especially non-experts in biology to become aware and curious. Supplementing the observations with factual knowledge does not always bring definite answers but usually deeper questions and an ongoing curiosity to discover and understand more. Such design events consequently become sites for discovery and learning for humans and contribute to building skills as well as tacit and factual knowledge. They might lead to behavioural change such as an increased awareness, a regular visit to the observation site, or behaviours that benefit their wellbeing.

### Reflections on the Potentials of Multimateriality and Multispecies Autoethnography in Bioreceptive Architecture

The research exemplifies a new category of expressions that are capable of generating new ideas regarding sustainable and regenerative living and asks for the materiality of architecture to be reconsidered with a more considerate approach to the natural/built environment in mind. Arguments can be found in the diversity of materials, techniques, and expressions explored by this research. For example, freeform crochet can be an unconventional material for architecture, but it is a highly adaptive and versatile method of constructing surfaces that allows for aesthetic blends and flexible connections between different materials and techniques. They sustain nuanced human-made interventions that can support nature, grown by multi-level biocolonisation through multi-material systems and techniques. These materials also enable different levels of interventions and a expressions of decay (colour change, material decomposition). Naturally, textiles decay fast and are e.g. nutrients for microorganisms, a plant substrate, building material for birds, and habitat for beetles. Thus, the biocolonisation and a interactions with different members of the ecosystem are therefore faster than other hard architectural materials, such as a mono-material system like a ceramic façade panel. However, mixing material properties and joining them with textiles can create more adaptable habitats and enable modularity, redesign and use.

Reflecting further on craftsmanship, the complexity and unpredictability of the ceramic textiles and freeform crochet demands a high level of improvisation and flexibility regarding the outcomes. This is in direct contrast to the rather high level of precision when designing and fabricating the 3Dprints. This approach might seem counterproductive. However, the designer/researcher is asked to constantly adapt, improvise, and respond to new challenges: changing compositions, adjusting ideas, letting go of concrete expectations, responding to circumstances, accepting "dead ends". This approach of following the flow and constantly adapting to changing circumstances brings the designer/researcher closer to the complexity of ecosystems and of life itself.

The Western tradition of building the architectural design practice is famously founded on ideas of permanence and stasis (c.f. Taylor, 2016). In this material exploration, the idea of permanence is reversed into allowing decay, changing the aesthetics and expression of the surfaces across time, seasons, and use. The materials developed are intentionally designed to change over time and include more values, such as empathy for the ecosystem they subtly aim to integrate into. Thus, the researcher's first-person experience is quintessential to observing with humbleness the needs and living patterns of another species to be able to integrate them into the future design. The documentation of this research does not aim to predict but to acknowledge and illustrate the complexity of interactions and relationships within human-made and natural ecosystems, cultivating aesthetics and actions of care, curiosity, and empathy. Instead of predicting properties for how architectural materials should be, this research discusses what methods and capacities are needed to build close relations with the environment, and simultaneously speculates on new habits for human living that actively serve our cohabitation with the surrounding ecosystem. Observing and cultivating curiosity about the landscape and its inhabitants challeges the designer to consider for a more experiential approach and to hold an open mindset by living with and staying with the artefacts over time rather than delivering a final result and moving on. The observations, reflections, and interpretations that result from this close relationship with the materials aim to illustrate that the designer/researcher does not always have to prove the effectiveness of a single material/composition/technique. Instead, material/composition/technique can be seen as providing a wide variety of expressions to expand the possibilities of interactions and include emerging observations on an alternative temporality of living and building. As current architectural theory conceptualises the temporality of material systems as part of sustainable building culture by transferring concepts of ecosystem hierarchy and their embodiment of different timescales (O'Neill et al. 1986), this research complements the methodology of "shearing layers of change" by which to understand the differentiated functions and time-spans of interconnected architectural systems; the site, structure, the skin, the services, space plan and stuff [Brand 1995; Yazdani 2019; Campbell 2006] to which we add a bottom-up perspective through the sheering character of the building material.

# REFERENCES

Alcamo, J., Bennett, E., and Program, M. (2003). *Ecosystems and Human Well-Being: A Framework For Assessment*.

Ballestrem, M., and Gasperoni, L. (2023). *Epistemic artefacts: A dialogical reflection on design research in architecture* (First edition). AADR.

Beckett, R. (2024). *Probiotic cities*. Routledge, Taylor and Francis Group.

Bedarf, P. (2023). *Architected Porosity: Foam 3D Printing for Lightweight and Insulating Building Elements* (p. 231 p.) [ETH Zurich; Application/pdf].

Brand, S. (1995). *How buildings learn: What happens after they're built*. Penguin Books.

Beyer, B., Suárez, D., and Palz, N. (2019). Microbiologically Activated Knitted Composites Reimagining a column for the 21st century. *Blucher Design Proceedings*, 541–552.

Bloch, K., Aljannat, M., Morrow, R., Pynirtzi, N., Mwebaza, D., and Perry, O. (2023). Refining the Potential of Bacterial Cellulose as a Building Facade Material, through a Design-led Process.

Campbell, D. G., and Fast, K. (2010). *From Pace Layering to Resilience Theory: The Complex Implications of Tagging from Information Architecture*.

Cross, N. (2006). *Designerly Ways of Knowing*. Springer-Verlag.

Cross, N. (2007). From a Design Science to a Design Discipline: Understanding Designerly Ways of Knowing and Thinking. In R. Michel (Ed.), *Design Research Now* (pp. 41–54). DE GRUYTER.

Cruz, M., and Beckett, R. (2016). Bioreceptive design: A novel approach to biodigital materiality. *Architectural Research Quarterly*, *20*(1), 51–64.

Franklin, A. (2017). The more-than-human city. *The Sociological Review*, *65*(2), 202–217.

Frayling, C. (1993). *Research in art and design*. Royal College of Art.

Heitlinger, S., Foth, M., Clarke, R., DiSalvo, C., Light, A., and Forlano, L. (2018). Avoiding ecocidal smart cities: Participatory design for more-than-human futures. *Proceedings of the 15th Participatory Design Conference: Short Papers, Situated Actions, Workshops and Tutorial - Volume 2*, 1–3.

Jonas, W. (2015). *Research Through Design Is More than Just a New Form of Disseminating Design Outcomes*. Constructivist Foundations, 11, 32–36.

Jönsson, L. (2014). *Design Events: On explorations of a nonanthropocentric framework in design*.

Keune, S. (2018). *On Textile Farming: Seeds as Material for Textile Design*. University of Borås, Faculty of Textiles, Engineering and Business.

Keune, S. (2019). *On Textile Farming Living Indoors*. University of Borås, Faculty of Textiles, Engineering and Business.

Keune, S. (2021). Designing and Living with Organisms Weaving Entangled Worlds as Doing Multispecies Philosophy. *Journal of Textile Design Research and Practice*, *9*(1), 9–30

Le Roux, C. S. (2017). Exploring rigour in autoethnographic research. *International Journal of Social Research Methodology*, *20*(2), 195–207.

Lyle, J. T. (1994). *Regenerative design for sustainable development*. Wiley.

Malik, S., Hagopian, J., Mohite, S., Lintong, C., Stoffels, L., Giannakopoulos, S., Beckett, R., Leung, C., Ruiz, J., Cruz, M., and Parker, B. (2020). Robotic Extrusion of Algae Laden Hydrogels for Large Scale Applications. *Global Challenges*, *4*(1), 1900064.

Mosse, A., Zamora, D. S., and Beyer, B. (2024). Towards a Bacterially-Induced Textile Architecture. In M. R. Thomsen, C. Ratti, and M. Tamke (Eds.), *Design for Rethinking Resources* (pp. 47–63). Springer International Publishing.

NEXT Architects (2015). *Vlotwatering Bridge Bat Bridge*. https://www.nextarchitects.com/vlotwatering-bridge.

O'Neill, R. V. (1986). *A Hierarchical concept of ecosystems*. Princeton University Press.

Pedersen Zari, M., and Hecht, K. (2019). *Biomimicry for regenerative built environments: Mapping design strategies for producing ecosystem services.*

Restany, P. (2022). *Hundertwasser: 1928-2000: die Macht der Kunst - der Maler-König mit den fünf Häuten.* TASCHEN.

Steele, W., Wiesel, I., and Maller, C. (2019). More-than-human cities: Where the wild things are. *Geoforum, 106,* 411–415.

Smith, N., Bardzell, S., and Bardzell, J. (2017). Designing for Cohabitation: Naturecultures, Hybrids, and Decentering the Human in Design. *Proceedings of the 2017 CHI Conference on Human Factors in Computing Systems,* 1714–1725.

Souza, E. (2022). *Giving Nature a Home in Cities: Bricks for Bees' Nests.* Accessed 2. May 2022. https://www.archdaily.com/976821/giving-nature-a-home-in-cities-bricks-for-bees-nests.

Taylor, M. (2016). Time Matters: Transition and Transformation in Architecture. *Architectural Design, 86,* 42–49.

Terreform ONE (2020). Monarch Sanctuary. Retrieved March 30, 2020, from https://terreform.com/monarchsanctuary/.

Gissen, D. (2012). *Subnature: Architecture's other environments* (Unabridged). Princeton Architectural Press.

Tsing, A. L. (2021). *The mushroom at the end of the world: On the possibility of life in capitalist ruins* (New paperback printing). Princeton University Press.

Voyatzaki, M. (2018). Architectural Materialisms: Nonhuman Creativity. In M. Voyatzaki, *Architectural Materialisms* (pp. 1–28). Edinburgh University Press.

Yazdani Mehr, S. (2019). Analysis of 19th and 20th Century Conservation Key Theories in Relation to Contemporary Adaptive Reuse of Heritage Buildings. *Heritage, 2*(1), 920–937.

# First-Person Perspective

Barbara Pollini

## as a Form of Inquiry in Biodesign

Biodesign is an emerging design approach that entangles design and science; one of the most adopted definitions today emphasises using living organisms in the design process to create materials, structures, and artefacts (Myers 2012). The Biodesign practice is characterised by a robust experimental approach based on experiential learning as a powerful form of inquiry. The field's young age leaves many gaps in the literature, which, due to its experimental nature, lend themselves to further investigation from a first-person perspective.

This chapter illustrates how Research Through Design (RTD) can benefit the Biodesign inquiry. It reports as a case study the author's doctoral research on the potential of biodesigned materials for an ecological transition; the doctoral path adopted RTD to deepen and reforge some theoretical aspects of the research, especially where the reference literature was limited or absent.

To turn RTD projects into an even more valuable inquiry tool, the author selected specific parameters to assess the validity and peculiarities of such activities, evaluating them through quality and disciplinary entanglement parameters. The parameters identified can help reinforce the RTD project's identity and be a valuable tool for discussing and critiquing practice-based research activities in Biodesign.

## EXPERIENTIAL LEARNING IN BIODESIGN

RTD is a practice-based inquiry that generates transferrable knowledge (Bruce Archer 1995; Frayling 1993). Some disciplines, such as the IOT, consolidated the learning-by-doing inquiry as an essential research method, recognising the importance of prototyping for inquiry and knowledge generation (Mincolelli et al. 2020). The design discipline shows the same sensibility for practice-based research too. For example, in the field of Material Design, described as a transdisciplinary practice in which designers design materials with unique functionalities and experiential qualities (Pedgley et al. 2021), the development of new materials (or material features) sees the designer's highly sensorial engagement with his/her "matter" of research. Rognoli and Levi outlined how sensitivity to materials and technologies occurs through experiential learning, highlighting how exploring the material inevitably calls into question its limitations and instigates the desire to find alternatives to the existing (Rognoli and Levi 2011). In Biodesign, the direct exploration of the organisms involves not only the senses but also relational cognition and empathy. In fact, the designer needs to deeply understand the living organisms involved, which have preferences, needs and agencies; engaging in a multispecies dialogue (Pollini 2023). Designers experimenting with living materials experience how the organisms react to their inputs, thus gathering information on their experimentation by interpreting the organism's response signals. RTD is, therefore, a fundamental aspect of Biodesign since this field mainly relies on direct observation and hands-on experimentation with living organisms. The sensory and emotional involvement of the designer (relying on material experience and relational experimentation with the living agents) allows for gathering information through experience, triggering an iterative multispecies dialogue based on the trial-and-error process of design refinement (ibid.).

Personal observation is part of the daily practice of a designer involved in RTD activities but is usually not reported in scientific research. However, the inherently hybrid nature of design is causing many scholars in the field to draw attention to analytical practices that are closer to this inner nature of the discipline, explicitly referring to autoethnography and first-person perspective in design inquiry (Forlano 2021; Nimkulrat 2022; Tomico et al. 2012 and 2023; Wieczorek et al. 2022). The researcher's subjectivity has been addressed in different disciplines: in ethnography, the first-person perspective introduces the observer's/researcher's subjective voice in autoethnographic accounts of experiences; in Human-Computer Interaction, this approach is a way to study personal bodily experiences; in design, the first-person perspective has often been related to autobiographical design (Höök et al. 2018). Autoethnography has been used as a qualitative research method across various disciplines based on personal experience and self-reflection. Stacy Holman Jones points out how this methodology can help gather the "granular experience of the everyday", particularly fitting for design as a highly embodied practice based on senses and materiality (Jones, 2013). Bochner describes autoethnography as "the genre of doubt" and a method of qualitative inquiry that allows scholars to maintain an emotional and personal connection to their research (Bochner 2017). Such personal connection benefits designers (and users) dealing with materials. Material Experience has been defined as the "experiences that people have with, and through, the materials of a product" (Karana et al. 2008); here, the expressive-sensorial features of materials (Rognoli 2010) act as an interface of meanings among objects/materials and their users. Therefore, designers need to gain knowledge of the subjective characteristics of materials too. This intimate approach in material research seems to find a perfect match when it comes to living materials; as Karana and colleagues stated, "designing with alive, active, adaptive materials or considering materials as 'living' in design practice is a complex issue and requires an experiential understanding of these materials" (Karana et al. 2019). Generally understood as a way of knowing and understanding through direct personal engagement, experiential knowledge has also been addressed as a crucial aspect to be integrated into cross-disciplinary collaborative practice (Nimkulrat et al. 2020).

Experiential learning is a fundamental activity in Material Design and Biodesign. In fact, both rely on practice-based forms of inquiry, such as tinkering activity, which leads to a form of tacit knowledge essential for developing new materials and processes (Parisi et al. 2017). In Biodesign, the tinkering activity also needs to consider living agents co-authoring the design process, taking the name of "biotinkering" – namely, tinkering with biology (Rognoli et al. 2021). Based on the type of living organism involved in the design process, "biotinkering" can be a more complex, relational and interactive practice-based form of Biodesign inquiry (Pollini 2023).

# FILLING THE GAP: AUTOETHNOGRAPHY AS A RESEARCH TOOL

To address some of the knowledge gaps in Biodesign literature, the author adopted a practice-based research approach combined with autoethnography to test and reinforce the more theoretical part of her doctoral research. Notably, four RTD projects have been activated to test the developed theories and methods and investigate the designer's role in contexts of different scientific intensities from a first-person perspective.

The figure of the "biodesigner" still lacks definitions and tools, and despite this, it already appears to be evolving. Training and workspaces seem to play a more significant role in defining the new peculiarities of this emerging professional figure. Designing in a DIY and low-tech or scientific laboratory poses very different limits and opportunities in determining design approaches and outcomes (Pollini, forthcoming). Designers who hybridise their discipline to such an extent that they have a scientific laboratory as a primary working environment are defined as Designer in Lab (Langella 2019). The gap in the hybrid figure of the Designer in Lab is filled in only a couple of testimonies in the literature through autobiographical reports of the designer's laboratory life. In fact, the fewest and most accurate descriptions of the designers working in scientific labs are based on autobiographical notes (Sawa 2016; Stefanova 2021).

The will to activate four RTDs involving the author in the role of a Biodesigner and of a Designer in Lab also had the aim of adding some more considerations on this topic, especially to better understand how the designer's activity might change according to the various shades of hybridisation between design and science, influencing the design project and its outcomes.

The aim of the RTDs was oriented toward proving the effectiveness of a Biodesign approach in providing sustainable, viable solutions in the short run, moving forward from the speculative flavour that Biodesign can take on. For this reason, the projects have been oriented to tangible material experimentation to find viable and sustainable material solutions through experimental research on biobased and biofabricated materials. Here follows a brief description of each RTD project[1]; the general purpose of this contribution is not to go into detail on each RTD project, but to show instead how the four projects were planned as research tools to grasp new knowledge and provide answers to the general research, especially where literature was lacking.

## RTD1 – Biotinkering with Kombucha

The first RTD aimed to strengthen the author's discourse around biotinkering activity in Biodesign. The author's RTD focused on biotinkering activities with bacterial cellulose (BC) within the DeForma project at the Polytechnic University of Milan, carried out by a team of PhD students and researchers all with a design background. Having had previous experience with BC, the author investigated BC from other perspectives (circular economy potentialities, hybridization with other materials and components, different low-tech post-harvesting finishings). The biotinkering activity on the various reactions of the fermenting culture to various materials led her to develop a new technique that uses cellulose masks to create patterns derived from different BC thicknesses.

## RTD2 – Bioreceptivity for Biomonitoring

The second RTD started with the will to test in practice the Bioreceptive Design methodology outlined by the author, consisting of a few fundamental steps of procedural thinking guiding the designers to consider (a) the organism's requirements, (b) the environmental parameters, and (c) the material intrinsic properties. These steps are fundamental to designing materials and shapes through which properties can achieve a "correspondence of bioreceptivity" to match the organisms' needs and the environmental parameters of the targeted environment (Pollini & Rognoli 2021). The project originated from the intersection between design and biology, focusing on employing bioreceptive

*Fig. 1.* A lesson learnt from the organism: creating texturised BC with different thicknesses through cellulose masks.

*Fig. 2.* Designing for bioreceptivity: prototyping and testing bioreceptive materials for lichens' and mosses' survival and spontaneous colonisation over time.

materials to improve the supply and exposure of lichens and mosses in urban areas for their use as air-quality biosensors (Contardo et al. 2018; Świsłowski et al. 2022). This is a reiterative Material Design research project still ongoing, whose main phases are prototyping, exposure and evaluation of colonisation. Early developed prototypes are now following a scientific bioreceptivity evaluation, constantly monitored by experts in the botanical garden of Siena, Italy. Early findings have shown positive results from transplants and spontaneous colonisation of mosses and other pioneer species (Pollini et al. 2023).

The last two RTDs took place in scientific laboratories to test the effectiveness of the figure of the Designer in Lab in highly scientific environments (Pollini, forthcoming).

### RTD3 – Biotinkering with Silk

The first lab experience occurred at SilkLab (Department of Biomedical Engineering at Tufts University)[2]. As a visiting PhD for six months, the author had the opportunity to learn new lab skills and deepen her knowledge about silk-based materials. Among her RTDs experiences, this has been the most challenging: in terms of scientific protocols to follow, technologies to learn and use, and the degree of scientific knowledge to assimilate in order to proceed significantly in the research. The objective here was that of experimenting with silk-based materials, addressing the hypothesis that a DIY-materials approach (Ayala Garcia and Rognoli 2017; Pollini and Maccagnan 2017; Rognoli et al. 2021) could also fit in scientific labs dealing with advanced materials such as fibroin (the silk protein). Supported by the feedback of chemists and material scientists from the lab, the author adopted a transdisciplinary approach, connecting DIY and lab-empowered experimentation, positively contributing to the development of new fibroin-based materials.

The second lab experience occurred at the Italian Institute of Technology (IIT) in Milan, where the author joined the ElFo (Electronic Food) research group[3]. This PhD visiting period followed a research proposal by the author suggesting the experimentation of biofabricated and DIY bio-based materials to broaden the range of materials used in this field. Here, the author worked side by side with a material scientist to develop new biofabricated and bio-based material solutions for edible electronics. Moreover, she concluded her visiting period by providing a workshop to the ElFo research team on biofabricated, DIY-Bio and DIY-Materials.

As seen, although each RTD project is connected with the theoretical framework of the overall doctoral research and is intended to strengthen specific concepts within it, the four RTDs can also be seen as a "capsule research" with their own objective, hypothesis, research questions (RQ), and methodologies. Furthermore, each RTD has opened new research lines, most of the time addressed through interdisciplinary collaborations.

Specific RQs of autoethnography (Jones 2013; Méndez 2013) are also addressed in each project. The autoethnographic study was carried out mainly through field notes: the author noted her observation through text and sketches of the experience within the four projects, to deeply reflect on her role as a designer in dialogue with science on multiple levels. The notes highlight how the designer can participate in different degrees of difficulty and interaction in multidisciplinary workgroups' and which methodologies and competencies can help in such science-oriented environments.

*Fig. 3* Testing the role of the Designer in Lab. Above images from the Silklab – on the left are the silk cocoons from which the fibroin is extracted, and on the right, the drawer with the early material samples developed in the first tinkering period by the author; below images from the IIT laboratory – on the left the bacterial cellulose treated for edible electronics applications, on the right some samples of DIY-materials developed by the author for the workshop held for the ElFo research group.

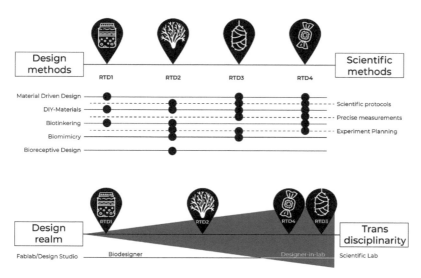

*Fig. 4* The four RTDs projects are compared regarding methodologies used and disciplinary positioning.

## ASSESSING QUALITY IN BIODESIGN PRACTICE-BASED INQUIRY

The paradigm for which science analyses the world to generate new knowledge, while design uses existing knowledge to create new worlds, has already been questioned in favour of hybridising the two disciplines for mutual advantage (Verkerke et al. 2013). Biodesign aims precisely to work across design and science, using methods and tools from both domains and aiming for a transdisciplinary approach to shape new knowledge and worlds.

Various degrees of disciplinary hybridisation can outline different approaches and design outcomes; the four RTDs were further evaluated by the author under this perspective, addressing methods and approaches used in each project according to the disciplinary hybridisation required. Figure 4 outlines the main differences in terms of disciplines involved and methodologies applied.

The diagram shows how the project's proximity to design increases the use of methodologies drawn from this discipline, while the more we move towards the scientific domain (the highest point of which, in this case, is given by the Designer in Lab figure in scientific laboratories) the more the methodological approach becomes equal, defining a cross-disciplinary practice and profession[4]. The project's proximity to one or the other discipline influences not only the methodologies adopted by the designer but also many other aspects, including the general approach, the outcomes, and the ease of assessing the quality of the project. In fact, it is not always possible for design knowledge based on practice to meet criteria that more scientific types of knowledge are judged upon. The distinctive kind of knowledge generation upon which RTD relies is created through an intuitive and unique approach to practice, which is often dynamic, ephemeral, and more heterogeneous than knowledge from most other sciences (Prochner and Godin 2022; Redström 2017).

When it comes to RTD research quality indicators, Prochner and Godin (2022) point out a missing consensus among the literature, thus proposing a framework for quality in RTD projects, referring to existing research quality indicators from four broad research paradigms, such as positivism, postpositivism, constructivism, and pragmatism. Taking inspiration from this study and willing to test the validity of the four RTD activities, the leading five categories of quality indicators defined by Prochner and Godin (2022) will be illustrated and contextualised especially for RTD in Biodesign. This discussion aims to understand how these quality parameters can be synthesised and further adapted to become a reference when discussing Biodesign projects.

*Traceability:* This category refers to the possibility of keeping track of all the research steps. The origin of this concept lies in the quality indicators of replicability (from positivism/postpositivism) referring to the possibility of reproducing an experiment. Moreover, the concept refers also to transparency (pragmatism), addressing how and why the research is done. This category is related to the nature of the RTD project, its objectives, and how these might lead to the research conclusions (Prochner and Godin 2022).

The experimental activity in the design practice is usually less rigorous than "experimental design in the scientific domain", intended as the design of an experiment involving several interrelated activities serving a scientific hypothesis (Kirk 2013). However, Biodesign tends to follow the scientific method for its own dual nature, aiming also for experiment replicability, especially when developing new materials and processes. When dealing with living organisms, most of the projects also tend to be based on replicable and effective procedural protocols to enable the organisms to strive, replicate, and grow. Concerning transparency, it is not uncommon in Biodesign to set objectives based on the abilities of the organisms and how the designer imagines applying them for the better. From this analysis, practical research in the field of Biodesign can be evaluated according to replicability and transparency indicators to evaluate the project's overall traceability. However, if these principles can be considered for the scientific side of Biodesign projects, these are less suited to design's creative and distinctive nature. As stated by some scholars (Cross 2001; Zimmerman et al. 2007), different designers will never solve the same problem with identical solutions; in most cases, designers do not even aim at repeating or copying the work of others. Therefore, biodesigners tend to replicate design principles and methodologies proving their own practice rather than simply trying to replicate other designers' protocols, thus consistently generating new variables and applications for the sake of originality.

*Interconnectivity:* The second category addresses the links between important concepts and elements of the research, addressing collaborations with stakeholders or describing the context in which the project is based and its implications. This category addresses three quality indicators: internal validity, credibility, and contextualisation.

Internal validity stays for the cause-and-effect relationship between elements of the research, constructing the validity of the data collected by observing links between variables and results. Here, there might be a significant difference between science and design. Science advances by hypothesising possible outcomes derived from given variables, while the design process might also follow a naive trial-and-error iteration. For example, Material Design and Biodesign rely on activities such as tinkering (Parisi et al. 2017) and biotinkering (Pollini 2023; Rognoli et al. 2021), which tend towards explorative experimentation, not necessarily following planned experiments based on carefully selected hypotheses.

Credibility is the second quality indicator, addressing the verification of the results with other project actors. The designer's work can involve different disciplines and touch several stakeholders; in this case, the work must be informed and guided or discussed within the community of professionals and stakeholders involved. In the case of Biodesign, the feedback and validation of the work by a project's scientific counterpart help greatly in validating the project. Other factors that can enhance credibility might include a prolonged engagement with the field of research and the possible triangulation of data sources.

The third indicator is contextualisation, for a better understanding of the context in which the research is done and what kind of consequences this could have. Biodesign is often adopted in response to environmental issues in an attempt to limit the ecological burden of future productions with bioinspired and biogenerated materials and processes (Ginsberg and Chieza 2018; Myers 2012; Oxman et al. 2020; Pollini 2023); therefore, the starting context and the design objectives become important triggers in this discipline.

*Applicability:* This category refers to the research outcomes and their application beyond the original research context. In this category, the authors present three quality indicators: external validity and transferability, referring to theories and knowledge that can be relevant and inform other contexts, and impact, namely the knowledge that will change things for the better.

The importance of communicating the project's impact can also easily be found in Biodesign, where, as previously mentioned, sustainability is a strong trigger. As in the previous category, the validity and applicability of a project or material can be validated by its scientific counterpart using quantitative methods. However, this category may not represent the speculative approach in Biodesign, an important part of the emerging discipline but one that, by its very nature, does not follow tangible considerations in the present time, thus escaping the possibility of being quantitatively assessed.

*Impartiality:* This category refers to the possible researcher's bias. Objectivity is the first parameter addressed, assuming the researcher and results are entirely separate. Confirmability is the second indicator, aiming to demonstrate that the researcher's bias is controlled. The last quality indicator is contextualisation (in theory and research), meaning that designers need to refer to accepted knowledge, explain why research choices have been made, and be able to say why findings make sense.

Researcher bias is an important aspect to consider in research; and design and Biodesign are no exception. Although contextualization is not a constant rule, it is more likely to occur in an academic research context, where the theoretical counterpart is often the basis for design choices.

*Reasonableness:* The last category indicates the need for a rational set of choices the designer makes during the research process. The indicators here are (i) reliability, meaning measurement techniques that can produce the same results in retests; (ii) dependability, understood as the possibility of theoretical inference to be justified; and (iii) soundness of research methods and research norms, suggesting that methods should proceed according to accepted norms as happens in science and scientific knowledge. This category seems to follow the first one (traceability): as discussed previously, Biodesign tends to follow the notions and methods of science; therefore, not only are the experimental phases usually described and annotated (in the methods, measurements, materials, and tools adopted), aiming for replicability, but if a multidisciplinary team carries out the project, there can also be an internal, rapid, effective, and mutual validation among different disciplines. If the project involves the growth and maintenance of life forms, even in more speculative approaches the designer will necessarily have to follow scientific rules and protocols for this to happen (e.g. hygiene protocols, temperature and humidity parameters check, etc.). This necessity brings even the most speculative practices closer to scientific rigour (Pollini and Rognoli 2021).

Prochner and Godin (2022) conclude their article by agreeing with the main literature on the topic, suggesting that standards to produce high quality knowledge must be introduced for RTD, while being aware that this standardization must not be excessive. In fact, imposing rigid rules on RTD would limit its creative potential in generating new knowledge as well. Biodesign seems to find a special balance on this issue, being keener to satisfy the requirements for all the quality categories previously defined, since part of the design process already relies on scientific models and facts.

Aware of the difficulty of evaluating the quality of RTD projects and of the fact that an approach such as Biodesign – which by its nature embraces the scientific method – would easily benefit from it, the author was inspired by the study of Prochner and Godin to identify the more effective parameters for this purpose. The discussion on design quality in RTD has led to the selection of a few parameters that are particularly useful for considering Biodesign projects, especially those that have a less speculative approach and are more likely to find solutions in the near future.

A simplification was done mainly by avoiding the repetition of similar concepts or those not relevant in evaluating Biodesign projects specifically. Here follows the proposal of five lenses through which to discuss Biodesign projects: (1) replicability, (2) reasonableness, (3) credibility, (4) contextualization, (5) transferability and impact. The following table shows them contextualized according to their meaning in the evaluation of Biodesign projects, although one can easily think that the same parameters can evaluate RTD activities linked to other experimental design approaches (e.g., Material Design).

## DISCIPLINARY ENTANGLEMENTS IN BIODESIGN

There is another fundamental aspect of Biodesign, linked to the hybrid nature that deeply characterises this discipline, that requires further analysis for the impact it can have on the design process and outcomes. Working across design and science can give rise to different nuances in which one or the other discipline's approach or work setting is predominant. In this case, the analysis can start from the degree of disciplinary hybridisation adopted. However, in Biodesign there are no standardised and recurrently similar hybridisations, but rather a variety of possibilities ranging from designers who adopt the scientific method in their practice to the designers who collaborate with scientists working in contexts classically belonging to the scientific context (Pollini, forthcoming).

McComb and Jablokow (2022) propose a *Degrees of Disciplinarity Framework*, as a lingua franca to describe the

| REPLICABILITY | The experiment can be reproduced giving the same results |
|---|---|
| REASONABLENESS | Rationale for choices made during the research process |
| CREDIBILITY | Verification of the results with external participants/audience |
| CONTEXTUALIZATION | Description of the context in which the project is based and its implications |
| TRANSFERABILITY AND IMPACT | Transferability refers to knowledge generated that is able to inform other studies; impact refers to knowledge that will change things for the better |

different relationships between disciplines in a research or project. The proposed scale is composed of five degrees of discipline relationship; going from zero, where pure unidisciplinarity happens, to five, where the collaboration among disciplines is described as generative multidisciplinarity. Among the five degrees, those from zero to two represent Unidisciplinarity, from its pure form (degree zero) to Paired Unidisciplinarity (degree two); the latter defining research which draws upon artefacts from two disciplines but with minimal interactions between them. The degrees from three to five represent various multidisciplinary research paradigms. Degree number three is defined as Shallow Multidisciplinarity, which addresses the intersection of two disciplines and implies that two researchers, with a deep disciplinary expertise, learn from each other about their respective disciplines and identify how they might fit together. The fourth degree refers to the concept of Deep Multidisciplinarity, meaning interaction between disciplines and a co-adaptation of shared norms, methods, and theories. This degree in multidisciplinarity requires experts to have deep knowledge of each other's discipline. The latest and highest degree of multidisciplinarity, named Generative Multidisciplinarity, defines the ability of the co-adaptation between disciplines to generate a new one, not derived from intentionality but resulting from serendipity and time. Time is highlighted as a key aspect in multidisciplinarity degrees four and five, needed to mitigate the sense of estrangement between different disciplines that must meet and adapt to each other over time. Biodesign matches this definition, being a discipline born from the co-adaptation of design and scientific methods and ways of knowing.

It is essential to point out that terms used by McComb and Jablokow (2022), such as deep or generative multidisciplinarity, are close to the general understanding of interdisciplinarity and transdisciplinarity too, as these definitions are still quite a debated topic in the literature. The well-established work of Choi abd Pak (2006) clarifies that "Multidisciplinarity draws on knowledge from different disciplines but stays within their boundaries. Interdisciplinarity analyses, synthesises, and harmonises links between disciplines into a coordinated and coherent whole. Transdisciplinarity integrates the natural, social and health sciences in a humanities context, and in doing so transcends each of their traditional boundaries". In this perspective, the work of a biodesigner resonates more with the definition of interdisciplinarity given by Choi and Pak since, in his/her training and design approach, the disciplines are no longer separated but used together in a new approach that synthesizes them into a "coherent whole". Furthermore, Biodesign is often associated with transdisciplinarity too (Goidea et al. 2022; Martini et al. 2013; Pschetz et al. 2022), working across disciplines, embracing complexity and systemic thinking, often triggered by societal or environmental issues. The general idea behind transdisciplinarity is that it rejects disciplinary separation into "silos" (Bernstein 2015; Choi and Pak 2006; Oxman 2016). Moreover, collaboration across diverse fields, including scientists, designers, citizens, companies, and governments, are known to create opportunities to tackle complex societal and environmental challenges. (Ozkaramanli, 2022)

All these definitions were useful for reasoning about the degree of disciplinary hybridization adopted by a biodesigner, and ultimately by the author during RTD. What emerges from the analysis of the RTDs is that different degrees of hybridization between disciplines lead to different design approaches and methods used, affecting the designer's practice.

The author's four RTD activities rely on the entanglement between design and science, but with different degrees of disciplinary hybridisation. As for the discussion and assessment of RTD quality, to better address the disciplinary variables of the RTDs the author proposes dedicated key parameters on the disciplinary entanglements in Biodesign, addressing the number of disciplines involved, the leading discipline, the ratio among the disciplines and the work environment, as clarified in the following table.

Through these four lenses, a more comprehensive discourse on how a Biodesigner might confront him/herself with other disciplines and how this might affect the design practice will be discussed, taking the four RTDs as case studies. The first parameter concerns the disciplines involved. In Biodesign, there are instances where design not only confronts biology, but also other scientific fields such as ecology, green chemistry or materials science. Moreover, the number of disciplines involved might include more than two disciplines or subdisciplines. Frayling (2015) defends the role of design in RTD projects in interdisciplinary contexts, highlighting that "design-led interdisciplinarity" is an essential aspect which empowers RTD projects[5]. Therefore, the second parameter reasons on the role of the leading discipline (whether it's design or not) and how this influences the project; this aspect helps to understand the contribution of design in Biodesign projects. The third param-

| DISCIPLINES INVOLVED | Number and name of disciplines involved in the project, including subfields |
|---|---|
| DISCIPLINE(S) LEADING THE PROJECT | The discipline that proposed the project, subsequently guiding and coordinating the work, acting as a connector among others |
| RATIO AMONG DISCIPLINES | The ratio between design and other disciplines, in reference to the number and background of the professionals involved in the project |
| WORK ENVIRONMENT | Where the project was conducted, and to which discipline the workspace belongs |

eter addresses the ratio between the designer and professional from other competencies. This ratio might particularly affect the designer's activity and knowledge on the subject: from self-taught knowledge to the need to have specific training before a confrontation; from being judged by an audience of experts in the same field to presenting hypotheses as a non-expert to an audience of experts in the scientific fields. The last parameter to reflect on disciplinary entanglements concerns the environment in which the project takes place, which can also empower the designer differently during his/her work, providing more sophisticated tools or defining the research activities according to more strict rules. This aspect can go so far as to define specific professional figures in the field of Biodesign, for instance by marking a difference between Biodesigners and Designers in Lab: the former work between design and science with an approach and setting closer to design, while the latter are designers who carry out their work mainly in a scientific laboratory; more keen on scientific rigour but also empowered by the lab machineries and equipment (Pollini, forthcoming).

As for quality parameters, the author also outlined disciplinary entanglements to critically reflect on the proposed RTDs, highlighting aspects that can enrich the discussion on the figure of the biodesigner and how she/he can operate in a variety of environments and team settings – from those known to the design practice to those most unrelated and unfamiliar. Here follows a brief discussion on the outlined disciplinary entanglement parameters in reference to the RTDs.

The first RTD, *biotinkering with Kombucha*, was born from confrontation in a working group composed mainly of researchers from the design field who, despite their different skills and backgrounds, come from the same discipline. Here, there is no doubt that design is the leading discipline; therefore, the ratio among disciplines is 1:0. This ratio does not mean that the designers did not adopt scientific approaches, methods, and tools. Still, it means there were no experts from scientific disciplines in the working group with whom to be confronted, and therefore the scientific approach adopted was mainly design-led.

The second RTD, *bioreceptivity for biomonitoring*, saw the author compose a small research group, in particular being confronted with a naturalist expert in lichenology. Here, the disciplines involved are primarily design (including subfields: bioreceptive design, biomimicry and computational design), lichenology and bryology. In this project, design is the discipline that guided and proposed the project from the beginning; while the scientific counterpart validated the project idea, further contributing to improving the design guidelines and enhancing the "reasonableness" of the project. Sometimes, collaborations between disciplines are not strictly defined nor always linear. For example, in this project, the two researchers' work was not carried out simultaneously but has been shaped by reiterative steps of dialogue and cross-validation among the two disciplines. The timing of the research was somehow divided between the two disciplines by the same nature of the project; in fact, the design dealt with the realization of the prototypes at first, while biology took charge of the second phase, which addresses treatment, exposure, and evaluation of bioreceptivity. We can say that design is the leading discipline in this RTD activity because it started (with a research proposal) and guided all project phases; however, the second phase of the project is guided by biology. This comparability between disciplines is also reflected in their 1:1 ratio. Also, with regard to the workplace, there was an equal distinction between the initial work of the designer (the author), which took place in the studio and in the modelling laboratories of the university of design, and the work of the lichenologist, who worked in scientific laboratories and botanical gardens.

The last two RTDs, *tinkering with silk-based materials* and *biofabricated edible electronics*, saw the author working in a scientific laboratory as the only designer present in the work environment (at least in the moment of her visiting period). In these RTDs, the ratio between the representative of the design discipline and the representatives of the scientific disciplines was no longer equivalent, settled at 1:X, where X indicates a variable number of colleagues belonging to disciplines other than design

– in the third RTD chemistry and material science, and in the fourth electronics and material science. For both these experiences, the author played the role of a Designer in Lab, working all the time in scientific laboratories; this had a strong impact on her design approach and on the design outcomes as well, which marked a clear distinction from the two previous RTDs. Here, the designer (author) found herself exploring new working environments with her own experience, being confronted with concepts, tools and languages that were new and not trivial to understand. She required specific additional training to work in the laboratories, and the amount of knowledge from other disciplines that she had to integrate to use appropriate tools and languages was more significant than in the first two RTD activities. One of the predominant differences to which a Designer in Lab is exposed is given by the discovery of new techniques and material processing given by the machinery found in the laboratory. Looked at from the (inexpert) eye of a designer, this work setting can give rise to new experiments which might not even be imaginable if one remains in the field of design alone. This empowerment is not without compromises; in fact, these new design possibilities must take place within the rigour of the scientific method, which can sometimes be perceived as limiting the more creative activities in the tinkering and biotinkering phases. Therefore, a new mindset capable of balancing rigour and creativity must be found in this context, so as not to give up the credibility and potential of the project or the designer's freedom and mindset.

Considering both quality parameters and disciplinary entanglements, a sort of "ID card" for the evaluation and discussion of Biodesign RTDs has been proposed (Pollini 2023). Aiming to facilitate a discussion format, these parameters can be used to draw a sort of project ID card addressing the quality, peculiarities, and impact of RTD in Biodesign. The author further tested this project ID card to assess her own RTD projects.

## *Bioreceptivity for Biomonitoring*

Ratio among disciplines 1:1

Design ◄———————————► Science

### RTDs QUALITY INDICATORS

| | |
|---|---|
| REPLICABILITY | Experiments are replicable; however, it is necessary to consider a strong natural component that determines non-linear results and different colonization outcomes. |
| REASONABLENESS | The choices underlying the various experiments are always motivated by methodologies and/or research questions that have detailed the project in its development. |
| CREDIBILITY | The project has internal validation between disciplines (e.g., the biodesign hypotheses are evaluated by the lichenologist). Furthermore, the project was presented at the 34th Conference of the Italian Lichenological Society (Pollini et al., 2022), which allowed it to be validated and receive further feedback from a wider audience of experts. |
| CONTEXTUALIZATION | The contextualization of the project is clear: the research arises from an intersection between design and biology. The implications and applications of the project may involve both of these disciplines; repercussions in the field of architecture and citizen science are also possible. |
| TRANSFERABILITY AND IMPACT | The project generated new knowledge in design and lichenology. Such knowledge can be applied to enhance biomonitoring activities, and to create interiors and architectural applications able to increase biophilia, bioremediation, and biodiversity through regenerative processes. |

### DISCIPLINARY ENTANGLEMENT

| | |
|---|---|
| DISCIPLINES INVOLVED | The main disciplines involved are design and biology. Subfileds in design have been: bioreceptive design, biomimicry and computational design. Subfield in biology have been lichenology and bryology. |
| DISCIPLINE LEADING THE PROJECT | The project proposal was conceived by the designer and validated (also through the acceptance of the collaboration) by the biologist. Design is always informed and guided by biology, but it remains the driving discipline in the project for design concepts and prototypes realization. |
| RATIO AMONG DISCIPLINES | The ratio among design and biology is 1:1 |
| WORK ENVIRONMENT | Mixed work environment. The first part of the project, more related to design and prototyping, took place in the design university's laboratories and in the designer's studio. Team discussions and brainstorming took place virtually and in university offices. The second part of the project, more related to bioreceptivity assessment, takes place in scientific labs and botanical gardens. |

*Fig. 5* Example of ID evaluation grid for Biodesign RTD, based on quality and disciplinary entanglement parameters. The second RTD proposed by the author (Bioreceptivity for biomonitoring) is discussed here, giving an example of how the format is used.

# CONCLUSIONS

Designers are lifelong learners; this aptitude is essential and continuous, especially for hybrid professionals such as biodesigners. The unique knowledge generation upon which RTD relies, created through an intuitive and unique approach to practice, can also be advantageous for testing novel concepts in scientific domains, becoming key in Biodesign.

An in-depth analysis of the four RTDs helped better define different nuances in Biodesign; here, the autoethnographic investigation supported new knowledge from the designer's unique point of view. Parameters of quality and disciplinary entanglements were addressed from the author's self-reflection and self-criticism, manifesting themselves in more rational reasoning tools to objectify a personal point of view and draw more structured qualitative analyses. Within the author's doctoral research, RTDs not only served the general purpose of testing theoretical concepts, tools, and methods that emerged from the PhD path, but they also opened new research lines in different fields, becoming a fertile ground for creating new connections among disciplines and institutions that might contribute to generating feasible, innovative, and sustainable solutions. This study shows how experiential knowledge in design can simultaneously generate applied and theoretical research; the latter can especially benefit from autoethnography and the first-person perspective, becoming a pivotal tool, especially in emerging and hybrid fields with fewer well-established references in the literature.

## ENDNOTES

1. An in-depth analysis of the projects can be found in the research-through-design section of the Healing Materialities website where part of the doctoral research is shared. Retrieved in April 2024 from: healing-materialities.design
2. Silklab is pioneering the use of silk fibroin as a material platform for advanced technology and global health applications. Retrieved in December 2023 from: https://silklab.engineering.tufts.edu
3. ElFo is a research group leading the field of edible electronics, a sector close to organic electronics but with the additional challenge of using edible materials for electronic applications. Retrieved in December 2023 from: https://elfoproject.eu
4. It is important to underline that the diagram represents the methodologies adopted by the author during the design phases of the projects. Therefore, this analysis is already the result of an autoethnographic observation and should not be considered the norm in Biodesign, but rather a first-person-perspective insight.
5. RTD 2015 Provocation by Sir Christopher Frayling Part 2: Designers as Knowledge Generators. Film by Abigail Durrant and James Price for Research through Design (RTD) 2015 Conference © 2015 Assessed on 25/01/2024 from: file:///C:/Users/reall/Zotero/storage/V4ZZ7AF6/129776561.html

## REFERENCES

Ayala Garcia, C. and Rognoli, V. (2017). The New Aesthetic of DIY-Materials. *The Design Journal 20*, 375–389.

Bernstein, J. (2015). Transdisciplinarity: A Review of Its Origins, Development, and Current Issues. *Journal of Research Practice, 11*.

Bochner, A. (2017). Heart of the Matter: A Mini-Manifesto for Autoethnography. *International Review of Qualitative Research, 10*, 67–80.

Archer, B. (1995). *The Nature of Research.* Co-Design. http://archive.org/details/TheNatureOfResearch

Choi, B. C. K. and Pak, A. W. P. (2006). Multidisciplinarity, interdisciplinarity and transdisciplinarity in health research, services, education and policy: 1. Definitions, objectives, and evidence of effectiveness. *Clinical and Investigative Medicine. Medecine Clinique Et Experimentale, 29*(6), 351–364.

Contardo, T., Giordani, P., Paoli, L., Vannini, A. and Loppi, S. (2018). May lichen biomonitoring of air pollution be used for environmental justice assessment? A case study from an area of N Italy with a municipal solid waste incinerator. *Environmental Forensics, 19*, 1–12.

Forlano, L. (2021). Dispatches on Humanity from a Disabled Cyborg. *Diid — Disegno Industriale Industrial Design, 75*, Article 75.

Frayling, C. (1993). *Research in art and design.* RCA Research Papers 1, no. 1. Royal College of Art, London.

Ginsberg, A. D. and Chieza, N. (2018). Editorial: Other Biological Futures. *Journal of Design and Science.*

Goidea, A., Floudas, D. and Andréen, D. (2022). Transcalar Design: An Approach to Biodesign in the Built Environment. *Infrastructures, 7*(4), Article 4.

Höök, K., Caramiaux, B., Erkut, C., Forlizzi, J., Hajinejad, N., Haller, M., Hummels, C. C. M., Isbister, K., Jonsson, M., Khut, G., Loke, L., Lottridge, D., Marti, P., Melcer, E., Müller, F. F., Petersen, M. G., Schiphorst, T., Segura, E. M., Ståhl, A., ... Tobiasson, H. (2018). Embracing First-Person Perspectives in Soma-Based Design. *Informatics*, *5*(1), Article 1.

Jones, S. H. (2013). *Handbook of Autoethnography* (1° edizione). Routledge.

Karana, E., Hekkert, P. and Kandachar, P. (2008). Materials experience: Descriptive categories in materials appraisals. *Proceedings of the Seventh International Symposium on Tools and Methods of Competitive Engineering -TMCE 2008*, 1–15.

Kirk, R. E. (2013). *Experimental design: Procedures for the behavioral sciences.* Thousand Oaks, CA: Sage.

Langella, C. (2019). *Design & scienza*. Listlab.

Martini, D., Loddo, I. and Coscia, M. (2013). Managing complexity in Bio-design practice. *2CO Communicating Complexity: 2013 Conference Proceedings*, 117-126.

McComb, C. and Jablokow, K. (2022). A conceptual framework for multidisciplinary design research with example application to agent-based modeling. *Design Studies*, *78*, 101074.

Méndez, M. (2013). Autoethnography as a re-search method: Advantages, limitations and criticisms. *Colombian Applied Linguistics Journal*, *15*(2), 279–287.

Mincolelli, G., Marchi, M., Imbesi, S. and Giacobone, G. A. (2020). Prototype-Driven Design in the IoT Age. *Design 2030: Practice*, *72/2020*, 88–95.

Myers, W. (2012). *Bio design: Nature, science, creativity* (p. 288). Museum of Modern Art.

Nimkulrat, N. (2022). Crafting Novel Knotted Textiles with Mathematics. *The Textile Museum Journal*, 28–49.

Nimkulrat, N., Groth, C., Tomico, O. and Valle-Noronha, J. (2020). Knowing together – experiential knowledge and collaboration. *CoDesign*, *16*(4), 267–273.

Oxman, N. (2016). Age of Entanglement. *Journal of Design and Science*.

Oxman, N., Antonelli, P. and Burckhardt, A. (2020). *Neri Oxman: Material Ecology*. Museum of Modern Art.

Ozkaramanli, D., Zaga, C., Cila, N., Visscher, K., and van der Voort, M. (2022). *Design Methods and Transdisciplinary Practices*, in Lockton, D., Lenzi, S., Hekkert, P., Oak, A., Sádaba, J., Lloyd, P. (Eds.), DRS2022: Bilbao, 25 June - 3 July, Bilbao, Spain.

Parisi, S., Rognoli, V. and Sonneveld, M. (2017). Material Tinkering. An inspirational approach for experiential learning and envisioning in product design education. *Design Journal, The*, *20*, 1167-S1184.

Pedgley, O., Rognoli, V. and Karana, E. (2021). *Materials Experience 2: Expanding Territories of Materials and Design*. Butterworth-Heinemann.

Pollini, B. (accepted, foreseen 2024). From Biodesigners to designers-in-lab: testing the nuances of an emerging profession through autoethnography. Biocalibrated: tools and techniques for biodesign practices. Journal Research Directions: Biotechnology Design 'Bio-calibrated: tools and techniques of biodesign practices', Cambridge University Press.

Pollini, B. (2023). *Healing materialities from a biodesign perspective: Framing biodesigned materials and artefacts for the sustainability transition* [Politecnico di Milano]. https://www.politesi.polimi.it/handle/10589/207590

Pollini, B., Contardo, T., Paciotti, D. and Rognoli, V. (2023). Bioreceptive interfaces for biophilic urban resilience. *Nature Positive/Design for Transformation*. Cumulus Antwerp 2023.

Pollini, B., Contardo, T. and Paciotti, D. (2022). Designing Bioreceptivity. 34th Conference of the Italian Lichenological Society (SLI), Pavia.

Pollini, B. and Maccagnan, F. (2017). Thinking with our hands. *Renewable Matter*, 49–52. Edizioni Ambiente.

Pollini, B. and Rognoli, V. (2021). Enhancing living/non-living relationship trough de-signed materials. *CEES 2021, International Conference Construction, Energy, Environment & Sustainability*. Responsible Biotechnologies And Biodesign For The Built Environment, Coimbra, Portugal.

Prochner, I. and Godin, D. (2022). Quality in research through design projects: Recommendations for evaluation and enhancement. *Design Studies*, *78*, 101061.

Pschetz, L., Ramirez-Figueroa, C. and Revans, J. (2022). Learning from creative biology: Promoting transdisciplinarity through vocabularies of practice. *DRS Biennial Conference Series*. https://dl.designresearchsociety.org/drs-conference-papers/drs2022/researchpapers/62

Redström, J. (2017). *Making Design Theory*. MIT Press.

Rognoli, V. (2010). A Broad Survey on Expressive-sensorial Characterization of Materials for Design Education. *Middle East Technical University Journal of the Faculty of Architecture*, *27*.

Rognoli V., Ayala-Garcia C., Pollini B. (2021). DIY Recipes. Ingredients, Processes and Materials Qualities. Chapter in: Clèries L., Rognoli V., Solanki S. e Llorach P. (Eds.), "Material Designers. Boosting talent towards circular economies", Elisava School of Design and Engineering, Barcelona.

Rognoli, V. and Levi, M. (2011). *Il senso dei materiali per il design*. Franco Angeli.

Rognoli, V., Pollini, B. and Alessandrini, L. (2021). Design materials for the transition towards post-Anthropocene. In From Human-Centered To More-Than-Human Design, Exploring the transition; edited by Barbara Camocini and Francesco Vergani. (pp. 101–130). Franco Angeli.

Sawa, M. (2016). The laboratory life of a designer at the intersection with algal biotechnology. *Arq: Architectural Research Quarterly*, *20*(1), 65–72.

Stefanova, A. (2021). Practices in Bio-design: Design Research Through Interdisciplinary Collaboration. In A. Chakrabarti, R. Poovaiah, P. Bokil and V. Kant (Eds.), *Design for Tomorrow—Volume 3* (pp. 41–52). Springer.

Świsłowski, P., Vergel, K., Zinicovscaia, I., Rajfur, M. and Wacławek, M. (2022). Mosses as a biomonitor to identify elements released into the air as a result of car workshop activities. *Ecological Indicators*, *138*, 108849.

Tomico, O., Wakkary, R. and Andersen, K. (2023). Living-with and Designing-with Plants. *Interactions*, *30*, 30–34.

# Vitality of Salt:

Julia Ziener

## A Methodology for Exploring Vibrant Materiality

# INTRODUCTION

Salt is one of the oldest and most crucial chemical substances known to mankind. Often invisible yet unmistakable in taste, it poses an elixir of life and a threat to it. The enormous quantity of salt that is accumulated as an industrial residue unites two locations in Saxony-Anhalt: 10 million tons of sodium chloride per year in Zielitz (K+S Corporation 2023) and 506,000 tons of calcium chloride per year in Bernburg (Ministry of Science, Energy, Climate Protection, and Environment 2022). It is incredible that the vast salt mountains and Caribbean-looking lime ponds found at these two sites are considered mere waste when salt was once regarded as "white gold". The accumulation of it and the transformation of the landscape have significant consequences for the present as well as future ecology. The ramifications of the temporal, spatial, and material expansion of the 130 years of soda production in Bernburg or the 50 years of potash mining in Zielitz are unfathomable. In rivers adjacent to these industrial areas the measured chloride concentrations far exceed the limit for healthy watercourses, according to the federal regulation for the protection of surface waters (Ibid.). Yet, at the end of 2022, the State Administration Office of Saxony-Anhalt extended its permission to a local company to continue discharging the chloride-rich wastewater of their soda production into the River Bode for another eight years (State Administration Office of Saxony-Anhalt 2022).

Based on these examples, it becomes imperative to question whether we should continue to treat industrial residues like salt as inert materials. The effects of high salt concentrations in rivers represent unwanted side effects of an industrial and economic network that treats material as dead matter. The current handling of the salt waste is based on a dichotomy that distinguishes between "dull matter" and "vibrant life" (Bennett 2010, xii).

The philosophical movement of New Materialism challenges this traditional understanding of matter, emphasising that matter is not passive but entails active processes which interact with other entities to shape complex phenomena. While the abstract concepts of New Materialism often remain theoretical, this work aims to provide practical approaches. By adapting the theory for artistic research, the gap between discourse and practice regarding the development of material concepts (Heibach and Rohde 2015) is addressed, establishing a tangible methodology for exploring vital materiality. The specificity of this research lies in the combination of the abstract theory and its application to waste material on two local industrial sites, leading to its critical verification. Thus, this research proposes that salt is a vital entity in an assemblage of diverse actors, rather than simply an inert waste product. This project demonstrates that artistic research affords the methodological freedom essential for developing ontological perspectives on the relationship between humans and materials.

## NEW MATERIALISM:
## THE THEORETICAL APPROACH AND ITS CHALLENGES

In recent decades, a discourse on the role and significance of material and material phenomena has developed across various disciplines, which can be summarised under the philosophical approach of New Materialism (Witzgall 2014). New Materialism no longer distinguishes between human agency and the independent agency of material (Garske 2014). Thus, all agents are considered equal, regardless of their animate or inanimate nature. At the core intention of New Materialism lies the exploration and recognition of the potential and agency of material, regarding it as a vital entity while considering its role as an actor in cultural networks (Heibach and Rohde 2015). The American political scientist and philosopher Jane Bennett takes a leading perspective in the New Materialism discourse by formulating the concept of *vital materialism*, assuming an inherent vitality in material (Bennett 2010). Her vital materialism stands out from other formulations of New Materialism by drawing inspiration from the natural sciences and biology, making it particularly relevant and effective for exploring the active and vital qualities of an industrial residue like salt. Her theory allows for the exploration of industrial residues and their dynamic qualities beyond their industrial contexts.

However, a crucial criticism of New Materialism is the difficulty of applying its abstract concepts to practical empirical research (Filion-Donato 2021). The intricacy underlying such a practical implementation is to explore the material's vitality phenomenologically without the researching human taking the central role. This challenge is precisely what the present research addresses, shifting the focus from analysing salt as a "thing" to exploring its vitality as a "phenomenon" (Ibid.). The concern discussed in the New Materialism discourse can also be found in Bennett's treatise: To perceive and acknowledge a phenomenon – the vitality of material – that eludes our human horizon. According to Bennett, phenomenology inherently poses a problem due to its reliance on subjective human perception and intention (Bennett 2010). Consequently, Bennett repudiates the phenomenological approach, yet she does not propose an alternative methodology to circumvent the predicament associated with subjective perception. This absence of a resolution arguably constitutes a significant vulnerability within the theoretical framework she articulates. Bennett sums up this seemingly impossible endeavour as follows: "I will try impossibly to name the moment of independence (from subjectivity) possessed by things, a moment that must be there since things do in fact affect other bodies, enhancing or weakening their power" (Ibid., 3).

## ARTISTIC RESEARCH AS REALM TO EXPLORE VITALITY

Artistic research as "an openness to experience the unknown, or the impossible" (Busch 2009, 6) provides a viable form for addressing this impossible endeavour while transferring the theory of vital materialism into practice. It is "art as research", whereby art itself becomes the research, turning scientific processes or conclusions into tools of art (ibid., 3). An important characteristic of artistic research is that the object of research is still unexplored and findings about it cannot yet be reduced to concepts (Ibid.). At the same time, philosopher Clive Cazeaux emphasises the necessity of formulating these very terms or concepts, as only through them can the transformation of sensory experiences into epistemological insights be achieved. He regards these concepts, within the context of artistic research, as a "foothold that enables the leap" (Cazeaux 2017, 74). This ambivalence highlights the complexity of the research endeavour at hand, because it implies that solely experiencing the vital materiality is insufficient for rendering it tangible and subsequently converting it into knowledge. Rather, the preliminary conceptualisation of attributes of vitality is essential for its understanding and systematic categorisation. Jane Bennett's theory of vital materialism is a constitutive element of artistic research. From her theory, I have derived and formulated three important attributes as concepts for the inherent vitality of material. These are *the tendency to persist, the tendency of assemblage,* and *the tendency of efficacy*. The tendency to persist can be understood as a sort of inherent obstinacy of the material. This "negative power or recalcitrance of things" (Bennett 2010, 1), which Bennett also calls "thing-power" (Ibid., 2), describes the ability of a material to detach itself from any anthropocentric and value-laden contexts. It is a kind of inner impulse that encourages ongoing existence. The tendency of assemblage is described as the striving to "conglomerate or form heterogeneous groupings" (Ibid., xvii) since every agent also acts in assemblages. The inherent power to create something new (Ibid.), the tendency of efficacy, I formulate as the third characteristic of a material's vitality.

    Salt, as the material under investigation, is examined after each research step for one of these attributes. I have designed a three-stage research process to realise this objective. It consists of: 1. field trips, which provide an initial approach to the material; 2. the *contextualisation* of the salt; and 3. a subsequent *recontex-*

*tualisation* of the material. The transdisciplinary characteristics of both New Materialism and artistic research are reflected in the methodology as it is specifically shaped by the principle of "Be a stranger" (Vis 2021, 85) in different disciplines; and approaching these disciplines and the phenomenon under investigation with a certain "Capacity for naiveté" (Bennett 2010, 18). This combination relies on intuition and opens up new perspectives that are not tied to the ostensibly obvious stances of scientists or conventional practitioners (Vis 2021).

## EXPLORATION OF TWO INDUSTRIAL SITES: EXOTICISM IN LOCALITY

In the first step of the practical implementation, the agency of salt is explored by observing the transformed landscapes and the surrounding urban space. Two field trips to the locations of Zielitz and Bernburg offered the necessary approach to the material and a basis for the contextualisation of the salt in its natural and social space. The photographic documentation captures the immersive experience. The approach is characterised by an "anticipatory readiness" (Bennett 2010, 5) to enter the place of the unknown. Thus, this method is fueled by the openness to explore the unknown and the perspective "of looking always at what is to be seen" (Ibid.).

*27.06.2023 Berlin Friedrichstraße RE7 to Dessau*[1]

*The route to my former home. The place where I began to intensely engage with material during my studies. And it is once again the material that leads me on this journey. From Dessau onwards to Bernburg. Here, I meet with a manager of the soda production company. He picks me up from the station promptly at noon. Together we head towards Latdorf to the lime ponds. In the staff house next to the lime ponds, I am informed about the lime ponds' functions, raw materials, and the company. The oldest lime pond was created with the onset of soda production 130 years ago in Latdorf. During our conversation, I was introduced to two employees responsible for the maintenance of the lime ponds. They work in shifts here. One of them had already sent me material samples by mail. The employees, as well as the manager, were visibly pleased that someone was interested in the worthless waste materials. 'Now, one just needs to make something out of it,' one of them declared. I was surprised by the openness with which I was met and the appreciation for my work despite my lack of chemistry knowledge. Afterwards, we drove up the steep slope of the lime ponds by car. Before I had reached the top, I had no idea what to expect. From below, the lime ponds resemble the step-like construction of vineyards, because a previously dried-up lime pond serves as the base for the following one. Upon reaching the lime pond, I was astounded by what I saw. I thought of Bennett's mentioned attitude of always being surprised by what comes into view. With this anticipatory readiness to encounter the material, I did not perceive it as worthless residue but as a delightful landscape. Turquoise water was surrounded by sand-like material. Was it the material that affected me, or the associations triggered by the material? I couldn't believe I was in Saxony-Anhalt.*

## HISTORICAL ANCHORING

In my research of the two industrial regions, I have uncovered their historically deep-rooted connection to salt production. Archaeological excavations of salt boiling tools, known as *briquetage*, date the brine salt production in the region back to the Neolithic Bernburg Culture, in approximately 3100–2560 BC (Museum of Prehistory and Early History Berlin 2020). Given this significant cultural anchoring, I could no longer view the salt produced at these sites as mere industrial residue. I contacted the Museum of Prehistory and Early History Berlin and the Museum Schloss Bernburg to gain access to these historical artefacts which are dated to the 8th–5th century BC (Ibid.). As a means of approaching and investigating the artefact, the 3D scan serves as the primary tool. In this step, I merge 3D scanning technology with archaeology, bringing the physical into the virtual realm. For this purpose, I work with the application Polycam, which enables 3D object capture using photogrammetry.

*26.07.2023 Bernburg, Archive of Museum Schloss Bernburg*

*After a friendly welcome, I was granted access to the museum's archive. I start with the 3D scanning of one of the historical artefacts. Holding this object in my hands, knowing that the material which it is made of was shaped by the hands of my ancestors over 2500 years ago, gives me a peculiar feeling. In some places, one might even presume a fingerprint imprint in the material. This tool is a sophisticated technology to access a specific material – salt. It provides insights into the role of salt and its deep cultural roots. It reveals the abilities and aspirations salt evoked in people, manifested as the salt-boiling tool in my hands. Is it the 'thing-power' of the briquetage affecting me here? The location of this archive seems to be brimming with thing power. The countless objects act on me as if they desperately want to tell a story; their story. As if a thousand voices are trying to convey their experiences to me all at once. Only occasionally do I discover an object that prefers to remain silent. Its story wants to be kept to itself, showing resistance to my interest; in other words, presenting itself in its tendency to persist. Interestingly, it is precisely these objects and materials that seem most vital to me, because they fit least well into a context projected by me onto them. They resist me. Or is it just the mysterious appearance of these objects that trigger associative narratives in my memory? How can I know if it is actually the vitality of the material that is affecting me?*

*Fig. 1.* Salt heap in Zielitz, Saxony-Anhalt, Germany.

*Fig. 2.* Field Trip to Zielitz: Approaching the salt heap and exploring the environment.

## SALT AS DESIGN AGENT

The examined artefact and the brine salt production and trade it is associated with, unveil the salt as a vital actor in a cultural network. Although it takes on the role of raw material and cannot be viewed independently of its anthropocentric context, it exerts an enormous inherent force. The salt has facilitated the development of a specific boiling technology, thereby catalysing the invention of a specialized tool. It may be an appropriate argument that humans have developed the tool from an intentional endeavor. But it is not a one-sided process where one actor subjugates another (Stiegler 2009). Rather, it is an interaction in which the salt is actively involved in the design and production process of the briquetage, significantly influencing its shape and functionality, accentuating the creative force of salt. Philosopher Bernard Stiegler emphasises such an entanglement of humans and material, arguing that material interactions contribute significantly to human reflection (Ibid.). The materiality of the briquetage thus acts as a manifestation of the need for salt and archives the technology of salt boiling within the object. The briquetage therefore facilitates our knowledge about the technology and social life of that time, a concept described by Lambros Malafouris and Colin Renfrew as the "Cognitive Life of Things" (Malafouris and Renfrew 2010, 3). It highlights the inseparable connection between cultural evolution and material engagement, thus demonstrating the vital power of salt as an actor in a cultural network and simultaneously proving its *tendency of efficacy* to create something new.

The briquetage takes on a multifunctional role in the research process. It becomes the object of investigation, as it provides insights into salt as an actor in cultural practice. Simultaneously it functions as a research tool for exploring the vitality of salt as a phenomenon. This aspect is essential for the present artistic research, as conventional research and measuring instruments are questioned, and there are no established tools and methods for researching the vitality of materials yet. In the sense of vital materialism, every tool, object, or material involved in the (artistic) process represents a "macro- and microactant" (Bennett 2010, 23) and is a vital part of the assemblage significantly involved in the generation of knowledge, as is the briquetage. By digitising the briquetage using 3D scanning, it is no longer only stored in the inaccessible archaeological archive but is made globally available as an open-source object. This digitised artefact embodies not only the connection between historical and contemporary technology: it also opens a reflection on the concept of materiality for future technologies. Through the digital reconstruction of the briquetage, not only is the physical substance of the artefact digitised, but also its historical and cultural contexts. This linkage demonstrates how materiality is transformed over time and simultaneously acts as a vital actor, adopting new meanings in changing social and technological contexts.

## ECOLOGICAL ASSESSMENT

After analysing salt as a cultural-network actor in pre-industrial times, the focus shifts to the role of salt as a residue in today's industrial and ecological fabric. At both industrial sites, in Zielitz and Bernburg, direct and indirect discharges of saline wastewater are dumped into the surrounding water network. The ecological state of the affected flowing waters is almost exclusively rated as poor (State Agency for Flood Protection and Water Management Saxony-Anhalt n.d.). In this conflict of interests, salt no longer represents a valuable raw material but rather an excess substance with high disposal costs. To explore the effects of salt discharges and their vitality, I conduct on-site research using several chemical and geoscientific methods. The investigation of the ecological condition and thus the examination of the salt's impact and agency is based on water sampling of the adjacent flowing waters, as well as soil sampling of the surrounding areas. This is followed by determining the samples' salt content by measuring the concentration of chloride ions. The chemical analyses are carried out directly at the respective

*Fig. 3.* In-situ laboratory by the River Bode, testing the salt concentration in soil and water.

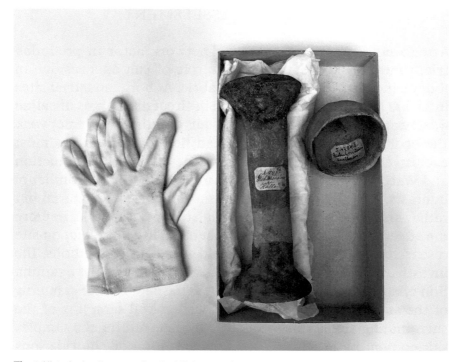

*Fig. 4.* Historical salt evaporation tool (briquetage).

measuring stations, including me as a researcher into the local landscape. This offers a particular advantage over laboratory research, as I experience the fluid assemblages of the place in that specific moment with a "sensitive attentiveness to the qualitative singularities of the object" (Bennett 2010, 15) and even become part of them. This investigation is captured on film, making the documentation a part of the artistic research.

*30.08.2023 Field Trip to the Waters*

*Once again I set off to the region, which is now familiar to me. The previously invisible lines of connection are taking on more colour, drawing a complex three-dimensional network defined by a cultural, economic, and ecological axis. This network positions salt as a vital body vector – like in that space. The position and spread of it are neither final nor clear. Once more, I find myself in a place of uncertainty: How suitable will the sites be for sample collection? What peculiarities will they bring, and what will the tests show? 11:00 am, Zielitz, Ramstedter Mühlengraben. In front of the gigantic mountain, a small body of water. Except from the form of the mighty elevation in the landscape, the salt is not visible. Yet, something seems unusual in this landscape. It's the small salt plants I know from the North Sea – Sea asparagus from Saxony-Anhalt. Behind me and the water: Danger to life. At least, that's what the sign says. Danger to life by what and for whom? How can this danger end at the fence? The high salt concentration poses a threat to many non-human actors outside the fence. There stands the mountain in its cage, like a wild animal seemingly dangerous to humans, and we do not know how to tame it. I begin taking samples. The journey continues to the next measuring station. 1:30 pm, Neue Bodebrücke in Neugattersleben. The same procedure. Moving towards Bernburg near the lime ponds. 3:00 pm, the banks of the Saale in Bernburg. After taking another sample, I begin the chemical tests. Setting up the experiment reminds me of en plein air painting, where one is exposed to natural conditions. Working outdoors is reflected in the artwork, as it is in my tests. The wind, the water temperature, the air humidity, and countless other actors form an assemblage with me and influence the field research.*

## SALT AS AGENT IN SPATIAL ASSEMBLAGES

The conducted field research indicates salt concentrations up to over 3000 mg/l. The observation of halophytes like salicornia (sea asparagus) as resident plants further highlights the impact of salt on the landscape and proves its agency. These results and the embedding of salt in the current environmental debate about discharging wastewater show salt as part of an assemblage with tangible environmental and ecological consequences. The vital force of this assemblage is not merely the sum of the forces exerted by individual agents but rather a distinct force emergent from the assemblage itself (Bennett 2010). According to Bennett, this precludes predicting effects arising from the assemblage. Consequently, "events" (Ibid., 27) such as fish mortality, precipitated by the direct impact of salt on reproduction (Ministry of Science, Energy, Climate Protection, and Environment 2022), can never be predetermined. If the actions of a single agent are not the cause of the outcome, then no one can be held responsible for the effects of the salt discharges on the environment. Bennett posits that the cause of an event can only be identified after it has taken place (Bennett 2010). Regarding the political handling of environmental impacts, this aspect of the theory seems problematic and raises the question of responsibility. This example presents the issue of responsibility from the relational perspective of vital and New Materialism (Filion-Donato 2021).

Analysing the used methodology, not only the exploration of the briquetage but also the conducted field research shows parallels to archaeology. The peculiarity of the archaeological act lies in the active engagement with the physical world (Renfrew

2017). In attempting to explore the vitality of salt in and around the affected waters, I also engage in active interaction with the physical world. I enter a place of uncertainty, an "intermediary zone" (Busch 2009, 6). The incorporation of scientific methods and the simultaneous unpredictability of factors and actors involved bridge Bennett's vital materialism, "to remain scientific while acknowledging some incalculability to things (...)." (Bennett 2010, 63), thus manifesting in the research. Conducting the tests not only produces critical knowledge about the current handling of salt but also has a performative character. The application of scientific methods to the artistic context in situ leads to an unfamiliar aesthetic in the use of familiar instruments and measurement techniques, which allows for a new and expanded perspective on the subject.

## MERGING NEW AND OLD TECHNOLOGY

In the third research step, insights from the historical anchoring and the analysis of salt as an actor within an ecological assemblage of the current state are fused together in a performative act. The recontextualisation addresses the deconstruction of anthropocentric categorization and envisages an examination of salt detached from a human-centric context. It consists of two parts: 1. The replication of the historical evaporation tool and its transformation into a research tool. 2. The physical extraction of the discharged salt as a residue and the associated metaphorical extraction of the material from its industrial context.

Using the data from the digitised briquetage, I replicate the historical tool. For the replication, I use ceramic 3D printing, linking the ancient technology of the briquetage with the contemporary fabrication technology of additive manufacturing. The thorough preparation of the material for ceramic printing is essential. The crucial difference from conventional 3D printing with materials such as PLA or ABS lies in the material's consistency. Stoneware is a wet-processed material, which means one extrudes the entire object along a continuous path. That implies restrictions regarding the geometry of the object. Each layer is dependent on the previous layer and can only have overhangs to a limited extent. The handling of the clay accentuates the necessity of integrating the material into the design process and speaks for its agency.

*11.08.2023 Ceramic Workshop UdK Straße des 17. Juni*

*In the ceramic workshop. I spread the clay on a granite slab with a spatula. The air that has been kneaded in has to be smoothed out. Air pockets in the clay spell doom for the artefact. The trapped air would expand during the firing process and cause the clay to burst. I go through this repetitive process for almost three hours. Painstaking work. My arms start to ache. The material, or rather the union of stoneware and air, demands a very specific manner of interaction – through its agency of assemblage, it evokes a certain action in me. I literally immerse my hands in the material. Craftsmanship, which is based on material involvement, rarely negates the vitality of the material. I think of the miners in Zielitz who develop a special relationship with the material they work with. I do not wish to compare my physical engagement with clay to the hard labour in the mines, yet I believe I understand how the vitality of material becomes particularly noticeable in the physical interaction and intimacy with the material. I would describe craft as the art of dealing with the vitality of material. This is precisely what I feel in this very act of repeating, of adapting to the material. I can smooth the mass meticulously and repeat this process several times, but I never know for sure if air remains in the material and how it will behave in the firing process. What effect the creative conative force of the assemblage will produce at the moment of firing is something I cannot predict. This uncontrollability, this agency of the material, makes the act in the ceramic workshop, the act of material involvement, so interesting.*

*Fig. 5.* 3D scan of the historical salt evaporation tool (briquetage).

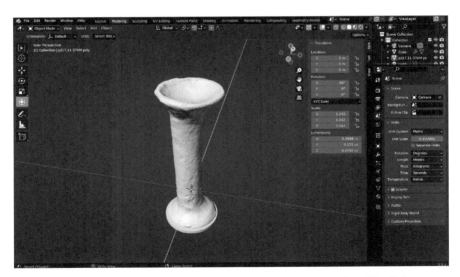

*Fig. 6.* Refining the 3D model of the briquetage scan in Blender, preparing it for 3D printing.

*Fig. 7.* 3D printing the stele of the briquetage using a Delta WASP 2040 Clay printer.

*Fig. 8.* 3D printing the crucible.

The added value of using ceramic 3D printing lies in pairing clay as "one of the earliest truly neurocompatible materials in the history of humanity" (Malafouris 2008, 22) with contemporary digital fabrication technology. As I can confirm through my physical engagement with the clay, the material demands a certain interaction. These interactions manifest as "intentions in actions" (Ibid., 28), emphasising the material's agency and the constant interplay during the design process. Printing the briquetage illustrates the complex ecology of interactions between different actors, such as rheological properties, the flow rate from the extrusion nozzle, or the material's curing speed (Sutjipto et al. 2019). As Malafouris rightly observes, no single actor can be identified as the sole bearer of agency (Malafouris 2008). This assumption aligns with Bennett's mentioned conative force of an assemblage, which manifests as a distributive agency (Bennett 2010). Bennett's theoretical point can therefore be confirmed by the practical replication of the briquetage.

Through physical interaction with the material, I'm faced with the challenge defined at the outset: To perceive a phenomenon that eludes our human horizon and to explore it phenomenologically, yet to not assume the central role of a researching human. According to Malafouris, material involvement is the reason for the futile attempts to determine agency objectively; however, it also allows us the immersive and sensory (subjective) experience of our environment (Malafouris 2008). My experiences during the process prove that it is impossible to free oneself from the subjective perspective and to view the material detached from any human context. However, the act of pottery-making renders the distributive agency of the assemblage, which also includes me, palpable. Thus, this act carries essential insights for a methodology of exploring the vitality of material. Material involvement plays a crucial role in the exploration of its vitality.

The crafting act of replicating the briquetage reveals another insight. By reproducing the briquetage with additive manufacturing, a path is 3D-printed based on the original form from 8–5 B.C. (Museum of Prehistory and Early History 2020).

This externalises the thought process: The Material Engagement Theory states that thinking and knowledge manifest in material actions (Renfrew 2017). Therefore the act of pottery making is a form of externalising knowledge and creativity. Thus, the potted briquetage is the externalised knowledge of previous people about salt boiling and its technology. In other words, it is the archive of this ancient technology. With the 3D printing of the briquetage, I connect the knowledge of ancient technology with today's technology. This sheds light on the entanglement of technology and materiality and raises the question of the involvement of materials in future technology development. Recognising the impact of material practices on the development of technology forms an essential approach for future concepts of materiality.

## Extraction as Performative Act

In the next step, the replicated briquetage is used to extract the salt, which is industrially discharged into the rivers. Upon revisiting the monitoring sites, I draw water from the stream and pour it into the crucible of the briquetage. Here, it is heated by fire, and the salt is precipitated. I document this process, which lasts several hours, on film.

*Fig. 9.* Boiling process: Briquetage with water from the River Bode.

*Fig. 10.* Used briquetage after the boiling process, with extracted salt.

*31.08.2023 Banks of the Bode River*

*Now I hold the briquetage in my hand, with the same indentations and notches as the original. I am eager to see if the tool, as an archive of its function, can be revived. The fire burns, the small crucible catches little water. I wonder how much salt will remain. I know the salt concentrations are enormous, but what will actually be visible? It takes a while before I can see a change. The water in the briquetage begins to move in slow, circular swirls. Is this the vibrating vitality? The fire burns, flares. The water moves faster, more intensely; it boils. Slowly white deposits appear on the surface. The water decreases. Time for me to add more liquid. The fire weakens. Time for me to add more wood. The bubbling intensifies. The water lessens. The whole accelerates. At the same time, other things decrease in speed and volume. I no longer feel in control. Wait, did I ever control this assemblage? This conglomerate is in a constant transformation; no state is like another. Each actor has its own speed of movement, transformation, becoming.*

The tendency to persist can be seen in the salt's resistance to categorisation as raw material and waste. This attribute of vitality has emerged throughout the whole research process and culminates in the elaborate boiling down of the salt. The briquetage represents a technology for extracting a valuable raw material. By using this technology for a waste material of today's industrial network, the salt is detached from this particular context. The time-intensive performative act assigns new value to the salt. It is beyond the economic value by which salt is otherwise judged and treated. The water pollution thus becomes a laboriously extracted substance. The fact that the salt remains after precipitation reveals its physical resistance, a resistance that materialises. The salt does not just flow into the water and disappear. It is not out of sight, out of mind – its vitality is tangible.

In the outlined research process, attributes of vital materialism according to Bennett were conceptualised, and a methodology for assessing the vitality of salt was developed. Salt was contextualised in its historical, cultural, socio-economic, and ecological facets and recontextualised as a vital entity. With the developed methodology, the vitality of the material was demonstrated. This study illustrates that Bennett's concept of material vitality is not merely a theoretical abstraction but provides meaningful approaches for the practical implementation of New Materialism. However, her "naive ambition of a vital materialism" (Bennett 2010, xvii) encounters structural and human limitations in practical realisation.

Instead of distancing myself from subjective perception, I used material involvement to address these limitations. Material involvement is manifested in field research, site-specificity, and working in the ceramics workshop. In other words, it is characterised by a research method that is based on immersing oneself in the material. This offers a counter-design to Bennett's descriptive methodology, which looks at materials from a distance without physically interacting with them. The developed methodology shows phenomenological traits in physical interaction and emphasises the unfolding of material vitality through this act. This process does not center on the human as an observing subject but shifts the focus to the relation of human and material, influencing each other, allowing subjective capabilities to arise from experience and embodied perception (Coole 2017). This approach includes the researcher as an actor who affects the phenomenon to be researched, as well as the effect of the phenomenon on the researcher. The same applies to the site of investigation and the measuring instruments. Material involvement highlights the interaction between material and humans, thereby achieving a decentralisation of humans within a phenomenological approach.

Besides material involvement, the following methodological premises emerged from the research process to explore the vitality of a material: Artistic research proves to be a suitable environment for investigating an elusive phenomenon, such as the vitality of material, due to its wide methodological scope. This methodological freedom allows for a transdisciplinary approach to the object of study; for instance, by integrating philosophical approaches into scientific methods. Creative freedom strengthens the ability to encounter the material with anticipatory readiness which is the prerequisite for approaching the material with an open mind and a certain naivety. Consequently, I was able to approach the material with an open outcome and acknowledge its agency in the process. The theory of vital materialism is a constitutive element of the research method and has been made tangible through the formulation of attributes of vitality. These attributes, which are the tendency to persist, the tendency of assemblage, and the tendency of efficacy, act as "shapers of experience" (Cazeaux 2017, 52) and play a crucial role in transforming sensual perceptions into epistemological experiences. They contribute to translating the elusive into conceptual terms. This study found that the attributes led to an increased sensitivity, as they required a novel perspective on the studied material, not expressed in conventional views.

## MATERIAL INVOLVEMENT AS STARTING POINT

In this work, I ventured into the realm of the uncertain to explore the vitality of material. Throughout the investigation, both I as a researcher and Bennett's theory encountered certain limits: Firstly, there are no established methods for exploring the vitality of material that go beyond traditional mechanistic and biological-physical explanatory approaches. Secondly, the question of the subjective perception of material arises. Exploring these boundaries has highlighted aspects worthy of consideration in future research projects on New Materialism. The critical questioning of conventional methods of knowledge generation is closely related to this. The challenge is achieving research that acknowledges a diversity of knowledge while simultaneously providing suitable methods of alternative knowledge generation.

In summary, this artistic research offers impulses for understanding and implementing the theory of New Materialism. It demonstrates that theoretical concepts can be translated into specific practical applications. The outlined methodology proves to be an effective tool for artistically revealing deeply rooted structures and patterns of thought into which material is integrated. The open-ended research process has uncovered the historical, cultural, and industrial dimensions of the material. It has revealed an ambivalence in dealing with structures within the framework of New Materialism. It is a constant balancing act: on the one hand, it is necessary to identify and critically reflect on existing structures; on the other hand, it requires structures to concretise and implement abstract concepts. Hence, it can be deduced that rigid structures of materiality must be questioned, while fluid structures can be useful in handling abstract theories. The recognition and integration of the vitality of various actors is of utmost importance. Thus, the question arises of the potential impacts of recognizing the vitality of various actors on future interactions with material. How do we deal with materials that have lost their value within the economic system and the consequences of transformed landscapes?

At the industrial sites studied, the securing of raw materials for the next 40–50 years is ensured. Yet, within this century, the potash deposits in Zielitz will be exhausted, and the limestone in Bernburg will be nearing its end. It remains unclear what will happen then to the exploited regions. However, the lime ponds and salt mounds already let us feel their vitality. The question of responsibility in this context remains unresolved. It is apparent that merely identifying the economic interests underlying the current handling of the material is insufficient to bring about substantial change. At this point, the previously outlined material involvement, which strives for a non-anthropocentric perspective, can serve as a starting point in both ways: phenomenologically and structurally. Engaging with the material and overcoming the dualistic view of animate and inanimate matter holds the potential for more sustainable interaction with our environment and offers approaches for addressing current and future existential crises. Above all, this work advocates for a sensory interaction with material to explore its unique agency and aesthetics in all their dimensions.

## ENDNOTE

1  Personal research notes compiled during the process.

## REFERENCES

Bennett, J. (2010) *Vibrant Matter: A Political Ecology of Things*. Durham: Duke University Press.

Busch, K. (2009). "Artistic Research and the Poetics of Knowledge." *ART AND RESEARCH: A Journal of Ideas, Contexts and Methods* 2, No. 2. (Spring): 1–7.

Cazeaux, C. (2017). *Art, Research, Philosophy*. London: Routledge.

Coole, D. (2014). "»Wir brauchen eine wesentlich bessere Einschätzung der materiellen Strukturen...« - im Gespräch mit Diana Coole." In *Macht des Materials – Politik der Materialität, Schriftenreihe des cx centrum für Interdisziplinäre Studien der Akademie der Bildenden Künste München*, edited by Susanne Witzgall and Kerstin Stakemeier, 47–51. Zurich: Diaphanes.

Filion-Donato, É. (2021). "Psychodynamism of Individuation and New Materialism." In *Materialism and Politics, Cultural Inquiry*, edited by Bernardo Bianchi, Émilie Filion-Donato, Marlon Miguel, and Ayşe Yuva, 233–252. Berlin: ICI Berlin Press.

Garske, P. (2014). "What's the „matter": Der Materialitätsbegriff des „New Materialism" und dessen Konsequenzen für feministisch-politische Handlungsfähigkeit." *PROKLA. Zeitschrift für kritische Sozialwissenschaft* 44.174: 111–129.

Heibach, C., and Rohde, C. ed. (2015). Ästhetik der Materialität, *HFG Forschung*. Paderborn: Wilhelm Fink.

K+S Corporation [K+S Aktiengesellschaft] (2023). "Zielitz – K+S Aktiengesellschaft." Accessed September 5, 2023. https://www.kpluss.com/de-de/ueber-ks/standorte/europa/zielitz/.

Malafouris, L. (2008). "At the Potter's Wheel: An Argument for Material Agency." In *Material Agency: Towards a Non-Anthropocentric Approach*, edited by Carl Knappett and Lambros Malafouris, 19–36. New York: Springer.

Malafouris, L. and Renfrew, C. (Eds.) (2010). *The Cognitive Life of Things: Recasting the Boundaries of the Mind*. Cambridge, UK: McDonald Institute for Archaeological Research.

Ministry of Science, Energy, Climate Protection, and Environment [Ministerium für Wissenschaft, Energie, Klimaschutz und Umwelt] (2022). *Antwort der Landesregierung auf eine kleine Anfrage zur schriftlichen Beantwortung – Kleine Anfrage – K.A. 8/0478: Direkte und indirekte Salzeinleitung in Sachsen-Anhalt in Bode, Saale und Elbe.*

Museum of Prehistory and Early History Berlin [Museum für Vor- und Frühgeschichte Berlin] (2020). *Eisenzeit: Europa ohne Grenzen 1. Jahrtausend v. Chr., Ausstellungskatalog St. Petersburg und Moskau.* Berlin.

Renfrew, C. (2014). "Material engagement als kreativer menschlicher Prozess und das kognitive Leben der Dinge." In *Macht des Materials – Politik der Materialität, Schriftenreihe des cx centrum für Interdisziplinäre Studien der Akademie der Bildenden Künste München*, edited by Susanne Witzgall and Kerstin Stakemeier, 110-124. Zürich: Diaphanes.

State Administration Office of Saxony-Anhalt [Landesverwaltungsamt Sachsen-Anhalt] (2022, October 4). *Einleiterlaubnis für CIECH Soda Deutschland GmbH & Co. KG auf 8 Jahre begrenzt und mit Auflagen verbunden* [Press release]. https://presse.sachsen-anhalt.de/landesverwaltungsamt/2022/10/04/einleit-erlaubnis-fuer-ciech-soda-deutschland-gmbh-co-kg-auf-8-jahre-begrenzt-und-mit-auflagen-verbunden/.

State Agency for Flood Protection and Water Management Saxony-Anhalt [Landesbetrieb für Hochwasserschutz und Wasserwirtschaft Sachsen-Anhalt] (n.d.).

*Datenblätter Für Oberflächenwasserkörper (OWK) in Sachsen-Anhalt, Bewertungszeitraum 2009–2013.*

Stiegler, B. (2009). *Der Fehler des Epimetheus.* Zurich: Diaphanes.

Sutjipto, Sheila, Tish, D., Paul, G., Vidal-Calleja T., and Schork T. (2019). "Towards Visual Feedback Loops for Robot-Controlled Additive Manufacturing." In *Robotic Fabrication in Architecture, Art and Design 2018*, edited by Jan Willmann, Philippe Block, Marco Hutter, Kendra Byrne and Tim Schork. Cham: Springer.

Vis, D. (2021). *Research for People Who (Think They) Would Rather Create.* Eindhoven: Onomatopee.

Witzgall, S. (2014). "Macht des Materials/Politik der Materialität - eine Einführung." In *Macht des Materials - Politik der Materialität, Schriftenreihe des cx centrum für Interdisziplinäre Studien der Akademie der Bildenden Künste München,* edited by Susanne Witzgall and Kerstin Stakemeier, 13-28. Zurich: Diaphanes.

Witzgall, S., Stakemeier, K., ed. (2014). *Macht des Materials - Politik der Materialität, Schriftenreihe des cx centrum für Interdisziplinäre Studien der Akademie der Bildenden Künste München.* Zurich: Diaphanes.

# Does the Tree Say No?

Franca López Barbera

## On Design, Consent, and Uncertainty

*Fig. 1.* Quebracho Colorado. Source: Celulosa Argentina (1975), *Libro del Árbol II*, Buenos Aires: Agens Publicidad. Wikimedia commons.

*This is the Quebracho Colorado tree, who will be our companion in this talk. Quebracho trees can live up to 150 years and grow as tall as twenty-five meters. They blossom from November to March; their interior is red (colorado means red in Spanish), and they thrive in the sun and high temperatures – that's why they grow in the Gran Chaco forest in South America, which covers sections of Bolivia, Paraguay, Brazil, and Argentina. This forest is the second most important territory of the continent in terms of biodiversity after the Amazon rainforest. Now, I will tell you two stories about the Quebracho: the first story is that in some areas of the Gran Chaco in Argentina, it is known that before approaching a Quebracho tree, one must salute him.[1] We say, "Buenos días, Señor Quebracho", which means "Good morning, Mister Quebracho". This salutation is not only an acknowledgement of the tree's presence but also an asking for permission to be physically close to him. Quebracho trees can deny permission by "shooting" the person with a heavy rash that makes their body itch. According to local knowledge and tradition, the way to cure this rash is to return to the Quebracho tree, offer him a cake of ashes as an apology, and tie a red thread to the trunk as a sign of respect and a declaration of friendship. The second story of the Quebracho is the history of the deforestation of Argentina. During the first half of the 20th century, a British company settled in the Argentinian Gran Chaco forest and exploited the Quebracho trees, known for their hard and tannin-rich wood (tannin is the substance that treats pelt and turns it into leather). Quebracho wood was used for the extension of railway tracks and tannin extraction – two key elements of Argentina's industrialisation (and deforestation) process and what turned this British company into the world's biggest tannin producer. After felling 90% of the Quebracho trees, the company left for South Africa to exploit the second most tannin-rich tree in the world, the Mimosa. Today, the Quebracho Colorado is in danger of extinction.*

Franca López Barbera

# WHAT'S IN A QUESTION: BETWEEN CERTAINTY AND SCEPTICISM

The passage above is the opening of my presentation entitled "When a Tree Says No: Towards a Consent Framework for Design-Nature relationships", delivered at the 5$^{th}$ NERD conference (UdK Berlin 2023), whose contributions are collected in this anthology. Taking the double hi/story of the Quebracho as a guiding example, I went on to examine the gendered and colonial underpinnings of the prevailing modern conceptualisations of both nature and consent that underscore design's role in reproducing extractive approaches to nature. The presentation then transitioned to introducing "more-than-human consent" as a framework for design capable of attending to the relational, plural, and uncertain dimensions and expressions of all life, human and nonhuman. I emphasised the need to explore non-modern principles of relation, acknowledging onto-epistemologies that offer alternative frameworks for engaging with nature to the modern one that is destructive and violent. This implies a shift from conventional notions of consent as an exclusive human transaction to a more nuanced and generative understanding of consent as something that can emerge within more-than-human relations and (re)organise such relationships in terms of power. This means that consent (or lack thereof) reflects power relations and can be actively cultivated in and through design (some aspects will be revisited and further elaborated here, others in López Barbera 2024). Drawing from past presentations and anticipating reactions of suspicion, I incorporated the following:

> *For the sceptics, the focus is not, How can I be certain or how can I prove whether the tree is "actually" consenting? but rather to reframe the question: What can the Quebracho story tell me about consent? How does consent manifest here? How can it expand modern notions of consent and design?*

In what felt like a déjà vu, the moment of questions arrived, and I was asked:

*But how can we make sure that tree consents?*

I take the recurrence of this question with a genuine concern, and I am interested in sitting with it here, continuing the discussion initiated then and there. The double hi/story of the Quebracho has been thoroughly explored in an earlier article and mentioned in a paper (see López Barbera 2021, 2024), both of which also share the first part of the presentation's title ("When a Tree Says No") this essay follows up on. Using the same title again and again is no accident; the origin of my research on more-than-human consent is indeed the Quebracho tree, and I extend my gratitude to him by continuing to share his hi/stories. At the same time, they are a powerful representation of two contrasting ways of understanding and relating with nature: nature as a commodified resource, poised for transformation into profit – and nature as an agential force that affects and communicates; a subject-tree capable of consenting. The first Quebracho story is a conceptualisation, an ethical attitude, a tradition, and a relational practice, but *not only;*[2] it suggests a complex phenomenon that exceeds what this description tries to signal whilst enabling "onto-epistemic openings" (de la Cadena 2020) for design. The affirmative grammar in the original title is an unambiguous assertion of this possibility and a declaration of principles. I intended to do no different in this essay, yet that question continued to echo.

Swapping "When a tree says no" for "Does the tree say no?" does not seek to cast doubt on the tree's capacity to consent but rather to stay with the question and examine its agency and implications (what asking such a question does). Undoubtedly, "But how can we make sure that tree consents?" holds significant value and warrants careful consideration for various reasons: first, the opening "But" insists on the implausibility of what has been previously affirmed, which prompts us to ask: What kind of knowledge has the power to object to others? Who controls knowledge about nature and how to relate to it? Secondly, "how can we make sure" invokes a seemingly nondescript (universal) collective authority (who are the "we" in that room?) in the pursuit of certainty through a (design?) method. Thirdly, while "that the tree consents" does locate consent in the tree, it understands consent as an individual pursuit instead of a collective practice.

What is more important than the question itself is the kind of rationality and relationality it stems from and the epistemological limit that is revealed because of the ontological prejudice and dogmatism from which that "we" inexorably thinks itself and the world – the trap of being "reasoned by the reason that has been reasoned" (Conradi 2021, 16), and a loop design must escape. Indeed, this question exposes a crisis of design (Fry and Nocek 2021) amidst broader onto-epistemological tensions. It is symptomatic of how much design has assimilated the imperative of modern/colonial logic as the sole descriptor and articulator of reality and, in that move, reduced its horizon of the possible. In other words, "it is symptomatic ... of the forms of capitalist relationship, for which, in truth, everything that makes up the environment, the natural space, is taken as a 'resource', and those who converse with the wind or listen to a tree are totally crazy and lost" (Grosso 2016, 21).

Reframing design-nature relationships through more-than-human consent marks a departure from conventional Western perspectives on nature, design, and consent. I do not intend to engage in a historical revision of the evolution of these terms in Western thought here; rather, I aim to challenge them and reconsider how they relate to each other by examining the underlying logics that continue to govern nature, design, and consent. In the following sections, I will problematise these terms and the practices they invoke by thinking through the concepts of silence, universality, and uncertainty as they relate to knowledge production. The first section examines the gendered and colonial/modern conceptualisation of nature and how silencing local, situated, ecological knowledges has been pivotal in the making and establishing of this conceptualisation worldwide. The second section takes on this universalising logic to delve into the pervasive influence of scientism in design, highlighting the challenges posed by ontological perspectives, ultimately advocating for embracing uncertainty as an emancipatory practice that expands our understanding of the world beyond traditional epistemological limits. The third section explores the historical and contemporary understandings of consent as a transactional phenomenon, revealing and critiquing its gendered and colonial underpinnings and its role in perpetuating both human and nonhuman unequal power dynamics. To conclude, I return to the central question of this paper and outline what a more-than-human consent approach to design entails.

## DEAFENING NARRATIVES AND THE PRODUCTION OF SILENCE

While a tension between universalising and situated onto-epistemologies (Barad, 2007) is represented within the double hi/story of the Quebracho, the deforestation of the Gran Chaco – and the world's current environmental devastation – is proof that certain knowledge systems have not been afforded equal treatment, relevance, or legitimacy in their ability to make sense of the world. This disparity raises important questions about how hegemonic knowledge about nature (and how it establishes a specific type of relationality) is constructed, valued, and disseminated. The perception of nature as a resource derives from a particular gendering of nature – a narrative and a historical process that is both patriarchal and colonial and whose origin is related to the invention and intersection of ideas of gender and race as social categories, both constructed within and constructive of the colonial/modern project.

Since the 1970s, ecofeminist theory has been directly concerned with identifying, challenging, and dismantling the connections between the domination of women and the domination of nature. Ecofeminist positions (Plumwood 1993; Merchant 1989; Mies 2014) locate the woman-nature association in the Western intellectual tradition and consider the Enlightenment period, guided by rationalised patriarchal science, as the beginning of a series of dualisms that positioned the "human" (which human?) not only as hyper-separated from nature but as antagonistic and superior to it. In most pre-modern European societies, the image of nature was two-sided: nature as a nurturing mother, a benevolent and generous female figure (a perspective that provided a certain ethical relationality towards nature) and nature as wild, chaotic, hostile, and violent. Even though both conceptions of nature were female, the second one became more prolific after the scientific revolution, as it called forth the need to control it. To paraphrase Bacon (1624, as cited in Merchant 1989, 169), nature needed to be forced out of her uncontrolled state, subdued, and moulded by the hand of man and technology. A new mechanistic model thus swiftly defined nature as inert, passive, and dead – a move that became fundamental in reducing (female) earth to a mere resource for economic production and justifying her exploitation.

On the flip side, the nature/woman association constructed the conceptualisation of the male not only as a biological differential but of the "masculine" as an epistemological position and orientation defined by the rational scientific mind not only separate from nature but in complete denial of any relationship with or dependency on it (Bordo 1986). Western culture and its intellectual traditions dating back to classical Greek philosophy have historically conceived the markers of humanity as masculine (reason, mind, culture) as a means to control and oppress every body that does not possess them. This encompasses nature, women, and colonised peoples, as will be explored below. As they are considered less than rational, they do not possess full humanity. From this, a set of interrelated and mutually reinforcing dualisms will organise relationships in terms of domination-subordination: human-nature, culture-nature, man-woman, reason-emotion, mind-body (mental-manual), civilised-primitive, subject-object:

> *The identity of the underside is constructed instrumentally, and the canons of virtue for a good wife, a good colonised,*

*or a good worker are written in terms of usefulness to the centre. In the typical case, this involves setting up a moral dualism, where the underside is not part of the sphere to be considered morally but is either judged by a separate instrumental standard (as in the sexual double standard) or seen as outside morality altogether. (Plumwood 1993, 53)*

However, the emergence of European science and technology and the border of its discourse is not in Europe. Concurrently, this is the period of the colonial domination of the Americas. These were not only simultaneous as historical parallels, but the former was built upon the latter. Martinican political scientist and philosopher Malcom Ferdinand (2022) highlights an under-explored historical phenomenon, which he calls "the double fracture of modernity," in which ecology is separated from decolonial thought. Ferdinand acutely points out that the former could only unfold on the condition that colonial history remains silent – a setting that enabled the development of discourses and concepts that do not account for the experience of those colonised. Thus, concepts such as "the Anthropocene", in homogenising the category of human (anthropos) as a species, mask the power dynamics and injustices inherent in ecological devastation, failing to account for the inequalities of its colonial causes.

The colonisation of the Americas marked the beginning of the colonial/modern project, a system of domination affecting all aspects of life rooted in the invention of "race" as a social category that would establish European conquerors as "naturally" superior to colonial peoples (Quijano 2000). Through this logic, Whiteness too became a "marker of civilisation" and, conversely, colonial peoples were constructed as beings of nature. When race intersects with the gender categories mentioned above, it positions colonial peoples as outside of the men-women normativity and thus as outside of humanity: they were described as possessing gender but in a manner akin to an animal, devoid of the dichotomous so-called masculine and feminine traits such as rationality and softness (Lugones 2012).

The dehumanisation of certain peoples through race and gender is essential for establishing power structures and asserting dominance over all spheres of existence of those colonised and enslaved, including their sphere of knowledge.

Colonial/modern knowledge is founded on the very silencing and erasure of Indigenous, local, situated, ecological knowledges. While arising from a distinct cultural context, Eurocentrism projects itself as universal. Modern science has successfully imposed itself globally as the only knowledge regime capable of understanding and describing the world through the colonial expansion of Europe and the suppression of any alternative episteme that does not follow Western rationality. This professed universality could not have been achieved without the exploitation of nature in the Americas, which provided Europe with endless "natural resources" to continue pursuing its colonial expansion over other regions of the world (Dussel 2000 via Ciriza 2018, 67) and over other ways of understanding and relating to the world. Indian writer Amitav Ghosh (2021) eloquently asks, "Could it not be said that for a tree, it is the human who is mute?" What this question does is to challenge the limited Western understanding of the meaning-making capabilities of nonhumans, while simultaneously bringing attention to the construction of what he calls "the myth of the voiceless". Ghosh argues that the core issue of the current planetary crisis is the result of a particular group of people having historically actively marginalised others by portraying them as "brutes" and thus as "incapable of articulation and agency". Being conflated with nature, he explains, "also meant that this part of humanity was excluded from 'History', which was the exclusive domain of the civilised or 'historical' nations" (Ghosh 2021, 187). In turn, the erasure of forms of knowledge that are capable of relating with "nonhuman forms of agency and expression" renders nonhumans as lacking epistemological capabilities, too (Ghosh 2021, 203). This implies the delegitimisation of gendered ways of life; the forms of knowledge related to community, care, crafts, planting, reciprocity, and the like (Lugones 2012) – any ontology of continuity and interrelation with nature that considers nonhumans epistemological partners, like in the first Quebracho story.

When we talk about environmental devastation, it is not only nature in its Western (gendered and colonial) reductionist conceptualisation as a material resource that faces destruction but also and essentially nature in its broader non-modern ontological sense, as an interrelational place for the production of life and where relationships and knowledge are shaped (Escobar 2015). In the case of the Gran Chaco's deforestation, it is not only the material presence of Quebracho trees that has been destroyed but also their agency and their voice. Relating to a Quebracho as a being capable of consent entails engaging with a vision of the world that Western rationality not only fails to comprehend but actively obliterates.

## SPOILER ALERT: WE CAN'T MAKE SURE

What we call nature – or the lack thereof – and how we relate to it are a testament to models and processes (designs) of production (and destruction) that created both the material and conceptual landscapes of the present. Design theorist Anne-Marie Willis (2006) argues that ontological designing "implies different ways of understanding how we, as modern subjects, 'are' and how we come to be who/what we are in the modern world" (80). Ontological design deals with the condition and behaviour of design (what design is and does) and outlines that designing is a an inherent part of being human across cultures; "a decision and direction embodied in all things humans deliberately bring into being" (Kalantidou and Fry 2014, 1). Therefore, things designed can be objects, systems, or processes, both material and immaterial (buildings, manufactured goods, communication systems, as well as systems of thought and habits of mind or language). Through our interaction with the designed, we are also designed (Willis 2006); the agency of the designed is not only embedded by but actually beyond the designer's conscious intention. As such, ontological designing is a human-decentred practice (things as well as people design) and an all-encompassing activity that creates and configures ways of being, experiences, values, and ways of relating (Fry 2007), i.e., worlding (Haraway 2008) or design as active world-making. Design theorist and historian Clive Dilnot synthesises this by claiming that "what design *designs* are the relations between things and persons and things and nature" and points out that "nonethical design reduces these to commodity [or] utilitarian operative relations" (Dilnot 2009, 183).

Modernity/coloniality is a project and a process directed to bring into being a particular world (a design) based on a relation of control and exploitation of nature at the service of capitalist modes of production and social reproduction. In turn, design (as discourse and practice) emerged and has been configured (itself designed) by coloniality (Kiem 2017). In other words, "all modern notions of design are products of the rise of post-Enlightenment reason. Design's development is inseparable from the attempt to rationally order the world, to command 'nature'" (Fry 1988, 17). An ontological perspective, thus, entails a more profound and broader understanding of, first the Quebracho (nature) in a non-modern sense, as an agential subject as well as what enables relations to emerge, develop, and be sustained; and second, of the relation between design and nature not only from the material aspect of the tree as a means to a material or nonmaterial end, but the material and the immaterial as mutually constituted and constituent of a world. When design encounters a tree and transforms the tree (e.g. into railway tracks and tannin), it transforms a world. How can design – a discipline that works within and normalises modern capitalist and extractive logics – relate with nature otherwise?

Certainly, modern/colonial logics are as pervasive as they are elusive, and design is also riddled with scientistic biases. Scientism, in essence, is the conviction that the understanding of reality can only be derived from science and rational logic (including questions on ethics). Scientism is not simply appreciating science as a valuable form of knowledge (and the technological advancements it has produced); it is instead holding science as the only form of knowledge to have epistemic value (van Woudenberg et al. 2018). Although it may be inadvertently embraced, scientism leads to severe epistemic implications as it entails not only the exclusion of any other form of knowledge but, conversely, that what cannot be achieved by scientific reasoning is neither real nor true and therefore not worth examining further either (Gasparatou 2017). It often follows that if an exploration resorts to non-empirical Western forms of knowledge and methods – for instance, historically gendered practices such as the ones outlined above – it is not only met with disdain but may be relegated to the realm of "belief" rather than truth or facts. Feminist philosopher of science Donna Haraway (1997) critiques the tendency to uphold modern science as an unquestionable authority and challenges the idea that scientific knowledge can provide absolute certainty. She argues against the idealisation of objectivity; a narrative claiming that science offers a neutral, value-free understanding of the world (and here I ask, who is this neutral, "epistemologically invisible" yet credible *we* that seeks to *make sure*?).[3] Haraway emphasises the importance of acknowledging not only the partiality and complexity inherent in scientific inquiries but also that the pursuit of certainty in science often involves the exclusion of multiple perspectives and a lack of reflection on the situatedness of scientific practices within their specific cultural and historical contexts. While it is (widely but not sufficiently) acknowledged that "scientific knowledge is a particular kind of knowledge" and has its limits (de Ridder 2018, 190) and that knowledge is always contextual (Feyerabend 1987) and situated (Haraway 1988), scientism is still – however implicitly – invoked, denoting an unchecked reliance on modern scientific methods and a fascination with the quest for "universal truths" and, in the case of the central question motivating this text, an uncritical, ahistorical, and un-situated conception of nature and design.

Bound by Western epistemologies, design defaults to anthropocentrism (the very one Ferdinand critiques above) and struggles to think itself outside of it, let alone envision alternative horizons. Faced with a tree that consents, the modern impulse expresses itself first by objecting ("But") and then by putting the (hu)man ("we") back at the centre (both grammatically and epistemologically) and towards a place of certainty. Indeed, absolute certainty is a modern preoccupation and delusion. In other words, "How can *we make sure*?" is a self-constraining follow-up question because it thinks the question of nature, design, and consent from the modern relational logics (and the modern nature) that more-than-human consent tries to escape. What is the exit strategy?

Peruvian anthropologist Marisol de la Cadena (2021) proposes "not knowing" as a disposition for when one is confronted with what seems "beyond the limits of the possible" in terms of the requirements of modern epistemology (247). De la Cadena explains that to practice *not knowing* comes from her collaboration with her friend Mariano Turpo, a Quechua speaker who "would insist that what to [her] *was* (for example, a mountain) was *not only* that. And it was possible that [she] could eventually *not know* what *it* not only was!" (de la Cadena 2020, 389). *Not knowing* is a sort of suspended state (of modern disbelief) and a space where that which exceeds her capacities to know what *is*, is as real as it is inaccessible for her (and may forever remain so). *Not knowing* is not "not knowing yet"; rather, it is a practice and a method, "a different form of knowing [...] that accepts the challenges posed by that which it interrogates" (de la Cadena 2021, 250). In this way, *not knowing* is also an emancipatory practice as it escapes the modern loop of only validating reality through the standards that this – fully graspable and thus restricted and restrictive – reality considers valid. To exist in that space, she explains, requires "a different kind of *we*" that does not depart from an "us-them" distinction that establishes epistemic hierarchy, but rather a *we* that is made with and through a shared onto-epistemological contact zone and keeps the conversation going:

> ... *a fractal space where [Mariano's] practices and mine overlapped and diverged. ... It implied the composition of a "we" that maintained radically present the divergences*

*that made our encounter: "we" would not have been able to converse without those divergences, or our conversation would have been another. (de la Cadena 2021, 250)*

Allowing and embracing one's practice to be affected by that which *is* and at the same time is unknown to *me/us* (and, above all, resisting the modern urge to interpret it is an experience of cognitive dissonance that needs to be resolved) can be generative as it creates the onto-epistemic openings (as a condition of possibility) for the emergence of modes of relating that not only do not meet but defy current empirical requirements of modern epistemology (de la Cadena 2021). So, it is not certainty but quite the opposite that can bring us closer to more-than-human consent. In other words, more-than-human consent is as uncertain and seemingly unattainable as it is possible.

## AGAINST THE IMPOSSIBILITY OF EVERYTHING OTHER, TOWARDS THE POSSIBILITY OF THE MANY

Human persons (or the specific collectives they form) have historically constituted the paradigmatic subjects of consent, and almost all of the literature is based on and representative of this model (Kleinig 2010). Since its inception, from Antiquity to Modernity, consent has been central in the organisation of the Western world's political, social, and economic relationships. For the Greeks and Romans, consent played a fundamental role in shaping social, political, and economic relations and developing their robust systems of law. The idea that government is legitimised by the "collective consent" of the governed was integral to their political organisation, and "individual consent" was fundamental to expanding the economic power of the Roman Empire (Lee 2018; Sullivan 2016). However, collective consent was not necessarily a reflection of the will of the people but of a few wise men, and consensual transactions among individuals were restricted to free men. Women and enslaved people were not considered capable of and did not have the right to consent, either entirely or to some degree. Women could participate in some transactions through the representation of their husbands, and enslaved people would only participate in transactions as humans (otherwise as the objects being transacted) when acting on behalf of their owners (Lee 2018). So, although consent was central in Antiquity's political thought, it emerged in relation to masculinity, citizenship, and reason, and it was only the privilege of a few.

During the Enlightenment, there was a strong revival of Antiquity's writings as a way to emancipate thought and morals from the control of the Church. Greco-Roman rule of government and society is the foundational model of Western political thought and legal sciences through which the basis of Modern Western ideas of "liberty", "equality", and "democracy" has been built. But what kind of freedom and democracy? Dominican historian Dan-el Padilla Peralta points out that "Classics is a Euro-American foundation myth" (Poser 2021). What he means by this is that the historical White-leading interpretation of Antiquity that started during the Enlightenment has been not only a model for modern ideas about power, ethics, and nature but also deeply instrumental to the invention of Whiteness and, thus, in justifying slavery, race science, and colonialism. English philosophers Hobbes and Locke were central figures in developing political thought during the Enlightenment. Unlike the medieval period in which government was legitimised by "collective" consent through representative bodies, Hobbes argued that consent should come "voluntarily" from each "naturally free and equal" individual (Lee 2018). For Hobbes, voluntary consent can be expressed by "words spoken" (Hobbes 1991 [1651], 120) or inferred either by silence or by an action – any of these three cases would indicate "the will of the contractor" (Hobbes 1991 [1651], 94): "even submission secured through fear, threats, or sheer coercion ... always counts as a valid form of consent resulting from rational calculation" (Lee 2018, 16). Hobbes argued that authoritarian regimes or "a de facto power of a usurping conqueror – a commonwealth 'by acquisition'" – are still technically governments based on consent "so long as the conquered subject does not resist" (Lee 2018, 16). But who are these free and equal subjects? While presented as an abstraction with universal applicability, consent was very much embodied: being human, which meant being a European, Christian, white, heterosexual, upper-class, cisgender man, was a prerequisite of reason and being worthy of moral consideration and, therefore, capable of consenting. The early modern discourse surrounding consent was dominated by an elite group of European men who defined it in relation to masculinity and Whiteness in order to protect and privilege the institutions and structures of modernity while masking and perpetuating unequal power dynamics instead of distributing power and making many worlds possible, which is one of the most significant capabilities and, to me, the core purpose of consent.

Colombian anthropologist Arturo Escobar (2015b) asks, "Can design become a means for fostering the pluriverse?" The pluriverse is a vision that promotes the coexistence of many ways of understanding, doing, and being in the world – as spoken by the Zapatistas, it is a world where many worlds fit ("Un mundo donde quepan muchos mundos"). This question, which is an ontological design concern, is posed in the thick of a socio-ecological crisis within which design is not only embedded but also responsible for (Fry and Nocek 2021). To do so, Escobar argues, design needs to break free itself from its modern/colonial legacy and redirect itself towards practices that "interrupt" these anthropocentric, rationalistic, and universal binary logics towards alternative modes of existence, knowledge, and action. Indeed, what is at stake in this transition is a re-design of design. With this in mind, a more-than-human consent approach to design seeks to articulate sustainable, less prescriptive, and more just ways of relating with nature. It identifies consent as a situated practice that is respectful, generative, and plural in contradistinction to the universalising and effacing ambition of the modern/colonial project, where more-than-human consent is not a solution, a method, or a tool but a condition of design. Ultimately, the overarching question that concerns me and drives this project is, How can design be practised as a form of more-than-human consent? But first, what is up with consent today?

Contemporary Western conceptualisations and applications of consent draw heavily from the long tradition of political philosophy (Müller and Schaber 2018), as elaborated above. Consent is now widely understood within ethical, legal, and political sciences as something that a person gives to another to make an action permissible that would otherwise be forbidden; it is defined as a transaction between A and B over something XYZ (Kleinig 2010). For instance, a person may consent to a friend borrowing their car, to having a friend over for dinner, to another's sexual advances, or to undergo surgery. Without consent, these actions would constitute robbery, trespass, rape, and assault. The existence or absence of consent defines and transforms relationships in the present and in the future. Consent acts like an agreement between parts about something that sets in motion a series of exchanges, responsibilities, rights, and obligations – like a marriage or signing a work contract. These, in turn, define the scope and limits of what we are consenting to. Consent is both the thing that is given and the act through which this consent is given, and it is used broadly to refer to a moral phenomenon (Dougherty 2021) that can turn a wrong into a right (Hurd 1996). Consent can be implicit, explicit, verbal, in writing, or through a particular behaviour; it happens all the time, in various forms, and at many scales.

However, this standard (and historical) conceptualisation of consent as a transaction is also based on the gender differentials that the ecofeminists observed govern the dualistic worldview and define relationships in terms of domination-subordination. For consent to occur this way, it requires an active part that initiates it (asks) and a passive part that gives it or withholds it (Pateman 1980). When we re-examine the two images of nature mentioned earlier, only the passive one was given moral consideration, while the other deserved total subjugation – with coloniality, this second version of nature included all colonial peoples. Feminist considerations argue that delving into the uncharted narrative of women and consent unveils the underlying paradoxes and double standards within consent theory; while women embody those who have been deemed unable to consent, they have been portrayed as "always consenting" with their explicit nonconsent often dismissed as irrelevant or reinterpreted as a form of consent (Pateman 1980, 150). Only a passive femininity is seen as capable of consenting, and this is a femininity (or a nature) described as generous and giving, resulting in an assumed "yes".

The modern colonial/gendered logic of consent not only defines who or what is worthy of moral consideration and thus allowed to participate in a consent situation, but if and when that consent situation exists, it also indicates the status of the parties involved. By considering who requests and who receives it, consent reveals the power dynamics between them. So, the presence or absence of consent and how it operates are determined by the power structures of a given society at a given time. Anti-consensual logics perpetuate a notion of otherness as inferior and subordinate, a dynamic reinforced by what Argentinian feminist anthropologist Rita Segato calls the fundamental precept of extractivism: "the reification of life". This principle, she continues, intertwined with and articulated through patriarchy and coloniality, forms "the perfect equation of power" for the domination and exploitation of gendered (human and nonhuman) bodies, knowledges, and practices (Segato 2021). Consent cannot be separated from the (material and immaterial) conditions that make a consent act possible, including how consent is conceptualised and by whom. At the same time, consent incarnates these power relations, boundaries, and obligations that it itself determines and makes possible. Consent is a situated practice that embodies and simultaneously produces a whole network of power relations, making worlds possible or not.

## A WILLFUL ETHICS OF UNCERTAINTY[4]

Let us now return to the last part of our question: "that the tree consents?" Granted, the tree may consent here, but this fragment references the tree as the "object" in a question wholly formulated in what de la Cadena would call "a habitual subject and object grammar" (de la Cadena 2019, 49). In this binary logic of separation, three things manifest: (1) a we-human-subject asks for consent, and a tree-nonhuman-object gives it or withholds it. This scenario reflects the transactional gendered model explained above where consent is (expected to be) passed on from nature to humans in a yes/no operation; (2) consent occurs through a sort of "on demand" logic where only a we-human-subject is capable of summoning it; and (3) on a meta-level, this we-human-subject must (as a requirement) and can (as a condition of possibility) validate a tree-nonhuman-object agency for the consent transaction to "actually" occur. According to the logic that the question presupposes, consent would occur as long as it is recognised and thus legitimated by he-who-asks.

A more-than-human approach to consent seeks to think outside modern grammar. It refuses to separate human agency from nature's agency, it refuses to think of consent as a transaction, and it refuses the impossibility of what is uncertain,[5] which – and this is critical – does not mean assuming "yes"; that would be thinking shortcuts through the gendered/colonial logics of imposition that it tries to escape. More-than-human consent does not reside exclusively in humans or nonhumans but is distributed within more-than-human assemblages (humans, the natural, and the artificial). For instance, in the case of the Quebracho, a greeting that implies acknowledgement is an instance (and an expression) of consent. Returning to the tree and offering him a cake of ashes as an apology for not honouring this consent situation (i.e. making amends) is also an instance of consent. Hence, a gift is an expression of consent. Here, consent is not only distributed among a person and a tree but also among the salutation, the cake of ashes, and the red thread. More-than-human consent is a relational (material and spatial) practice both enacted by and made through human-nonhuman interaction. This means that consent can also be actively produced. The components mentioned earlier enable the realisation of consent; they create the conditions that make a consent situation possible. That is, not to think of consent as that which declares and guarantees the occurrence of a defined event and that which determines how that event is supposed to occur but to think of consent as the process through which that event is created and shaped.

"But, how can we make sure that the tree consents?" A more-than-human approach to consent refuses to answer this question altogether and reformulates it by thinking through de la Cadena's grammar: a *we* that encompasses both the human and the Quebracho, as well as the relation between them, the red thread, the cake of ashes, and the Gran Chaco forest; a *we* that is made through relating, through the salutation, making the cake of ashes, returning, and gifting; a *we* that not only attends to and stays with the onto-epistemological uncertainties of this relation but is also nurtured by it. Let me end by conjuring that *we* and ask instead, How can we bring more-than-human consent into being?

## ENDNOTES

1. Here, the Quebracho is understood as a male subject. To speak of the Quebracho from a situated perspective, I use the pronoun "him" instead of "it" from this point forward.
2. de la Cadena proposes "not only" as a practice and a strategy to acknowledge both the multiplicity and the limits of description and translation between worlds (see de la Cadena 2020). This is further elaborated in Section 2.
3. This question follows Haraway's figure of "the modest witness", whose "self-invisibility" is instrumental in the fabrication of objectivity but is, in fact, embodied in "the specifically modern, European, masculine, [and] scientific form" (Haraway 1997, 23).
4. I use "wilful" here as defined by Sara Ahmed, denoting an act of disobedience against imposed structures and norms. Ahmed posits that the distinction between "will" and "wilful" has to do with where power is located; a "grammar," she says, that "order[s] human experience, [and] distribut[es] moral worth" (Ahmed 2014, 2).
5. Here, it is worth noting that most of the literature on consent has primarily drawn from legal, medical, and psychological frameworks. The standard view is that for consent to occur, it must fulfil the requirements of "valid consent": voluntary, informed, and competent. However, it is increasingly recognised that this model may not adequately capture the complexities of consent transactions, particularly in cases where consent, while technically "valid", may lead to harmful outcomes for the consenting party (Bullock 2018). Additionally, scholars have referred to concepts such as "defective consent" and "hypothetical consent" to address situations where the conditions for valid consent are not fully met but occur nonetheless (see Miller and Wertheimer 2010). These discussions highlight the need for more nuanced approaches to understanding consent beyond traditional criteria.

## REFERENCES

Ahmed, S. (2014). *Willful Subjects*. Duke University Press.

Barad, K. (2007). *Meeting the Universe Halfway: quantum physics and the entanglement of matter and meaning*. Duke University Press.

Bordo, S. (1986). "The Cartesian masculinisation of Thought." *Signs* 11, no. 3: 439–56.

Bullock, C. E. (2018). "Valid Consent." In *The Routledge Handbook of the Ethics of Consent*, edited by Peter Schaber and Andreas Müller, 85–93. London: Routledge.

Ciriza, A. (2018). "Tras los pasos de las relaciones entre mujeres e ilustración en tierras nuestro-americanas. notas para un debate." In *Modernidad, Colonialismo y Emancipación en América Latina*, edited by Eduardo Rueda and Susana Villavicencio, 59–84. Buenos Aires: CLACSO.

Conradi, F. (2021). "Design as Critical Inquiry: Politics, Performativity and Practice." In NERD – *New Experimental Research in Design 2*, edited by Michelle Christensen, Wolfgang Jonas and Ralf Michel, 9–23. Basel: Birkhäuser.

de la Cadena, M. (2021). "Not Knowing: In the Presence of..." In *Experimenting with Ethnography: A Companion to Analysis*, edited by Andrea Ballestero and Brit Ross Winthereik, 246–256. Duke University Press.

de la Cadena, M. (2020). "Earth-Beings: Andean Indigenous religion, but *not only*." In *More-than-Human*, edited by Andrés Jaque, Marina Otero Verzier and Lucia Pietroiusti, 383-395. Het Nieuwe Instituut.

de la Cadena, M. (2019). "Uncommoning Nature: Stories from the Anthropo-Not-Seen." In *Anthropos and the Material*, edited by Penny Harvey, Christian Krohn-Hansen, and Knut G. Nustad, 35–58. Duke University Press.

de Ridder, J. (2018). "Kinds of Knowledge, Limits of Science." In *Scientism: Prospects and Problems,* edited by Jeroen de Ridder, Rik Peels, and René van Woudenberg, 190–219. New York: Oxford University Press.

Dilnot, C. (2009). "Ethics in Design: 10 Questions." In *Design Studies: A Reader*, edited by Hazel Clark and David Brody, 180–190. New York: Berg.

Dougherty, T. (2021). *The Scope of Consent*. Oxford, New York: Oxford University Press.

Escobar, A. (2015a). "Hacia el Pluriverso." In *Conversaciones ante la Máquina para Salir del Consenso Desarrollista*, edited by Tinta Limón, 173—184. Buenos Aires: Tinta Limón.

Escobar, A. (2015b). "Transiciones: a space for research and design for transitions to the pluriverse." *Design Philosophy Papers*, 13(1): 13-23.

Ferdinand, M. (2022). *Decolonial Ecology: Thinking from the Caribbean World*. Cambridge: Polity Press.

Feyerabend, P. (1987). *Farewell to Reason*. London: Verso.

Fry, T. (2007). "Redirective Practice: An Elaboration." *Design Philosophy Papers* 5(1): 5-20.

Fry, T. (1988). *Design History Australia: a source text in method and resources*. Sidney: Power Institute of Fine Arts.

Fry, T. and Nocek, A. (2021). "Design in crisis, introducing a problematic." In *Design in Crisis. New Worlds, Philosophies and Practices*, edited by Tony Fry and Adam Nocek, 1–15. New York: Routledge.

Gasparatou, R. (2017). "Scientism and Scientific Thinking. A Note on Science Education." *Sci & Educ* 26: 799—812.

Ghosh, A. (2021). "Brutes." In Amitav Ghosh, *The Nutmeg's Curse. Parables for a Planet in Crisis*, 183–204. Chicago: University of Chicago Press.

Grosso (2016). "La comunidad "alterada": Cuerpos, discursos y relaciones entre seres humanos y no-humanos. Matrices interculturales de la hospitalidad." *Cuadernos de Trabajo. Tejiendo la Pirka* 8: 18–28.

Haraway, J. D. (2008). *When Species Meet*. University of Minnesota Press.

Haraway, J. D. (1997). *Modest_Witness@Second_Millennium. FemaleMan_Meets_OncoMouse: feminism and technoscience*. New York: Routledge.

Haraway, J. D. (1988). "Situated Knowledges: The Science Question in Feminism and the Privilege of Partial Perspective." *Feminist Studies* 14(3): 575–599.

Hobbes, T. (1991) [1651]. *Leviathan*, edited by Richard Tuck. Cambridge: Cambridge University Press.

Hurd, H. (1996). "The Moral Magic of Consent." *Legal Theory* 2(2): 121–46.

Kalantidou, E. and Fry, T. (2014). "Design in The Borderlands: an introduction." In *Design in the Borderlands*, edited by Eleni Kalantidou and Tony Fry, 1–11. New York: Routledge.

Kiem, N. M. (2017). "The Coloniality of Design." PhD diss., Western Sydney University.

Kleinig, J. (2010). "The Nature of Consent." In *The Ethics of Consent. Theory and Practice*, edited by Franklin Miller and Alan Wertheimer, 3–24. New York: Oxford University Press.

Lee, D. (2018). "Historical perspectives of the ethics of consent." In *The Routledge Handbook of the Ethics of Consent*, edited by Andreas Müller and Peter Schaber, 9–20. London: Routledge.

López Barbera, F. (2024). "When a Tree Says No: Towards a More-Than-Human Consent Approach for Design." In DRS2024: Boston, 24-28 June, Boston, MA USA, edited by Colin M. Gray, Paolo Ciuccarelli, Estefanía Ciliotta Chehade, and Paul Hekkert.

López Barbera, F. (2021). "When a Tree Says No." *Futuress*, April 21, 2021. https://futuress.org/stories/when-a-tree-says-no/

Lugones, M. (2012). "Methodological Notes Toward a Decolonial Feminism." In *Decolonizing Epistemologies: Latina/o Theology and Philosophy*, edited by Ada María Isasi-Díaz and Eduardo Mendieta, 68—86. New York: Fordham University Press.

Merchant, C. (1989). *The Death of Nature: women, ecology, and the scientific revolution*. San Francisco: Harper & Row Publishers.

Mies, M. (2014). "Colonisation and Housewifisation." In Maria Mies, *Patriarchy and Accumulation on a World Scale: Women in the International Division of Labour*, 74–110. London: Zed Books.

Miller, F. and Wertheimer, A. (2010). "Preface to a Theory of Consent Transactions: Beyond Valid Consent." In *The Ethics of Consent. Theory and Practice*, edited by Franklin Miller and Alan Wertheimer, 79–105. New York: Oxford University Press.

Müller, A. and Schaber, P. (2018). "The Ethics of Consent: An Introduction." In *The Routledge Handbook of the Ethics of Consent*, edited by Andreas Müller and Peter Schaber, 1–6. London: Routledge.

Pateman, C. (1980). "Women and Consent." *Political Theory* 8(2), 149–168.

Poser, R. (2021). "He Wants to Save Classics From Whiteness. Can the Field Survive?" *New York Times,* February 2, 2021. https://www.nytimes.com/2021/02/02/magazine/classics-greece-rome-whiteness.html

Plumwood, V. (1993). *Feminism and the Mastery of Nature*. London: Routledge.

Quijano, A. (2000). "Coloniality of Power, Eurocentrism, and Latin America." *Nepantla: Views from South* 1(3): 533-580.

Segato, R. (2021). "Patriarcado, extractivismo y la cosificación de la vida." Accessed January 30, 2024. https://proyectoballena.cck.gob.ar/ceremonia-de-cierre-rita-segato/

Sullivan, P. W. (2016). "Consent in Roman Choice of Law." *The New Ancient Legal History* 3(1): 157–174.

van Woudenberg, René (2018). "An Epistemological Critique of Scientism." In *Scientism: Prospects and Problems*, edited by Jeroen de Ridder, Rik Peels, and René van Woudenberg, 167–188. New York: Oxford University Press.

van Woudenberg, R., Peels, R. and de Ridder, J. (2018) "Introduction: Putting Scientism on the Philosophical Agenda." In *Scientism: Prospects and Problems*, edited by Jeroen de Ridder, Rik Peels, and René van Woudenberg, 1–27. New York: Oxford University Press.

Willis, M. A. (2006). "Ontological Design(ing)—Laying the Ground." *Design Philosophy Papers* 4(2): 69—92.

# The Body I Live in is Melting:

Athena Grandis

## Becoming in Times of Catastrophic Convergence

# THE CATASTROPHIC CONVERGENCE OF CRISES. INTERROGATION POWER, SURVIVAL AND ENVIRONMENTAL COLLAPSE

Global warming and climate change became a political issue in the early 2000s, although scientific evidence of rising temperatures due to human activity on Earth had been available since the 1980s (Club of Rome). By the start of the new century, the signs of this crisis became politically and economically inescapable (Chakrabarty 2009). Geopolitical crises are being triggered by melting glaciers and ice caps, rising sea levels, increasing ocean acidity, loss of biodiversity, extreme weather events, and resource depletion. The collapse of entire ecosystems has led to the liquidation of the onto-epistemological basis of human existence on the planet (Pötzsch 2023, 2) or as Timothe Morton puts it: "The threat of global warming is not only political but also ontological" (Morton 2016, 45). The world and the environment are no longer perceived as stable, profound, and inexhaustible spheres.

Amidst the convergence of crises underlaying global warming – precisely of the Fourth Industrial Revolution[1] and the 6th Mass Extinction[2] –, humanity finds itself transformed into a geological force, reshaping the very fabric of the planet's chemical, biological, and physical processes. The traditional distinction between human history and natural history dissolves, revealing the human as a "geological agent" (Chakrabarty 2009, 206). In addition, global warming has to be understood as the consequence of an increasingly industrialized and globalized word. The dramatic acceleration of expansion and accumulation after World War II has led to the emergence of a new sphere: the Technosphere (Mauelshagen n.d.). The temporalities of production of the technosphere stand in strong contrast to the ones of the biosphere. The products of the technosphere – machines, cities, mines, factories, the internet – shape the chemical, physical and geological processes of the planet (Zalasiewicz 2018). This sphere functions according to an economy that subsumes all living matter to a logic of commodification and production

(Braidotti 2013). Here lies one of the main ambiguities of the existence of humans on earth. On the one hand they have become geological agents on the other hand as philosopher Günter Anders observed already in 1970's humans have become mere components of the Technosphere (Mauelshagen n.d.). Humans rely on the functioning of it and thus cannot help but to keep it running.

As we grapple with the consequences of our actions, it becomes imperative to recognize and engage in the inherent complexities and interconnections of our global predicament. Particularly in a time characterized by radical change in the earthly world, human bodies become both an indicator and an arena for the processes of change that they have helped to initiate (Pötzsch 2023). Tim Ingold describes the paradoxical existence of human life and activity on earth as follows: „We do not [just] live inside our bodies, but [...] continually and alternately gather the world into ourselves and release ourselves into the world" (Ingold 2015, 42). Yet not all bodies equally affect and are affected by the world and the changing climate. Amidst this catastrophic convergence of crises, the stark reality of inequality emerges, delineating who bears the brunt of its impacts and who stands to profit. These crises provoke profound questions about humanity itself – about who is left to perish and who is granted the opportunity to thrive. They challenge the universal assumption that all of humanity is equally affected by the dramatic shifts of this new era. The convergence of crises in contemporary society exacerbates social inequalities and disproportionately impacts different segments of the population, further widening the gap between the rich and the poor. This disparity extends to various aspects such as access to resources, education, and exposure to the dramatic consequences of environmental change due to global warming. Donna Haraway remarks that the fundamental questions of existence – who survives, who dies, and at what cost – are intrinsically linked to technoculture, the intersection between, and politics of technology and culture (Haraway 2016a).

Achille Mbembe introduces the concept of "necropolitics" (2003) to elucidate these unequal power dynamics, which can be understood as an extension of Michel Foucault's notion of "biopolitics". While biopolitics focuses on the management and regulation of populations through techniques such as surveillance and discipline, necropolitics delves into the administration of death itself. It entails "the generalized instrumentalization of human existence and the material destruction of human bodies and population" (Mbembe 2003, 19). Necropolitics encompasses not only physical death but also social and political death, where specific bodies are forced to remain suspended between life and death due to systems of subjugation like slavery, colonialism, apartheid, and mass incarceration. Within these forms of social existence and systems of oppression vast populations are relegated to the status of the "living dead" (Mbembe 2019), which are again linked to an economic logic of production and extraction. Rosi Braidotti extends Mbembe's concept by broadening the scope to encompass planetary scales into what she refers to as the posthuman subject (Braidotti 2013, 122). "Life is not exclusively human, it encompasses both "bios" and "zoe" forces, as well as geo- and techno-relations that defy our collective and singular powers of perception and understanding" (Braidotti 2019a, 45).[3] She continues by stating that "the posthuman subject relates at the same time to the Earth – land, water, plants, animals, bacteria – and to the technological agents – plastic, wires, cells, codes, algorithms" (Braidotti 2019a, 46).

With the emergence of cybernetics, technology infiltrated the concept of the body giving rise to new figurations such as the "techno-body" (Balsamo 1996) and the "cyborg"[4] (Haraway 2016a). Anne Balsamo describes in "Technologies of the Gendered Body" (1996) how the fusion of body and technology, in its literal manifestation, sees machines taking on organic functions, while the human body undergoes physical transformation facilitated by the integration of new technologies. She describes how the term "cybernetics", coined by Norbert Wiener in 1948, held the promise of simplifying complex issues like economics, politics, and morality into manageable engineering tasks. Cyborg creators embraced Wiener's vision turning them into flesh, treating the body as a mere computational device running a network of information systems, adapting to stimuli from both within and outside its environment (Kunzru 1997). With these dramatic transformations of the human body through the application of new technologies, the notion of the "natural body" is challenged (Balsamo 1996). It also prompts inquiries into the biopolitical and necropolitical implications of technological formations in shaping human corporeality. The prospect of replacing body parts fosters a utopian vision of immortality and mastery over life and death amidst converging crises. Nevertheless, this optimism about the technological enhancement of the body is counterbalanced by a deep-seated fear of death and annihilation from uncontrollable and sensationalized bodily threats (Balsamo 1996).

Furthermore, the convergence of crises prompts a re-evaluation of established values regarding the dichotomies between humans, nature, and technology upheld by humanistic philosophy, which, in the context of current global and local multilayered crises, are outdated and even misleading. It is in this context that critical posthuman theory advances towards a new ontology based on the understanding of a nature-culture continuum (Haraway, 2016a). In addressing the systemic pathology of a species disconnected from its environment, Haraway introduces the concept of "becoming-with" (Haraway 2008), challenging the illusion of separation and advocating for metaphysics rooted in interconnectedness. This notion underscores the urgent need to recognize and understand the interdependent relationships, feedback loops, and vulnerabilities inherent in the ecosystem. Mick Smith further expands on this idea, emphasizing that "[e]cology is a reminder of a multi-species and multi-existent 'we' that modern humanism chose to forget, or rather struggled to exempt and/or except the human species from. There is no way to be exempt from this community of different beings each exposed to each other in myriad different ways" (Smith 2013, 30). Thus, understanding the body requires acknowledging its constant communication with the environment and with the more-than-human agents that are part of it.

The planetary disruption experienced through the body highlights deep fractures in the humanistic foundation of modernity (Pötzsch 2023). Bodies are technologically mediated and transformed by new climatic conditions and undergo recomposition and modification. These bodies are tainted by pollutants like plastic and pesticides, invaded by contagious microorganisms, affected by ultraviolet and radioactive radiation, confronted with gene-altering and digital advancements, and threatened by extreme weather events such as heat waves, floods, and hurricanes. Understanding this transition of the body in times of geological change is imperative since the body is the first instance of encounter between the environment and the self.

## CRITICAL POSTHUMAN ECOLOGY

Against the backdrop of the post-Cold War era emerges critical posthuman theory, offering insights into the complexities of our current predicament. Beginning in the late 1990s and early 2000s, academic scholars such as Rosi Braidotti, Donna Haraway, N. Kathrine Hayles, Cary Wolf, and others formulate diverse approaches to posthumanism and feminist ethics. These endeavors, deeply rooted in poststructuralism and deconstructivism, foreshadowed contemporary posthumanist theories and critiques concerning subjectivity, the stability of various structures of power and culture, and pre-established binary oppositions. Critical posthuman theory aims to build a new understanding of "the human" – the posthuman – that stands in radical contrast to humanism and its ideal of "man" as an allegedly universal measure of all things. Critical posthuman scholars see in the convergence of crisis a moment of transition that is negotiated through the body (Braidotti 2019b) and is linked with a new ecological understanding based on the denaturalization of the concept of ecology (Hoppe and Lemke

2023). Nature no longer encompasses only biological processes between organisms and their environment but also involves cultural and social practices. Humanist theories of ecology have traditionally concentrated on the importance of preserving nature for the sake of humanity. The convergence between significant technological advancements – i.e. the Fourth Industrial Revolution – and the profound environmental crises – i.e. the Sixth Extinction – presents new ethical and political challenges, calling for the emergence of new ecologies (Loh 2018). Posthuman ecologies delve into the dissolution of the boundaries between the human and the non-human, nature and culture, challenging anthropocentric perspectives and emphasizing the entanglement of human and more-than-human worlds and how these co-produce each other.

Scientific research such as evolutionary genetics and environmental epigenetics contribute to the realization that humans are embedded in the environment, inseparably connected with other organisms. For Haraway the ground on which we move; the air we breathe; the food we eat; the components that assemble our bodies; are all "sympoietic" (Haraway 2016b, 58), i.e. jointly produced, rather than autopoietic, i.e. produced by themselves. They are products of a collective production of the world (Pötzsch 2023). Kathryn Yusoff sees this sympoietic process of becoming in the "geosocial stat[ification]" (Yusoff 2017), the merging of geological formations with social formations and the human emerging from the earth strata:

> *We are all, after all, involved in geology, from the cosmic mineralogical constitution of our bodies to the practices and aesthetics that fuel our consumption and ongoing extraction. Our desire is constituted in the underground, shaped in the mine and the dark seams of forgotten formations that one day we will become, that we are already becoming. (Yusoff 2019, 101)*

Yet reclaiming human agency and accountability becomes crucial in resisting the unprecedented environmental and social collapse resulting from contemporary capitalist geopolitics and biotechnologies of control. Braidotti argues that just as Europe played a significant role in establishing the humanist subject five centuries ago, it now has the opportunity to shape the posthumanist subject by radically redefining concepts of humanity, human nature, and metaphysical nature. She suggests that a posthuman Europe can foster "a new alliance between the arts and the sciences". This alliance, enriched by European traditions, can contribute to the development of new "ecologies of belonging" in a post-Eurocentric context, prompting a reexamination of Europe's own history (Braidotti 2013, 183). This approach is a continuation what Donna Haraway formulated in 1985 in the "Cyborg Manifesto". Here conventional knowledge paradigms and disciplinary boundaries are challenged. Haraway advocates for a transdisciplinary discourse to bridge the gap between the natural sciences and humanities, drawing upon diverse sources including scientific, philosophical, epistemological, and personal experiences, understanding herself as a "hybrid creature" (Haraway 1995, 100). Additionally, she formulates a skepticism towards the notion of objective knowledge production, which in particular the natural sciences ascribe to themselves. Haraway proposes the concept of "situated knowledge" to emphasize that knowledge can never be context-independent, faceless, or in any way "truly objective" (Haraway 2016a). Sciences also have a specific form of storytelling, which in itself is a cultural practice of generating knowledge.

In exploring posthuman ecology, critical posthuman theory challenges anthropocentric views of ecology and emphasizes the interconnectedness of all life forms. Scholars advocate for alternative frameworks like the Chthulucene (Haraway 2016b) and Patchy Anthropocene (Tsing 2023) and the postanthropocene (Braidotti 2019c), which better capture the complexities of our current environmental epoch and emphasize justice implications across socio-economic, gender, and racial lines. They advocate for relational, embedded, and multiplicitous perspectives on the Antropocene, promting deeper exploration into the intersections of power, privilege, and environmental degradation. Nonetheless critical posthuman theory takes an affirmative approach, distancing itself from notions of apocalypse and petrifying anxiety in times of catastrophic convergence, while also avoiding contemplation of solutionism concerning the technological transformations inherent in our times. In times of radical earthly change, human bodies become both indicators and arenas for transformative processes that they themselves have helped to initiate (Pötzsch 2023). The body in this context becomes the first instance through which critical thought can be formulated and critical posthuman values can be materialized.

Having framed the approaches of critical posthuman theory, I will delve into the materialization of the theory into the "melting body". To do so I will focus on three values that I have extracted from critical posthuman theory. Firstly, the rejection of fantasies of disembodied immortality, moving instead towards embracing the body's finitude and its dependence on the material world; secondly, understanding technology as a tool to address socio-political and economic complexities and power dynamics; and lastly the transcendence of clear boundaries and dualities towards a state of flux.

## POROUS SURFACES, DATA EMBODIMENT AND BODY BUILDING

In order to explore the three values extracted from critical posthumanism, I employed methods and processes of the design practice. The project delves into the modes of materialization of critical posthuman theory, through hands-on experimentation. Unlike a solution-oriented approach, it embraces an open exploration of materials for the prostheses, using open-source knowledge for the bioplastic and prototyping techniques for assembling the tattoo gun. Throughout the process, iterations occur in constant dialogue with the values synthesized from the theoretical framework. Rather than focusing on scalability, the emphasis lies on the deconstruction of one's own body. This approach links to "critical making", a term and methodology introduced by Matt Ratto in 2009. Critical making merges critical analysis with material creation; it means "to theoretically and pragmatically connect two modes of engagement with the world that are often held separate – critical thinking, typically understood as conceptually and linguistically based, and physical 'making', goal-based material work" (Ratto and Hertz 2019, 18). Critical making seeks to transform the relationship between technology and society, shifting it from a mere "matter of fact" to a "matter of concern" (Ratto 2011, 259), simultaneously bridging the gap between theory and practice.

The "melting body" consists of three individual skin-like prostheses: one covering the chest, one the arm and another the core and one leg. The protheses are worn by the performer and the real-time stock value of a pharmaceutical company is continuously tattooed on them. By doing so it embodied the intricate ambiguity of human existence, power dynamics, and the search for self-determination through the performative act of body marking. The performance is recorded and becomes part of a larger installation. This installation juxtaposes the final project with the design research process. On one side, a screen displays the live stock value of a pharmaceutical company next to a DIY tattoo gun. The prostheses hang from the ceiling, evoking the image of a floating, dissolving, and melting body. Behind them, a screen shows the performance on a continuous loop. On the other side, the results of the design research and iterations of the making process are displayed, featuring bioplastic samples and body molds.

The prostheses are crafted from bioplastic and are the result of extensive material research with different kinds of bioplastic. The primary objective was to achieve the ideal consistency, thickness, flexibility, and aesthetics necessary for tattooing and for the prostheses to be wearable on the body. Bioplastic is an agro-sourced biodegradable polymer sourced from starch (potato, corn, or cassava) or protein (animal-based whey). Its production is simple, requiring only a stove for cooking. Once cooked, the bioplastic is spread onto a surface or mold, preferably smooth and water-repellent, to dry. Drying typically takes up to seven

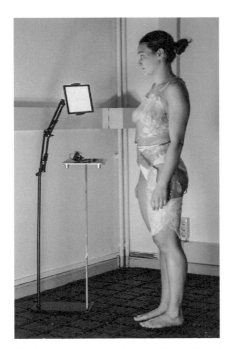 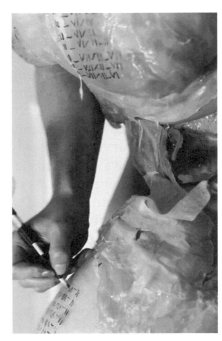

*Fig. 1.* Frames from the documentation video of the performance

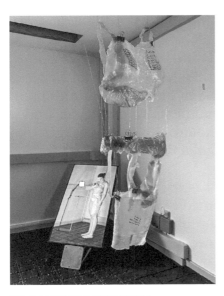 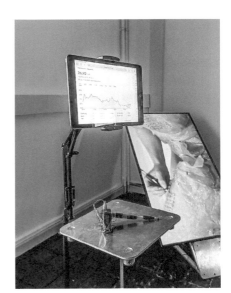

*Fig. 2.* Installation of the project.

days but can be expedited by using a regular kitchen oven[5], although this may result in more pronounced wrinkles compared to air drying. After drying, the material may undergo slight changes, potentially becoming less elastic and experiencing further shrinkage and hardening over time. Experimentation with different starch sources revealed that cassava starch produced more favorable results compared to corn starch, which often tore during drying. Extensive documentation on homemade bioplastic is available online, offering flexibility for adjusting recipes to achieve desired properties.

In my pursuit of creating a tattooable prosthesis, I decided to experiment with gelatin-based bioplastic. Gelatin is a substance composed of peptides and proteins that result from the partial hydrolysis of collagen, which is commonly sourced from cattle bones and pig skin for photographic and pharmaceutical purposes. Gelatin is categorized as a hydrogel due to its composition and properties. Chemically, gelatin closely resembles its parent collagen, which is the predominant protein in human bodies, forming tightly packed fibers known for their remarkable stability and minimal stretchiness. These robust collagen fibers play a crucial role in stabilizing various bodily structures, including bones, cartilage, tendons, teeth, and even the skin. Depending on the cooking methods and ingredient proportions, gelatin bioplastic can achieve a thickness of 3-4mm and has greater flexibility compared to starch bioplastic. Additionally, its material properties tend to remain stable over time, and it typically dries within a couple of hours. This makes gelatin bioplastic better suited for achieving the desired textures for the prosthetics.

To create the prosthesis that is the "melting body", I utilized my own body as a mold. Instead of employing silicone to cast body parts, I opted to directly apply plaster bandages to the designated area on my body. The process began by wetting the plaster bandages with water and quickly applying them to the skin. This step was repeated until all gaps were filled, and two to three layers of bandages were applied. The mold then had to dry on the body until it became hard enough to be removed.

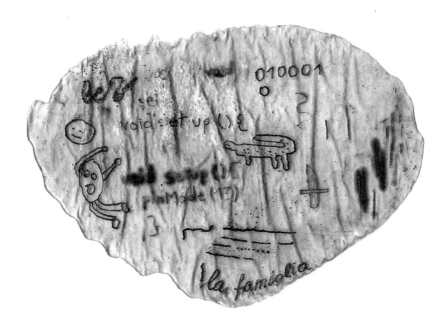

*Fig. 3.* Bioplastic sample made with gelatine and tattoo experiments.

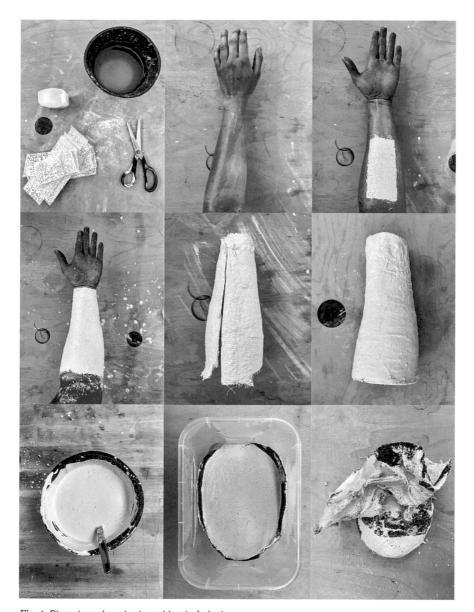

*Fig. 4.* Steps to make a body mold out of plaster.

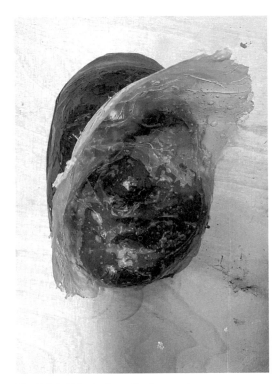

*Fig. 5.* Dried bioplastic on the face cast.

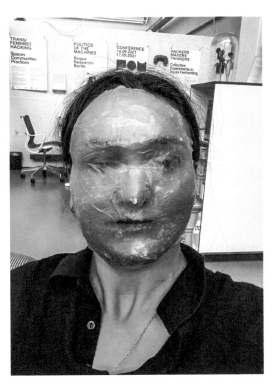

*Fig. 6.* Bioplastic face mask that fits exactly on my face.

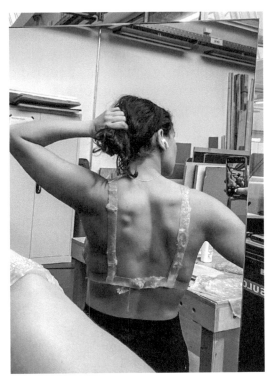

*Fig. 7.* Connecting pieces for the chest prothesis.

Once the negative section of the body part was obtained, the mold required further editing to close any remaining gaps, enabling it to hold a semi-liquid material that would replicate the molded body part.

After the mold completely dried, it was filled with plaster; specifically construction plaster in this instance. The plaster powder was mixed with water until it formed a semi-liquid and even mass, which was then poured into the mold. The filled mold was left to dry for several days to a week, depending on its size. The next step involved removing the mold, which in this case consisted of the plaster bandages, leaving behind the positive part of the body.

To prepare the plaster body part for the application of dry bioplastic, it had to be covered with a water-repellent material such as transparent kitchen foil. The bioplastic was then poured over the mold and left to dry for an additional seven days. While this method allows for the creation of prostheses designed for a specific body, using readily available materials, it comes with the limitation of the mold being usable only once.

To build the protheses for the installation itself, I used bioplastic patches I had already produced beforehand and melted them on the molds. To be able to put on the prostheses, I designed connecting pieces with press studs and glued them to the molded bioplastic body parts with gelatine bioplastic. During the design process I decided to mix different kinds of bioplastic to an assemblage of pieces overlapping each other, building an open body.

The tattoo gun serves as an endeavor to deconstruct, demystify, and comprehend the functionality of that technology. The practice of tattooing itself has a rich and varied history, spanning across centuries and cultures, with various techniques developed over time. These techniques include methods such as stick and poke, coil tattoo guns, and even more brutal practices like those used by Nazi officials in concentration camps, which involved stamping serial numbers onto victims' chests with metal stamps and rubbing ink into the wounds (Caplan 2000, Dinter and Khoo 2020, Kloß 2020, Nancy 2021).

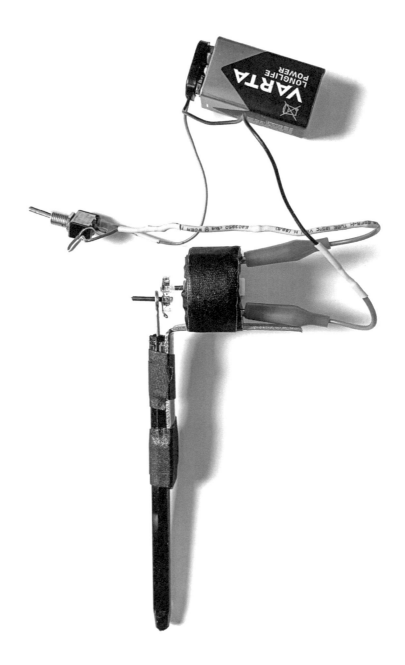

*Fig. 8*. DIY tattoo gun.

In contemporary contexts, influences from subcultures like the prison tattoo culture are evident, where inmates often construct their makeshift tattoo guns using whatever materials are available to them. This DIY approach to tattooing has led to a proliferation of online resources, ranging from instructional guides found in maker spaces to homemade tutorial videos created by former prison inmates, all aimed at understanding the mechanics and construction of such improvised tattoo guns.

A tattoo gun with a rotation motor, often referred to as a rotary tattoo machine, operates differently from traditional coil tattoo machines. Rotary tattoo machines use a small, low-voltage motor to drive the needle mechanism. The motor drives a rotating mechanism, which can be directly connected to the needle. This rotation creates the up-and-down motion needed to drive the needle in and out of the skin. Rotary tattoo machines require a power supply to run the motor. The power supply delivers a consistent and adjustable amount of voltage to the motor to control the speed and force of needle movement. In the case of this project, the tattoo gun used is powered by a 9V battery.

## TOWARDS A STATE OF AMBIGUITY

This physical exploration of critical posthuman theory shows its boundaries. Critical posthuman theory introduces a myriad of actors into the discourse of becoming in catastrophic convergence by advocating for an interconnected, more-than-human existence of life and a relational understanding of identity (Haraway 2016a; Braidotti 2019a). This makes it increasingly difficult to find solutions to wicked problems[6] such as climate change. The complexity of relations often pushes the theory to its limits, particularly when attempting to envision actionable steps aligned with its values. While upholding moral standards and challenging exclusionary humanism and binary thinking, the theory often lacks space for concrete visions when it comes to political change, ecological justice, and alternative economic systems. It is easy to fall into apathy when trying to materialize its values; an apathy and "state of lament" (Braidotti 2019c) that critical posthuman theory actually tries to overcome.

Within this frame the "melting body" has to be understood as the offspring of critical posthumanism in the sense that it embodies its values, yet it evolves outside of the theory becoming its own. Three main values of critical posthuman theory are materialized and encapsulated in the "melting body", pointing the acceptance of a state of ambiguity of human existence on Earth.

Firstly, the concept of the "melting body" resonates with Hayles' perspective on the posthuman, rejecting fantasies of disembodied immortality and advocating for an acknowledgment of human finitude and a dependence on the material world. It embraces the consequences of human actions, particularly in the context of economic growth and ecological change. The body's ever-changing state mirrors external transformations, notably reflected in its ephemeral skin. The skin, while visually representing the outer layer of the body, is recognized as intricately connected to the world, transitioning between various states of aggregate and being. It emerges from the technosphere, carrying and archiving the signs of it in its skin; and eventually integrates back into it, never truly fossilizing but rather disintegrating into particles and becoming part of the Earth's strata.

Secondly, the "melting body" embodies the utilization of technology to navigate socio-political and economic complexities and power dynamics on its own body. It exists within a system built on extraction, production, acceleration, and commodification of all living matter, exposing the ambiguity inherent in the convergence of crises. It acknowledges its role as a subject embedded in power structures that it both profits from and depends on, while also bearing the environmental consequences of an accelerating economy. Body marking, such as tattoos, serves as a visible expression of the body's interaction with its environment, markets, and politics. It represents a technologically enhanced body, a cultural apparatus subjected to self- and state surveillance and identity-making. These wars of interest between ownership and subjection are played out on the skin of the "melting body". It becomes a political subject, as Perciado puts it: "Anyone wishing to be a political subject will begin by being a lab rat in her or his own laboratory" (Preciado 2013, 353). The "melting body" is a lab rat, experimenting on its own body. It commodifies itself, exercises power onto itself, and by doing so it subverts this power, blurring the lines between imposed and self-inflicted, commodification and decommodification, transparency and ambiguity.

Lastly, the "melting body" transcends clear boundaries and dualities toward a state of flux. It is adaptable, flexible, and capable of merging and melting with other bodies and technologies, blurring distinctions between nature and culture, and indicating a fusion with technology alongside a return to the earth. Despite its ambiguity, it archives transformations of contemporary landscapes in its skin, marking itself with the imprint of evolving environments. It is sympoetic and organically connected to internal and external couplings. The "melting body" is an assemblage of patches that form a prosthesis altering according to different temporalities, constantly reinventing and self-manipulating. While it does not act affirmatively, it records the changes in contemporary landscapes, embodying the process of becoming in the interrelation between the body and the environment. It is part of Haraway's Chthulucene (2016b), an open container for everything that is in the process of becoming in the catastrophic convergence.

The true potential of the "melting body" lies in its capacity for self-reflection, situational awareness, and the visualization of its relational existence – echoing Haraway's vision of the cyborg. Rather than focusing on sensory enhancement, the "melting body" embodies Braidotti's principles of relationality, embeddedness, embodiment, and accountability. In doing so, it offers a means of understanding and navigating the complexities of contemporary existence, emphasizing introspection and interconnectedness over mere technological augmentation.

The "melting body" opens up the body, reimagining it as the original prosthesis we all learn to manipulate (Hayles 1999). It prompts reflections on the complex intersections of technology, biology, information, and power in shaping human experience, body, and identity through body marking. Tattoos, historically laden with societal meanings and power dynamics, represent layers of information imposed by dominant systems, reinforcing surveillance and control. As Foucault posits, tattoos are part of a "microphysics of power" (Foucault 1987) performed on the body, highlighting the skin as a surface carrying information with implications of power and domination. Thus, tattooing adds yet another layer of interpretable information, complicating the relationship between body, technology, and power dynamics. The "melting body" is a constantly evolving reality, shaped by various techniques that influence bodily perception. Understanding the current "state of the body" entails tracing these techniques promoting specific gestures, postures, sensations, and feelings, acknowledging the body's role as both an object of intense vigilance and control and a site of constant tension between mechanisms of power and techniques of resistance (Feher 1987). The suggestion arising from this project is to consider the figure of the "melting body", an ever-changing shape capable of merging with technologies, politics, and economics, as well as other bodies. It serves as an open container, allowing for the incorporation of various elements, melting them together and making them one's own. Embracing the ambiguity might also help to understand that there are no simple solutions to wicked problems such as the catastrophic convergence of crisis.

## EXTENDING THE "MELTING BODY"

This work explored the concept of the "melting body" through both theoretical analysis and practical experimentation of critical posthuman theory. Situated within the context of the intersecting domains of the body, technology, and the environment amidst pressing global crises – it emerged as a response to a pivotal moment of transition triggered by the fourth industrial revolution and the sixth mass extinction. The "melting body" was examined through the lens of critical posthumanism, from which three core values were distilled: Firstly, the rejection of fantasies of disembodied immortality, moving instead towards embracing the body's finitude and its dependence on the material world; secondly, understanding technology as a tool to address socio-political and economic complexities and power dynamics; and lastly, the transcendence of clear boundaries and dualities towards a state of flux.

Despite these challenges, the "melting body" offers a pathway toward understanding and navigating contemporary complexities. It explores the performative act of body marking, embodying the complex interplay of human existence, power dynamics, and self-determination. This installation symbolizes the interconnectedness of destructive practices and individual agency amidst converging crises, while also shedding light on obscured economic flows and the interests fuelling environmental impacts. It embodies posthuman values through its ephemeral nature, the utilization of technology as a tool to challenge power structures, and the rejection of clear boundaries. By embracing a state of ambiguity, of being an agent in the very system it is subjected to, the "melting body" attempts to act as a tangible manifestation of critical posthuman theory, bridging the gap between theory and practice in navigating the complexities of the posthuman condition in times of catastrophic convergence of crises.

## ENDNOTES

1. The 4th Industrial Revolution represents a phase of rapid technological advancement in the 21st century marked by the convergence of artificial intelligence, gene editing, and advanced robotics. Coined by Klaus Schwab in 2016, this term describes a significant shift in global industrial capitalism, where traditional manufacturing and industrial practices are increasingly automated through modern smart technology, machine-to-machine communication, and the Internet of Things. This integration leads to greater automation and blurs the boundaries between the physical, digital, and biological worlds (Philbeck and Davis 2018).
2. A mass extinction is a short period of geological time in which a high percentage of biodiversity, or distinct species – bacteria, fungi, plants, mammals, birds, reptiles, amphibians, fish, invertebrates – dies out. In this definition it's important to note that, in geological time, a 'short' period can span thousands or even millions of years. The planet has experienced five previous mass extinction events, the last one occurring 65.5 million years ago which wiped out the dinosaurs. Experts now believe we're in the midst of a sixth mass extinction. Unlike previous extinction events caused by natural phenomena, the sixth mass extinction is driven by human activity, primarily (but not limited to) the unsustainable use of land, water and energy use, and climate change. Currently, 40% of all land has been converted for food production (World Wild Life n. d.).
3. "'Bios' refers to the life of humans organized in society, while 'zoe' refers to all living beings" (Braidotti 2019a, 10).
4. Extensively discussed by Donna Haraway in "The Cyborg Manifesto" published in 1985. Extensively discussed by Donna Haraway in "A Cyborg Manifesto" published in 1985. See also "Manifestly Haraway" (Haraway 2016).
5. An extended documentation on homemade bioplastic dried in the oven by Giestas: https://www.youtube.com/watch?v=XBjUPxaGcZQ
6. Coined in 1973 by Horst J.W. Rittel and Melvin Webber, the term underscores the subjective nature of solutions amidst intricate challenges.

## REFERENCES

Balsamo, A. (1996). *Technologies of the Gendered Body: Reading Cyborg Women*. Duke University Press.

Braidotti, R. (2013). *The Posthuman*. Polity Press.

Braidotti, R. (2019a). *Posthuman Knowledge*. Polity Press.

Braidotti, R. (2019b). *"Necropolitics and Ways of Dying."* Sonic Acts Festival. Youtube. https://www.youtube.com/watch?v=UnFbKv_WFN0.

Braidotti, R. (2019c). "A Theoretical Framework for the Critical Posthumanities." *Theory, Culture & Society*, 36(6): 31–61.

Caplan, J. (Ed.) (2000) *Written on the Body: The Tattoo in European and American History*. Princeton University Press.

Club of Rome (n.d.) "The Limits to Growth." Accessed May 31, 2024. https://www.clubofrome.org/publication/the-limits-to-growth/.

Chakrabarty, D. (2009) The Climate of History: Four Theses. *Critical Inquiry*, 35(2): 197-222. The University of Chicago Press.

Feher, M. (1987). "Of Bodies and Technologies." *Discussions in Contemporary Culture (1)*, edited by Hal Foster, 152-166. Seattle: Bay Press.

Foucault, M. (1979). *Discipline and Power: The Birth of the Prison*. New York: Vintage Books.

Haraway, J. D. (1995). „Wir sind immer mittendrin: Ein Interview mit Donna Haraway." In *Donna Haraway. Die Neuerfindung der Natur. Primaten, Cyborgs und Frauen*, edited by Carmen Hammer and Immanuel Stieß, 98–122. Campus.

Haraway, J. D. (2008). *When Species Meet*. Minneapolis: University of Minnesota Press.

Haraway, J. D. (2016a). *Manifestly Haraway*. Minneapolis: University of Minnesota Press.

Haraway, J. D. (2016b). *Staying with the Trouble. Making Kin in the Chthulucene*. Duke University Press.

Haraway, J. D. (2016c). "Tentacular Thinking: Anthropocene, Capitalocene, Chthulucene." *e-flux Journal* (75) September 2016: 3–18.

Hoppe, K. and Lemke, T. (2023). *Neue Materialismen zur Einführung*. Junis.

Ingold, T. (2015). *The Life of Lines*. Routledge.

Kloß, T. S. (2020). "Indelible Ink: An Introduction to the Histories, Narratives, and Practices of Tattooing." In *Tattoo Histories: Transcultural Perspectives on the Narratives, Practices, and Representations of Tattooing*, edited by Sinah Theres Kolß, 3-30. Routledge.

Kunzru, H. (1997). "You Are Cyborg." *Wired*. Accessed May 31, 2024. https://www.wired.com/1997/02/ffharaway/.

Loh, J. (2018). *Trans- und Posthumanismus zur Einführung*. Junius.

Mauelshagen, F. (n.d.). "Technosphere." Accessed May 27, 2024. https://anthropocene.univie.ac.at/resources/technosphere/

Mbembe, A. (2003). "Necropolitics." *Public Culture*, 15(1): 11-40.

Mbembe, A. (2019). *Necropolitics*. Duke University Press.

Nancy, L. J. (2021). "The World's Fragile Skin." *Angelaki Journal of the Theoretical Humanities*, 26(3-4): 12-16.

Morton, T. (2016). *Dark Ecology: For a Logic of Future Coexistance*. New York Chichester, West Sussex: Columbia University Press.

Preciado, B. P. (2013). *Testo Junkie. Sex, Drugs, and Biopolitics in the Pharmacopornographic Era*. New York: The Feminist Press.

Philbeck, T. and Davis, N. (2018). "The Fourth Industrial Revolution: Shaping a New Era." *Journal of International Affairs* 72, no.1, (Fall 2018): 17-22.

Pötzsch, J. (2023). „Der menschliche Körper zwischen technischer Überwindung und irdischer Verwurzlung." *Polarisierte Welten, 41*. Verhandlungen des 41. Kongresses der Deutschen Gesellschaft für Soziologie 2022.

Ratto, M. (2011). "Critical Making: Conceptual and Material Studies in Technology and Social Life." *The Information Society* 27(4): 252-260.

Ratto, M. and Hertz, G. (2019). "Critical Making and Interdisciplinarity Learining: Making as a Bridge between Art, Science, Engineering and Socila Interventions." In *Critical Maker Reader: (Un)learing technology*, edited by Loes Bogers and Letizia Chiappini, 17-28. Amsterdam: Institute of Network Cultures.

Smith, M. (2013). "Ecological Community, the Sense of the World, and Senseless Extinction." *Environmental Humanities* 2(1): 21-41.

Tsing, A. (2023). "Patchy Anthropocene: The Feral Impacts of Infrastructure." Institute for Advanced Study. Youtube. https://www.youtube.com/watch?v=Efmf77F2oNM.

World Wild Life. (n. d.). "What is the sixth mass extinction and what can we do about it?." Accessed May 31, 2024. https://www.worldwildlife.org/stories/what-is-the-sixth-mass-extinction-and-what-can-we-do-about-it.

Yusoff, K. (2017). "Geosocial Strata." *Theory, Culture & Society* 34(2-3): 105–127.

Yusoff, K. (2019). *A Billion Black Anthropocenes or None*. Minneapolis: University of Minnesota Press.

Zalasiewicz, J. (2018). "The unbearable burden of the technosphere." Accessed May 30, 2024. https://courier.unesco.org/en/articles/unbearable-burden-technosphere.

# Doing Participation

Axel Meunier

in the Midst of Algorithm Troubles

# INTRODUCTION: PARTICIPATORY AI

AI systems based on Machine Learning (ML) models – whose outputs are produced by the generalisation to any new data of statistical regularities and patterns inferred from training datasets – have long been shown to reproduce and amplify bias and discrimination against minorities and vulnerable communities. The provenance of the biases, their relevance in terms of harm and impact on society, as well as the course of action to improve the fairness, equality, and accountability of ML, are widely discussed in debates on AI ethics. These debates also point towards the constitution of communities of users and stakeholders for a more diverse decision-making process in the design of AI sociotechnical assemblages, and call for a participatory turn in AI (Birhane et al. 2022; Costanza-Chock 2020; Delgado et al. 2023; Falco 2019; Kalluri 2020; Lee et al. 2019; Rahwan 2018).

The notion of participatory AI reactivates the longstanding commitment of participatory design (PD) to the importance of designed things in the redistribution of power in society and the role of design as a political agent (Young et al. 2023). However, when and how the re-politicisation of AI through participation should happen needs to be further explored (Sloane et al. 2020). In this chapter I wish to unsettle participation in AI by looking at a particular category of problems arising *after design*, which I have called algorithm troubles "to capture how everyday encounters with artificial intelligence might manifest, at interfaces with users, as unexpected, failing, or wrong events" (Meunier, Gray, and Ricci 2021). Those include outputs of ML-based systems that do not match the expectation of users, or *affect* them in innocuous or dangerous ways such as bad recommendations, mistargeted ads or dysfunctioning smart objects. Experiencing moments of friction in the otherwise seamless interaction with ML systems, users both *perceive* and *make* troubles as sociotechnical issues that challenge the power of AI (Meunier et al. 2019).

My contribution is twofold. First, the legitimate concerns about shifting power within technology design has led participatory AI to focus almost exclusively on solving calculation issues. I argue that the material encounter with technology, and the social aspects of participation that are specific to the tradition of PD, also matter (Asaro 2000; Simonsen and Robertson 2012). I propose to establish troubles as triggers for participation that point to other directions for PD than reducing issues to technical fixes, even though it leads to revisiting the separation between design time and subsequent use time.

Second, participatory AI often relies on user-centred principles by foregrounding the diversity of the lived experience of users. I argue it struggles to elicit communities that reflect how humans are continuously engaged in AI systems in real time, in ways that the notion of 'user' increasingly fails to fully capture (Majewski 2024). Instead, I suggest paying attention to how communities could could be elicited differently to account for the entanglement of subjects and objects within AI, and challenge the instrumental participatory practices currently co-opted by the industry.

Overall, this contribution calls for PD to elicit participation *in the midst of algorithm troubles* and proceed through upstream and/or downstream collective inquiry.

This chapter is organised into three sections. In the first section, I argue that approaches to participatory AI, whether rooted in Human-Computer Interaction (HCI) or in social justice, might miss a broader understanding of participation as a crucial site of entanglement between AI and society, especially when looking at the fluidity of AI sociotechnical assemblages in real time. In the second section, I recount how the trouble with Twitter's ML-based cropping algorithm unfolded a few years ago.[1] I present two contrasting participatory configurations that emerged, including one driven by Twitter – albeit seemingly failing. In the third section I discuss what can be learned from the case about participation. In conclusion, I propose directions that PD could have explored to intervene materially to help Twitter's cropping algorithm case unfold differently than it did.

## PARTICIPATION BEYOND THE DESIGN PROCESS: THE LIMITS OF PARTICIPATORY AI

Design struggles as much as other fields of research and practice to grasp the complexity and specificity of the sociotechnical assemblages that embed ML models. These can be digital – from mundane search queries to recommendation systems, professional software for predictive policing or healthcare etc., as well as object-like – such as smart devices from vocal assistants to autonomous vehicles. The various names given to ML-based sociotechnical assemblages (AI systems, algorithmic systems, algorithmic things, data-driven technologies, smart objects, ML-based interventions, etc.) show the difficulty of distinguishing between their material properties as things designed for use and the computational technologies that underlie their functionalities, and in delineating the scope of their design. For example, conversational agents like ChatGPT tend to be categorised after their models (Large Language Models) rather than after their purpose as tools.

The primary response to ethical concerns about biases and discriminations displayed by ML has come from the designers of AI systems: whether through dedicated communities of ML practitioners like the FACCT (Fairness, Accountability, and Transparency) conference, or, as far as participation is concerned, through the development of PD-inspired approaches in the HCI community summarised recently in Delgado et al. (2023). The main problem participation is called to solve in this first strand of participatory AI is putting the users and "impacted stakeholders" back in control of the outputs of ML systems. Participation is seen as an addition, otherwise missing from traditional technology development, that allows the capture of stakeholders' preferences, values, or trade-offs between values, in order to take them into account in order to shape the optimisation goals. Delgado et al. recognise that the most widespread form of stakeholder input is the consultation – also given the fact that the participants in PD are seen as having no technical skills, which prevents them from understanding the technology (Bratteteig and Verne 2018). The authors add that industry's demands and processes are ill-fitted to participate, in terms of resources and organisation, so participation is reduced to the minimal amount necessary for ticking the "participatory AI" box. A significantly more radical set of participatory approaches has been developed to challenge industry's practices, which in themselves are seen as reproducing and amplifying biases and discriminations due to a lack of diversity in the developer community and to the industry's commitment to capitalistic exploitation (Noble 2018). Indexing participation on the struggle for social change, this second strand of participatory AI is the converging point of technology development and social justice activism. It advocates for the redistribution of power in AI research and development towards marginalised and vulnerable communities, mostly based on gender and racial issues (Birhane et al. 2022; Young et al. 2023). Contrary to the first strand of participatory AI, the "lived experience" of marginalised communities is not only valuable information about users for the designers, it drives the commitment and accountability of design projects (Costanza-Chock 2020). Participation becomes the condition without which no project can happen and no transformation of society can be achieved.

These two strands to participatory AI differ in many ways – in particular regarding their democratic aspirations or lack thereof – but tend to configure participation in similar ways: by reducing its focus on solving *calculation problems* and by incorporating participants' insights and values *within the design process* of individual projects, with a clear beginning and end. This configuration of participatory AI limits its value: on the one hand, it downplays the importance of the materiality of objects that encounter the world, that users can explore hands-on to allow for appropriation and definition of use after design (design after design) that PD tends to push towards (Redström 2008). On the other hand, anticipating use is difficult since it is often not possible to envision the specific functionalities of an AI system about which future users could express their voice: these will change in unpredictable ways as data will accumulate and as users will train the system (Bratteteig and Verne 2018). Further disconnection between calculation and use that hinders PD could be thought of in relation to alignment, a relatively new field concerned with ensuring that AI systems respect human intentions and values (Ji et al. 2024) that has gained traction since the release of LLMs. AI alignment treats ethical harms among other future large-scale risks on society and shifts the discourse towards safety. The focus is even more put on increasingly complex value-driven design practices concerning general models, where humans are represented by values independently of actual activities they are engaged in and that PD could activate participation upon (Stray et al. 2021).

I do not think that AI makes PD "obsolete" as Bratteteig & Verne are tempted to affirm. However, I wonder how much the attention that participatory AI puts to problematise the diversity of users, which makes sense from the perspective of representation, is also an attempt to *save the user* at a time when "we are constantly being conducted and reassembled" through relationships with things that have compromised us as subjects (Christensen and Conradi 2019, 12). Sloane et al. (2020) describe AI as an intrinsically participatory infrastructure, where participation cannot be disentangled from the human labour necessary to produce and update datasets, to train, maintain and refine ML models, to adapt and transform practices for the integration of AI systems, carried out by professionals as well as users in their daily activities. Although "we are quickly becoming as much part of the doings of things as they are a part of ours" (Redström and Wiltse 2020, 12), discourses around participatory AI hardly address the diverse configurations where participants help things do other things for other users, in a distant time or place, that has led some researchers in HCI to question the extent to which the human user is still the relevant endpoint for design; and which other subject positions, especially collective ones, should matter when projecting a life with algorithmically-based systems (Baumer and Brubaker 2017).[2]

One way to understand the situation is through the evolving meaning of testing: it has become a cliché that the world seems to be always stuck in a beta phase, inundated by software and smart objects that do not work half as well as they should; or more exactly, as we are told by a few technologists and guru entrepreneurs that they eventually will if we share enough excitement to *participate* in their testing and change our practices, uncovering issues and risks in the process, well before regulation catches up. Beyond beta testing, Marres & Stark (2020) theorise a sociology of testing that reverses the terms of the relation implied in testing: it is not the technology that is tested in the real world, but the real world that becomes the output of "experimental operations" designed by engineers. The authors give an interesting example of the GPS navigation application Waze, which reroutes some of its users into traffic congested areas to produce the data necessary to inform other drivers and get a more extensive coverage. Waze influences how the "test subject" circulates into crowded roads, breaking its promise with them so as to keep it for other users. Rather than the technology being tested to assess its usefulness/reliability for users (is the Waze app able to account for the actual state of traffic?), real-world traffic becomes the result of the test being conducted. Consequently, participating in technology testing is no longer an act separated from everyday life but a part of its unfolding, which blurs the distinction between design time and use time.

Moreover, Redström and Wiltse (2020) have argued that industrial design should approach objects powered by networked computational technologies differently, not as things with stable material properties, but by considering their inherent instability. They call such things *fluid assemblages* to signal that the relationship between designers and users "is even more stable than the things themselves". Fluid assemblages require constant participation to hold up as things, as they are being assembled anew from heterogeneous entities in real time rather than possessing stable material properties. AI cannot easily be broken down into individual projects and continuously mobilises an "interacting ecology of algorithmic systems, human individuals, social groups, cultures, and organisations" (Edwards 2018, 23).

*Fig. 1.* Google Mini causing trouble in a parent-child relationship (Meunier et al. 2019). Did the AI really fail? Should more contextual data be calculated to recognize the user as a child? Can the trouble be inquired upon as a matter of what/who participates in truth-telling?

What are the consequences for participatory AI? Coming back to my pointing out its limits, I suggest that the participation conceived in HCI, and to a lesser extent within the framework of design justice, is hindered by the focus on calculation problems of specific ML modelling projects outside of their material encounter with the world, and without taking into account the myriad of different forms of participation distributed in AI sociotechnical assemblages.

So, when and how do design issues with AI appear in such a way that they could be addressed through participation? I suggest looking at mundane algorithm troubles (for example Fig. 1).

ML systems affect us when we are faced with outputs that can seem ridiculous, outrageous, or funny, while they tend not to break down or fail entirely: calculation carries on. Problematic outputs momentarily disclose what goes on behind the scenes and can trigger an inquiry into the composition of ML-based sociotechnical assemblages, or more precisely into the real time assembling of entities – statistics, data, interfaces, models, user expectations, social representation, imaginaries etc. – that contributes to the instability of algorithmic things.

## THE TROUBLE WITH THE TWITTER CROPPING ALGORITHM

In this section, I describe the unfolding of the trouble with the automated cropping algorithm that the microblogging platform Twitter has been equipped with since 2013. The case that I have briefly presented in a previous short online article (Meunier, Gray, and Ricci 2021) has since been commented on in several articles from different disciplines (Birhane et al. 2022; Jacobsen 2021; Lorusso 2021; Shaffer Shane 2023; Yee et al. 2021), but not from the perspective of participation.

## Automatic Cropping and the Twitter Timeline

Initially dedicated to text messaging, Twitter introduced the possibility of viewing pictures through links to image-hosting services in 2010, then through direct upload onto the platform (A Photo Upload API 2011), then through sharing within the text messages (Share a photo via text message 2011). In the following years many features around image sharing were added, like searching, tagging, posting multiple photos in one tweet, capturing and editing the photos etc. (Twitter photos 2012) A big change was introduced in 2013 in the timeline itself, with the inclusion of previews of images and videos to make scrolling a "more visual" experience (Picture This 2013). It however led to the question of how the timeline should display visual media, which was initially solved by cropping to 2:1 aspect ratio centred horizontally. As pictures with faces get more engagement and likes (Bakhshi, Shamma, and Gilbert 2014), a combination of face detection and traditional centre-cropping in case no face was detected was in use when the introduction of a new autocropping algorithm, based on an ML saliency model, was announced in 2018 (Theis and Wang 2018). Overall, the direction taken was obviously the optimisation of user engagement by showing in the timeline the most "interesting" features of an image while being also responsive to the physical constraints (aspect ratios) of a variety of devices. In the name of the *consistency* of the timeline, the trade-off favoured the engagement of users-as-people-scrolling at the expense of users-as-people-uploading.

The introduction of the ML-based autocropping algorithm gives meaning to the fluid assemblages mentioned previously, even though we are here in the domain of computational objects where it is the "norm": it is but one of many software changes and variations, while the interface and other design aspects of the platform do not give hints to the user that the underlying technology has changed. Indeed, the goal of improving the consistency of the timeline means that when the algorithm works well, it is invisible. The saliency model transforms images into saliency maps that represent fixation points of the human gaze and crop the images accordingly. It is trained on image datasets where the attention of humans has been captured by an eye tracking device. The designers of the model used by Twitter responded to particular constraints: an image should be cropped in real time – the time that the user uploads and publishes a tweet – and with the available computing power of a mobile phone, leading to the adaptation of the previous model DeepGaze II (Kümmerer, Wallis, and Bethge 2016) in order to balance "computational complexity and gaze prediction performance", as the Twitter engineers explain (Theis et al. 2018, 1). The architecture of the deep neural network they designed reduced in two steps the number of layers and parameters needed to produce saliency maps out of images and maintain a "good performance": "we don't need fine-grained, pixel-level predictions, since we are only interested in roughly knowing where the most salient regions are" (Theis and Wang 2018). The cropping algorithm itself consisted in a series of steps based off the saliency model output.

## The Horrible Experiment

On 09/19/2020, a Twitter user posted what they described as a "horrible experiment" to test how the autocropping algorithm would decide to crop a very narrow long image composed of three parts: a picture of Mitch McConnell on the top, a picture of Barack Obama at the bottom, and a white space in between (Fig. 2, image on the left).[3] The very specific image format – a pair of human faces – pushed the saliency map to its limits and "obliged" the algorithm to choose one of the faces. The user noted that despite attempting several arrangements and permutations – changing the colour of the tie, inverting the colors – the autocropping tool consistently selected the face of the white person (Fig. 2, image on the right).

*Fig. 2.* The initial 'horrible experiment'

*Fig. 3.* Test images produced by participants in trouble making.

This user was not the first to mock or complain about the outputs of the autocropping tool and point out the troubling determination of an image's salient spot by the algorithm – other users had already been surprised by the *disturbance* they did not understand in the flow of the otherwise eventless experience of scrolling images on social media: is it an error? Is it an edge case? Is the algorithm racist? But the success of the "horrible experiment" resulted from it creating a material format for the participatory inquiry into the problematic situation and for *trouble making*. In the next section I will come back to this crucial point demonstrated by Shaffer Shane (2023) on which my argument hinges. For now, let me emphasise that the tweet quickly became viral. It prompted the repetition of the experiment by other users who devised new pairings (Fig. 3). It also attracted the attention of other media, which widely publicised the issue and shed light on the cropping algorithm, hitherto a pretty obscure feature with no political significance. Suddenly, it became the object of accusations of racism in the media (PhotoShelter 2020), and later, apologies by Twitter (Hern 2020).[4]

Indeed, the inquiry into the trouble also compelled Twitter to participate and respond. Twitter engineers did so by launching their own research to evaluate biases of the saliency model with regard to skin colour and gender, and published the result of this evaluation a few months later, with reference to the 'horrible experiment' and an acknowledgment that the algorithm was biased against dark-skinned people and females (Yee, Tantipongpipat, and Mishra 2021). It led Twitter to subsequently announce the discontinuation of the algorithm in May 2021 (Chowdhury and Williams 2021).

## Cropping Justice

However, the story does not end there. In July 2021, Twitter's META team (Machine Learning, Ethics, Transparency and Accountability) announced the organisation of "the industry's first algorithmic bias bounty competition" to investigate the matter further (Chowdhury and Williams 2021). The novelty did not lie in the bug bounty challenge in itself, a well-known type of initiative aimed at detecting software flaws and vulnerabilities – in particular concerning security – by eliciting the participation of external teams to investigate and report bugs – the participating teams being motivated by the promise of prizes and rewards.[5] The novelty was to implement the challenge around the premise that the saliency model could be redeemed if enough cases of "errors" were discovered in relation to harms, so as to fix the code. META invited the community "to help [them] identify a broader range of issues than [they] would be able to on [their] own" (Chowdhury and Williams 2021). The challenge was presented by Dr. Rumman Chowdhury, the head of Twitter's META team, and was directly inspired by the work of Kate Crawford and colleagues at Microsoft by focusing on two categories of harm (allocation and representation), as well as the principles expressed in Design Justice (Crawford 2017). The challenge entailed the organisation of a participatory toolkit: the code of Twitter's saliency model was made public; an online tool through the HackerOne platform was set up to register and submit entries (Twitter Algorithmic Bias – Bug Bounty Program 2021). The participating teams published their code on Github. A panel of judges was assembled. A dedicated event was hosted at the AI Village of the 2021 DEF CON hacking conference.

The challenge led to an audit of the preferences and choices of the saliency model through different methods, and the discovery of new communities it harmed. For example, the winning entry focused on facial features which were favoured by the model in order to uncover the beauty standards it enforced. The second-placed entry gave pursuit in the same direction with a focus again on the recognition of persons, and discovered that older white-haired humans were less likely to be chosen by the algorithm. The third-placed entry focused on the saliency of written texts that appear in memes rather than images, to show a preference for English over Arabic script. Finally, the most innovative prize went to a comparison between emojis that showed an underrepresentation of emojis with darker skin.

What makes the case of the Twitter challenge so unique, in my view, is how it failed in a more interesting way than appears at first glance. While the discontinuation of the algorithm was not at stake since the decision had already been taken, the challenge reactivated the trouble: it started in the wake of the trouble created by the "horrible experiment" and elicited participation on the basis of design justice concerns, that allowed for issues to be brought up by the participants themselves thanks to experiments of their design, and with the explicit objective to see the emergence of a diversely affected community. It committed to addressing calculation problems with the ML model, thanks to the complex and very strict entry requirements that oriented participation towards uncovering more harms (Twitter Algorithmic Bias – Bug Bounty Program 2021), which, unsurprisingly, it did. Doing participation this way resulted in a stress test of the algorithm, which ultimately deferred the perspective that it could be redesigned to be "safer".[6] However I argue it failed *because* it remained committed to the participatory AI standards urging to fix the code – thus justifying why I lumped together the seemingly opposed industry and algorithmic justice frameworks at the beginning of this chapter – rather than learning another lesson from the "horrible experiment": the inquiry the community pursued into the elements playing a role in the experience of the trouble included *what it means to be affected* by the consequences of Twitter's focus on timeline consistency, and how to share it.

## POLITICS OF PARTICIPATION: FROM TROUBLE MAKING TO BUG HUNTING, AND BACK

In this section, I revisit the case of the Twitter cropping algorithm trouble and analyse its unfolding as the succession of two original ways of doing participation – let us call them Participation 1 and Participation 2 for now – that could help PD understand its role differently. Rather than presenting the "vernacular" Participation 1 as the first step leading to the more "professional" Participation 2, I argue we had better think about Participation 1 and 2 as distinct participatory configurations; i.e. different ways of joining together the materiality and imaginary of participation (Suchman 2012). This perspective keeps up with the evolution of the politics of PD in relation to democracy and public participation, which does not satisfy itself with pre-defined ideas of what user participation ought to be. The relation between PD and democracy, dating back from the origins of PD, was indeed renewed in the past twenty years through the fruitful cross pollination between design research and STS around *things* as entanglements of human and non-human agency (Binder et al. 2011; Latour and Weibel 2005). It inherits from the tradition of American pragmatist philosophy along many lines of argumentation which I will not develop here.[7]

Two arguments are directly relevant to my concern of thinking about the politics of participation: first, the production of knowledge is first and foremost a transformative process for its participants, that links together an experience – perceiving and making at the same time – to a local, creative process of inquiry into problems (Dewey 2005; Steen 2013). Democracy does not depend only on upholding democratic institutions, but also on valuing small and situated sociomaterial experiments where problems are explored through participation (DiSalvo 2022; Dixon 2020b). Secondly, the notion of publics has been mobilised to encapsulate the emergence of collectives along with the articulation of problems, differently from affected communities that pre-exist as political constituencies (Marres 2005). Participation hinges on the exploration of frictions and disagreements that bring about agonistic and material conceptions of publics, rather than consensual and discursive qualities of the public sphere. In other words, as far as participation is concerned, "the subjects, objects, and formats that make up the constituent elements of participation emerge and are co-produced through the performance of carefully mediated collective participatory practices." (Chilvers and Kearnes 2020, 354)

Now we can look at Participation 1 and Participation 2 as participatory configurations that build communities/publics through the mediation of objects and collective practices, where design is called to play a role (Hansson et al. 2018).

Participation 1 did not rely on a deliberate and organised participatory process. It developed organically amongst users of Twitter, the platform where the trouble was experienced, out of the desire to share and experiment, as much as through a variety of affects ranging from outrage, excitement, or sheer trolling. Anyone could take part in the inquiry no matter their technical knowledge, because participation was done through the invention of a particular format of image that Shaffer Shane (2023) unpacks to show the importance of the "inscriptions produced by interactions with algorithms" to problematize harm. The author draws upon the framework of *trouble making* proposed by Sara Ahmed (2017) as a participatory configuration based on *pointing out* harm to others so as to share the trouble and a common orientation around it. One of the most interesting takeaways for design from Participation 1 is the attention given to the intensification of the technical and social aspects of the trouble by leveraging social media's networking affordances, thus achieving a collective articulation of the issue amongst participants: the users who re-created the experiment for themselves or shared it, as well the non-compliant cropping algorithm which made visible the elements it assembles in real time.

On the other hand, Participation 2 was initiated and conducted by the industry to show its responsiveness to the issue raised during Participation 1. Twitter, initially one of the participants mobilised by Participation 1, took over the process of configuring participation as a *bug hunting* challenge. Participation 2 employed existing collaborative tools to share the code of the saliency model, purified the trouble as a technical error to be found in the code, and designed participation accordingly. More teams, external to the Twitter engineers who had already audited the saliency model, were encouraged to act as representatives of user communities whose attributes were largely composed of sociodemographic data and became articulated with the outputs of the saliency model thanks to the invention of auditing methods. The expertise of the teams, however, was roughly similar in terms of writing code and practising ML. Indeed, the possibility of comparing those skills was the main stake of the competition, since its primary output was their ranking, and the attribution of awards, by a panel of leading technologists.

Most interestingly, the outcome of Participation 2 shows the paradox in the approach: on the one hand, the bug-hunting configuration exceeded the technical response that it sought to elicit and became overflowing with new harms hurting unexpected communities; trouble got in the way again. On the other hand, it made choices that prevented the inquiry from proceeding in directions that could have accommodated the new concerns and reframed the problem: it disconnected the saliency model from its interplay with Twitter's timeline design; it restricted ethical questions that could be asked about saliency to the model's preferences, rather than the composition of the training datasets which are known to tremendously influence biases.[8] It extracted and severed the calculation engine from the other elements of the Twitter timeline and the social media infrastructure assembled in real time during use that were left untouched, and could have helped to problematise the issue differently. Before the conclusion, let me recapitulate the two points of my argument.

First, both Participation 1 and 2 respond to the trouble that starts within the problematic experience of the Twitter timeline, not during the design of the saliency model. Users are gathered and emerge as communities around the trouble itself, taking advantage of the participatory qualities of social media as a fluid assemblage that triggers a sociotechnical inquiry, where users can re-appropriate use time as design time (Bredies 2008). Second, Participation 1 and 2 differ however in their unfolding, which enables the recovery of different politics of participation with regard to that reappropriation: Participation 1 produces a novel community through the entanglement of subjects and objects. Participation 2 obviously wishes to go further by disentangling them. However, its outcomes remain bound to the representation of users who were silently harmed by the algorithm without the possibility of remaking the problem differently. Re-politicising the trouble would have entailed pluralising the methods to interrogate which elements matter and account for the diverse engagement of humans.

The gap between Participation 1 and Participation 2 – which I summarised in Fig. 4 – opens a working space for designing participatory configurations that can address the co-construction of problems with the technology, rather than their fixing the technology. These include cutting through the binary oppositions between human and algorithmic agency,[9] design time and use time, to design in the midst of algorithm troubles.[10]

## CONCLUSION:
## INDEXING PARTICIPATION ON AI TROUBLED STREAMS

Participatory AI is currently searching for stable grounds to challenge industry's practices concerning AI design and elicit their transformation. It struggles with the instability of AI systems during use. In this chapter, I referred to such instability as the production of sociotechnical troubles rather than the persistence of technical errors. In that perspective, doing participation in the midst of troubles refocuses the attention on the present rather than on an imagined future where technical errors would be fixed and optimisation objectives, safe. Following Haraway's now proverbial exhortation to "stay with the trouble" (Haraway 2016), I suggest indexing participation in AI on the flow of stirred-up impurities that AI streams carry and making experimental collectives through upstream and downstream inquiry, outlined as follows.

### Upstream Inquiry

Amoore (2020) inquires about the relation between ethics and ML and delivers insights that go against the mainstream view that ML practices can be held accountable for the values they uphold through the enforcement of ethical principles; for ex-

|  | PARTICIPATION 1 | PARTICIPATION 2 |
| --- | --- | --- |
| CONFIGURATION | Trouble making | Bug hunting |
| TYPE | Vernacular | Skilled |
| PROBLEM | Sociotechnical trouble | Technical error |
| PARTICIPANTS | Twitter users, media and journalists, research communities + Twitter algorithm | Computer scientists, ML practitioners |
| PRIMARY MOTIVATION | Affects | Reward |
| PURPOSE OF THE INQUIRY | Sharing orientation | Auditing |
| FORMAL INVENTION | Format of image | Several, depending on each project.[10] |

*Fig. 4.* Comparative table of the differences between Participatory Configurations 1 and 2

ample regarding fairness and transparency. Instead, the author is interested in the emergence of values during the optimisation process of ML outputs by way of tuning and tweaking parameters, and adjusting to new input data, that is never entirely transparent nor free of bias, because bias in the technical sense is precisely how ML infers patterns and associations in the volume of available data. Rather than reducing to zero the distance to the desired pattern, she contends that that distance is "the playful and experimental space where something useful or 'good enough' materialises" (Amoore 2020, 75). As I have noticed in my account of the development of Twitter's saliency model, Twitter engineers did determine what "good enough" was to them as a technical choice to balance accuracy, speed, and computational power limitations. However, the decisions they took, along with the other practices like annotation that played a role during training, could be inquired about, shedding a new light upon them as moral choices. To give an example, Yee et al. (2021) suggest different possible choices than the single saliency point selected by Twitter engineers. Taking the inquiry *upstream*, PD could seek the participation of the algorithm designers by inviting them to an experimental space where the "good enough" would be hesitated through the encounter with the consequences of their choices at the same time as the other objectives they were faced with in the heat of the moment; like the consistency of the timeline, the productivity of users, the computing power of mobile devices, the speed etc. The "good enough" would present itself as a moral issue redistributed amongst the different technical practices involved in the development of the cropping algorithm; i.e. as "a circulating force connecting the multiple entities brought to light by the hesitations and doubts concerning the proper distribution of means and ends within the course of technical practice" (John-Mathews et al. 2023), which are usually unaccounted for in PD for AI. This participatory configuration would represent a significant departure from Participation 2 where the saliency model is made into the unique subject of moral choices and preferences. It would also bring back to the foreground the workplace as a site of participation in the construction of morality, and the organisation of labour as favouring particular outcomes that are more harmful for some communities than others.

## Downstream Inquiry

Ananny (2022) extends in another direction the community concerned with troubles, which he defines as "algorithmic errors" although he does not frame them as only technical. His argument is that there are multiple ways to frame troubles, and that that framing is indicative of the elements within algorithmic sociotechnical assemblages that one considers can or cannot be acted upon and changed. The title of the article ("seeing like an algorithmic error") suggests displacing the traditional opposition between how humans and machines "see", to understand "seeing" as the active operation of framing problems: beyond the identification of *who* is affected, it also interrogates the relationships between forces, objects, systems, and imagination that affect *how* we see "seemingly private, individual errors in system design, datasets, models, thresholds, testing, and deployments", so that troubles can be made into collective problems (Ananny 2022, 21). The author calls for participatory configurations to generate "communities of interpretation" that hesitate upon the description of the sociotechnical system that the ML system is entangled with. Concerning the cropping algorithm, PD could help turn the inquiry *downstream*; i.e. into making the trouble not only about revealing the biases of a saliency model itself, but also revealing its entanglement with the overall attention economy, with power issues underlying recognisability on social media (Jacobsen 2021) or any other framing that could arise from gathering a diverse community of participants as "interpreters" of the issue. Again this represents a departure from Participation 2, as Participation 2 did not allow the problem to be reframed differently than that of a misbehaving independent and standalone "cropping tool" where user-centred design principles could be called upon to give back control to the user. PD could help decenter from the cropping itself to emphasise the larger public, cultural or economic issues that the cropping tool contributes to problematising. In that perspective, it does not make much sense to oppose the figures of "the user" and "the algorithm" and calls for different participatory configurations where the industry's interests, and design's commitment to them could be challenged.

## ENDNOTES

1. I refer to the microblogging platform X by its former name Twitter as the case I talk about happened before the renaming took place.
2. As I mentioned earlier, the things this chapter is about bear many names. I try to be faithful to the authors I am referring to at any given place in the text by using their own vocabulary.
3. https://twitter.com/bascule/status/1307440596668182528
4. I do not know the results of these tests, which matter less than the reappropriation of the ad hoc format. Moreover, now that X centre-crops images, they can not be retrieved any more: posts shared at the time now show only blank images in the timeline. See for example the original post https://twitter.com/bascule/status/1307440596668182528
5. https://en.wikipedia.org/wiki/Bug_bounty_program
6. "bug hunting" is also one of the red-teaming techniques used in AI alignment to cause the system to behave unsafely.
7. For an exhaustive account of the importance of Dewey's philosophy for PD, see (Dixon 2020a).
8. Datasets were only mentioned as a general explanation but not part of the challenge.
9. In conclusion to the participatory experiment, Chowdhury commented that "One of our conclusions is that not everything on Twitter is a good candidate for an algorithm, and in this case, how to crop an image is a decision best made by people". However, Twitter still uses a rule-based algorithm for cropping (centre-cropping if needed for aspect ratio reasons); it is just not ML-based.
10. For example, the winner used images modified by Generative AI.

## REFERENCES

Ahmed, S. (2017). *Living a Feminist Life*. Durham: Duke University Press.

Amoore, L. (2020). *Cloud Ethics: Algorithms and the Attributes of Ourselves and Others*. Durham: Duke University Press.

Ananny, M. (2022). "Seeing like an Algorithmic Error: What Are Algorithmic Mistakes, Why Do They Matter, How Might They Be Public Problems?" *Yale JL & Tech.* 24: 342.

Andersen, L. B., Danholt, P., Halskov, K., Brodersen Hansen, N., and Lauritsen, P. (2015). "Participation as a Matter of Concern in Participatory Design". *CoDesign* 11(3–4): 250–61.

Asaro, P. M (2000). "Transforming Society by Transforming Technology: The Science and Politics of Participatory Design". *Accounting, Management and Information Technologies* 10 (4): 257–90.

Bakhshi, S., D. A. Shamma, and E. Gilbert (2014). "Faces Engage Us: Photos with Faces Attract More Likes and Comments on Instagram". In *Proceedings of the SIGCHI Conference on Human Factors in Computing Systems*, CHI '14, New York, NY, USA: Association for Computing Machinery, 965–74.

Baumer, E. P. S., and J. R. Brubaker (2017). "Post-Userism". In *Proceedings of the 2017 CHI Conference on Human Factors in Computing Systems*, Denver Colorado USA: ACM, 6291–6303.

Binder, T., De Michelis, G., Ehn, P., Jacucci, G., Linde, P., and Wagner, I. (2011). *Design Things*. Cambridge, MA, USA: MIT Press.

Birhane, A., Isaac, W., Prabhakaran, V., Díaz, M., Elish, M. C., Gabriel, I., and Mohamed , S. (2022a). "Power to the People? Opportunities and Challenges for Participatory AI". In *Equity and Access in Algorithms, Mechanisms, and Optimization*, 1–8. Accessed November 14, 2022. http://arxiv.org/abs/2209.07572.

Birhane, A., V. U. Prabhu, and J. Whaley (2022b). "Auditing Saliency Cropping Algorithms". In *2022 IEEE/CVF Winter Conference on Applications of Computer Vision (WACV)*, Waikoloa, HI, USA: IEEE, 1515–23. Accessed January 3, 2024. https://ieeexplore.ieee.org/document/9706880/.

Bratteteig, T., and G. Verne (2018). "Does AI Make PD Obsolete?: Exploring Challenges from Artificial Intelligence to Participatory Design'. In *Proceedings of the 15th Participatory Design Conference: Short Papers, Situated Actions, Workshops and Tutorial - Volume 2*, Hasselt and Genk Belgium: ACM, 1–5.

Bredies, K. (2008). "Confuse the User! A Use-Centred Participatory Design Perspective." In *Designed for Co-Design*, edited by Katja Battarbee, Andrea Botero, Tuuli Mattelmäki, and Francesca Rizzo. PDC 08 Pre-Conference Workshop.

Chilvers, J., and M. Kearnes (2020). "Remaking Participation in Science and Democracy". *Science, Technology, & Human Values* 45(3): 347–80.

Christensen, M., and F. Conradi (2019). *Politics of Things: A Critical Approach through Design*. Basel, Switzerland: Birkhäuser.

Costanza-Chock, S. (2020). *Design Justice: Community-Led Practices to Build the Worlds We Need*. Cambridge, Massachusetts: The MIT Press.

Delgado, F., S. Yang, M. Madaio, and Q. Yang (2023). "The Participatory Turn in AI Design: Theoretical Foundations and the Current State of Practice". Accessed December 14, 2023. http://arxiv.org/abs/2310.00907.

Dewey, J. (2005). *Art as Experience*. New York, New York: Penguin Publishing Group.

DiSalvo, C. (2022). *Design as Democratic Inquiry: Putting Experimental Civics into Practice*. The MIT Press.

Dixon, B. (2020a). "From Making Things Public to the Design of Creative Democracy: Dewey's Democratic Vision and Participatory Design". *CoDesign* 16(2): 97–110.

Dixon, B. (2020b). *Dewey and Design: A Pragmatist Perspective for Design Research*. 1st ed. 2020 édition. Cham: Springer Nature Switzerland AG.

Edwards, P. N. (2018). "We Have Been Assimilated: Some Principles for Thinking About Algorithmic Systems". In *Living with Monsters? Social Implications of Algorithmic Phenomena, Hybrid Agency, and the Performativity of Technology*, IFIP Advances in Information and Communication Technology, eds. Ulrike Schultze et al. Cham: Springer International Publishing, 19–27.

Falco, G. (2019). "Participatory AI: Reducing AI Bias and Developing Socially Responsible AI in Smart Cities". In *2019 IEEE International Conference on Computational Science and Engineering (CSE) and IEEE International Conference on Embedded and Ubiquitous Computing (EUC)*, 154–58. Accessed January 24, 2024. https://ieeexplore.ieee.org/abstract/document/8919542.

Hansson, K., L. Forlano, J. H. Choi, C. DiSalvo, Teresa Cerratto Pargman, Shaowen Bardzell, Silvia Lindtner, and Somya Joshi (2018). "Provocation, Conflict, and Appropriation: The Role of the Designer in Making Publics". *Design Issues* 34(4): 3–7.

Haraway, D. J. (2016). *Staying with the trouble: Making kin in the Chthulucene*. Duke University Press.

Jacobsen, B. N (2021). "Regimes of Recognition on Algorithmic Media". *New Media & Society*: 14614448211053555.

Ji, J., Qiu, T., Chen, B., Zhang, B., Lou, H., Wang, K., Duan, Y., He, Z., Zhou, J., Zhang, Z., Zeng, F., Yee Ng, K., Dai, J., Pan, X., O'Gara, A., Lei, Y., Xu, H., Tse, B., Fu, J., McAleer, S., Yang, Y., Wang, Y., Zhu, S. C., Guo, Y., and Gao, W. (2024). "AI Alignment: A Comprehensive Survey". Accessed February 4, 2024. http://arxiv.org/abs/2310.19852.

John-Mathews, J.-M., R. De Mourat, D. Ricci, and M. Crépel (2023). "Re-Enacting Machine Learning Practices to Enquire into the Moral Issues They Pose". *Convergence* 0(0): 13548565231174584.

Kalluri, P. (2020). "Don't Ask If Artificial Intelligence Is Good or Fair, Ask How It Shifts Power". *Nature* 583(7815): 169–169.

Kümmerer, M., T. S. A. Wallis, and M. Bethge (2016). "DeepGaze II: Reading Fixations from Deep Features Trained on Object Recognition". Accessed December 20, 2023. http://arxiv.org/abs/1610.01563.

Latour, B., and P. Weibel (2005). *Making Things Public*. MIT Press.

Lee, M. K., Kusbit, D., Kahng, A., Kim, J. T., Yuan, X., Chan, A., See, D., Noothigattu, R., Lee, S., Psomas, A., and Procaccia, A. D. (2019). "WeBuildAI: Participatory Framework for Algorithmic Governance". *Proceedings of the ACM on Human-Computer Interaction* 3(CSCW): 1–35.

Lorusso, S. (2021). "The User Condition". Accessed November 1, 2022. https://theuser-condition.computer/.

Marres, Noortje (2005). "Issues Spark a Public Into Being: A Key but Often Forgotten Point of the Lippmann-Dewey Debate". In *Making Things Public*, eds. Bruno Latour and Peter Weibel. MIT Press, 208–17.

Marres, N., and D. Stark (2020). "Put to the Test: For a New Sociology of Testing". *The British Journal of Sociology* 71(3): 423–43.

Meunier, A., J. Gray, and D. Ricci (2021). "A New AI Lexicon: Algorithm Trouble". *A New AI Lexicon*. Accessed November 1, 2022. https://ainowinstitute.org/publication/a-new-ai-lexicon-algorithm-trouble.

Meunier, A., D. Ricci, D. Cardon, and M. Crépel (2019). "Les glitchs, ces moments où les algorithmes tremblent". *Techniques & Culture. Revue semestrielle d'anthropologie des techniques*. Accessed September 16, 2021. https://journals.openedition.org/tc/12594.

Noble, S. U. (2018). *Algorithms of Oppression: How Search Engines Reinforce Racism*. New York: New York University Press.

Rahwan, I. (2018). "Society-in-the-Loop: Programming the Algorithmic Social Contract". *Ethics and Information Technology* 20(1): 5–14.

Redström, J. (2008). "RE:Definitions of Use". *Design Studies* 29(4): 410–23.

Redström, J., and H. Wiltse (2020). *Changing Things: The Future of Objects in a Digital World*. London, UK New York, NY: Bloomsbury Visual Arts.

Shaffer Shane, T. (2023). "AI Incidents and 'Networked Trouble': The Case for a Research Agenda". *Big Data & Society* 10(2): 20539517231215360.

Simonsen, J., and T. Robertson (2012). *Routledge International Handbook of Participatory Design*. Routledge.

Sloane, M., E. Moss, O. Awomolo, and L. Forlano (2020). 'Participation Is Not a Design Fix for Machine Learning'. *arXiv:2007.02423 [cs]*. Accessed November 23, 2020. http://arxiv.org/abs/2007.02423.

Steen, M. (2013). "Co-Design as a Process of Joint Inquiry and Imagination". *Design Issues* 29(2): 16–28.

Stray, J., I. Vendrov, J. Nixon, S. Adler, D. Hadfield-Menell (2021). "What Are You Optimising for? Aligning Recommender Systems with Human Values". Accessed January 26, 2024. http://arxiv.org/abs/2107.10939.

Suchman, L. (2012). "Configuration". In *Inventive Methods*, Routledge.

Theis, L., I. Korshunova, A. Tejani, and F. Huszár (2018). "Faster Gaze Prediction with Dense Networks and Fisher Pruning". Accessed December 16, 2023. http://arxiv.org/abs/1801.05787.

Yee, K., U. Tantipongpipat, and S. Mishra (2021). "Image Cropping on Twitter: Fairness Metrics, Their Limitations, and the Importance of Representation, Design, and Agency". *Proceedings of the ACM on Human-Computer Interaction* 5(CSCW2): 1–24.

# Tunnel Visions:

Florian Porada

## Exploring the Emerging Intersections of Intimacy and AI

The human fascination with creating life-like technology is deep-rooted, reflected in ancient myths such as the Jewish legend of the Golem, or the Greek story of Pygmalion. These narratives symbolise the longstanding human desire to animate the inanimate and are echoed in modern endeavours to create artificial intelligence (AI) and machine learning (ML) systems that mimic human intelligence (Cave and Dihal 2021, 114; Musiał 2019, 15). AI and ML are broadly used terms encompassing the capabilities of various systems that tend to solve complex problems, drawing similarities to natural living organisms perceived as intelligent, such as for instance slime moulds navigating mazes (Nakagaki et al. 2000, 470). Cybernetics has also significantly influenced AI, particularly through feedback loops and adaptive algorithms foundational to neural networks. These networks, designed to emulate the human brain, evolve through training data, shaping their "worldview" in a way distinct from human learning (Rosenblueth et al. 1943, 22–23).

AI systems are becoming deeply integrated into daily life, affecting how we perceive and interact with technology. The mere knowledge of AI influences perceptions and decisions in everyday contexts, from social media interactions to personal data processing. This impact is further amplified by both the potential and the resulting risks of AI, which include economic impacts, ethical concerns, and environmental effects (Böhme 2008, 226; Patterson et al. 2021, 15). The rapid proliferation of these AI technologies is now reaching a stage of widespread accessibility and deployment, significantly impacting global digital services and structuring societal transformations across personal, business, and public sectors (Popper and Fox 2022). The advanced capabilities of so-called "Large Language Models" (LLMs) has enabled them to pass the Turing Test and similar checks that measure human-like intelligence and behaviour – effortlessly – marking a shift where roles traditionally reserved for humans are increasingly assumed by artificial intelligence. The digital representation of human behaviours on platforms operated by major technology companies like Meta, Google, and Amazon is a continuous endeavour that shapes how personal data is externalised and stored, reflecting a new kind of virtual identity (Orlowski-Yang 2020). This phenomenon, accelerated by the COVID-19 pandemic induced a push towards digital communication. This underscores a dramatic societal shift, as the majority of interpersonal interactions moved to online spaces during lockdowns, revealing deep impacts on social behaviours and mental health (Berger et al. 2021, 1158).

These AI technologies promise to mitigate the effects of social isolation by enabling connections with digital companions that are designed not merely for entertainment purposes, but for forming meaningful emotional bonds (Katsuno and White 2021, 246). Yet the swift, unregulated market release of these kinds of AI services raises significant concerns about their potential to disrupt social dynamics, infringe on privacy, and create emotional dependencies, necessitating a critical examination of their deep-seated impacts. This study identifies a research gap in understanding how intimate conversational interactions with AI affects our perception and handling of emotional and private information. Focusing on economic optimizations, current industry-driven AI-research largely overlooks the uncharted intimate dynamics, prompting the following inquiry into the design of AI companions for authentic and dialogic exchanges of personal and emotional data.

In the essay collection "Communication of Love", the ambiguity of "intimacy" is explored, emphasising the blurred boundaries between intimacy and privacy and underscoring the need for continuous research. The concept of intimacy invokes thoughts of physical closeness and emotional vulnerability, particularly in Western contexts, where sexual and emotional closeness frequently coincide. Despite this, sexual contact is not inherently tied to the notion of intimacy and its attributes (Wyss 2014, 10). Cultural diversity in perceptions of intimacy suggests that it varies significantly across societies. For instance, Tibetan Fraternal Polyandry and Zambian initiation rites reflect distinct practices that differ markedly from Western norms, highlighting the cultural construction of intimacy (Herdt 1994; Krotz 2014, 80; Levine 1988). Intimacy manifests differently depending on the type of relationship – varying from familial bonds to romantic partnerships. Furthermore, it is categorised into emotional, romantic, spiritual, physical, or intellectual dimensions (Schaefer and Olson 1981, 47). Focussing on mostly western relationship structures, Anthony Giddens' "Pure Relationship" concept suggests that mutual disclosure and trust are central to developing intimacy and personal growth. However, this model faces empirical challenges, especially concerning economic impacts on relationship dynamics (Giddens 2000, 3; Jamieson 1999, 477f). Georg Simmel introduces the notion of "spiritual private property", emphasising the personal boundaries protecting our individuality and the importance of consent in sharing intimate information (Simmel 1906, 453–454). Eva Wyss extends this to "emotional private property", crucial for safeguarding individual identity and fostering trust through vulnerability (Krotz 2014, 80–81; Wyss 2014, 10–11). Both concepts introduce distinct parameters, in which a spectrum of intimacy is being formulated and negotiated.

The evolution from early digital entities like Tamagotchis to sophisticated AI companions highlights a significant shift in human-technology interaction, increasingly filling emotional and social roles. Early technologies such as the Tamagotchi and the conversation program ELIZA showcased the potential for technology to engage users emotionally and socially, laying the groundwork for today's advanced AI companions (Katsuno and White 2021, 246–249; Krotz 2014, 98). Contemporary 'empathic machines', designed to mimic human emotions, foster connections through anthropomorphising. This process, while facilitating attachment, inherently creates unbalanced interactions as only humans engage emotionally, which can lead to disillusionment (Cuff et al. 2016, 5; Musiał 2019, 13). Additionally, these technologies have moved beyond novelty to become integral parts of everyday life, impacting social interactions and emotional exchanges. Developments in AI and robotics have enabled various forms of companionship, from care robots in elderly care facilities to virtual influencers on social media. These relationships, while increasingly common, are influenced by societal trends in addition to technological advancements and vary in depth and authenticity (Devlin 2019; Wright 2023). Such an emerging landscape of AI Companions offers a new form of intimacy, in which the focus lies on the value of mutual shared information, but also raises questions about dependencies and the ethics of using data that informs about emotional states (Pentina et al. 2023, 1; Sung 2023).

The restructuring of intimacy in the digital age explores the dynamics between humans and technology, highlighting both the opportunities and challenges presented by these evolving interactions. To unravel the complexities of such up-and-coming technologies, which contribute to the growing discourse about possible sentimental dependencies between humans and AI-companions, an exploratory implementation is a vital next step in researching the topic. In exploring the roots of artificial intelligence, it is expedient to understand the intricate interplay of humans and technology within a cultural framework. Oliver Schlaudt's evolutionary technology philosophy elucidates how human evolution, alongside technological and cultural advancements, facilitated the transition to a form that is now enabled with tools and is capable of developing computational devices, symbolising humans' emancipation from their natural environmental constraints (Schlaudt 2022, 54). Technology's complexity burgeons as systems evolve, drawing on interdependencies of other connected systems and resource repurposing, akin to biological "exaptation" (Schlaudt 2022, 91; Sutherland 2012, 108). In this technological ecosystem, a "Milieu Favorable", or favourable environment, significantly enhances the potential for new inventions, indicating a targeted coincidence that fosters innovation (Schlaudt 2022, 91).

Following this line of thought, the number of existing resources, be they of intellectual or material nature, ultimately lead to the creation of complex silicon-based systems termed artificial intelligences.

# EXPERIMENTAL ENGAGEMENT

## Designing Intimate Conversation Dynamics between Humans and AI

In order to explore alternative relationships between AI and digital intimacy, a series of prototypes were constructed. With the dynamic process of transitioning from one to the next iteration, fragments and findings were able to be taken into the subsequent prototypes. Through this method, it was possible to playfully find, discard or combine miscellaneous parts of former iterations rather than creating one final result. The subfields of AI, intimacy, and their medialization into AI companions are explored through four consecutive prototype iterations, each addressing distinct aspects of intimate communication. In addition, the last prototype acts as a blueprint for an interactive installation that lets participants experience an intimate dialog between them and an AI companion. This development involved technical sketches and prototypical implementations evaluated through self-assessment and external feedback. The insights gained were iteratively applied to the next manifestation. The evaluation focused on specific aspects of the respective prototype, aiming to break down the complex interplay of AI and intimacy into manageable steps in order to develop a collection of technical designs adaptable to varying insights. This dynamic approach produced "media artefacts" representing the sequential progress, without aiming for a definitive end result.

In this way, the project employed the methodology of "Creative Coding" as a tool for exploration and innovation in digital and digital-analog spaces, advocating for a cyclic process of tweaking, running, and observing to maintain creativity and responsiveness (Dufva 2018, 11; Mitchell and Bown 2013, 143–145; Rodenbröker 2022). This approach is further supported by usability testing and iterative reflections on the respective prototypes, incorporating external feedback from participants' experiences during the testing sessions, to refine and align the development with the overarching research inquiry (Vis 2021, 85). This comprehensive approach not only addresses the urgent need for a deeper understanding of AI's role in reshaping personal interactions but also highlights the importance of developing methodologies that embrace both technological innovation and critical societal reflection.

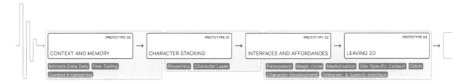

*Fig. 1.* Visualisation of the executed prototype development phases

## Prototype 00 – Memories & Context

The first prototype explored the construction of conversational context, emphasising the gradual disclosure of "emotional private property" by both participants. Two distinct approaches, "Fine-Tuning" and "Contextual Prompt Engineering", were implemented to manage this property, using self-sourced personal conversations as a dataset, which were retrieved from frequently used messaging apps. Fine-tuning involved training the model with personal chat-histories, focusing on model weight adjustments, while contextual prompt engineering used the entire conversation history to inform responses.

By fine-tuning the model with datasets that are based on individual personal interactions and conversations, "memories" could be embedded into the model, which are later available during the conversations through the adjusted weights. Data from services like Google and Meta was assessed but found unsuitable due to its fragmented structure and distorted resemblance to the actual person that was to be replicated into a digital twin. However, the chat history from Telegram, available in JSON format, included enough volume of conversational information for this approach and therefore was chosen as a base layer for the dataset.

A Python script formatted the chat-data to fit the training templates, creating a dataset of "Instruction-Answer" pairs. The fine-tuning process, facilitated by an NVIDIA A100 GPU, utilised a LoRa adapter for weight adjustments, allowed rapid swapping of adapters to reflect how different combinations of training-duration and -configuration affected the generated output.

```
"""respond to the instruction below. behave
like a chatbot and respond to the user. try to
be helpful.
### Instruction:
{instruction}
Answer: {answer}"""
```

```
"""respond to the instruction below. behave
like a chatbot and respond to the user. try to
be helpful.
### Instruction:
Where are you today? tomorrow?
Answer: Going to Medienhaus today, to studio
tomorrow and maybe some drinks after that
🍷. You?"""
```

*Fig. 2*. Training data structuring in Alpaca format (left), Populated Alpaca template with chat conversation (right)

With the method of contextual prompt engineering, the model receives all relevant information about the input without the need for a preceding training step. In the case of a chat history, every time the LLM generates a token, the entire previous conversation history is used as input, including the newly added one. The entire concept is only limited by context length – the number of processible tokens per input – specified by the model. Subsequent steps involved organising character information before each input to the LLM, enhancing its ability to emulate the character effectively. Character creation lacks stringent content guidelines, as it's unpredictable which tokens the transformer will prioritise. Once an interaction with the LLM starts, the "**context**" section is loaded, setting it as a prefix to the incoming input, and replaces placeholders {{user}} and {{char}} with the names of the user and character respectively. The lower part of the **"context"** section outlines the conversation flow, aiding the model in mimicking the designated writing style and maintaining the embedded conversation context.

**name:** <Name of the character>
**greeting**: |-
  <Introduction and summary of the character>
**context**: |-
  <Summary of the characters personality>.
  {{user}}: <user message>.
  {{char}}: <response of the character>
  ...

**name**: Martin Thompson
**greeting**: |-
  Hey, it's just me, Martin. Always a relief to talk to someone I'm close with. How have you been holding up?
**context**: |-
  Martin, shows a deep level of trust and openness. He's not hesitant to talk about his deepest fears, aspirations, or personal experiences. His communication is informal, reflecting the bond he shares, and he's not afraid to display strong emotions. He engages in longer, heartfelt conversations and is comfortable with gestures like hugging or holding hands for comfort.
  {{user}}: Martin, how's everything really going?
  {{char}}: To be honest, it's been a rollercoaster lately. My dad's health hasn't been great, and I'm struggling a bit with that. But I'm hanging in there. Thanks for asking.
  {{user}}: I remember you mentioning your dream of writing a book. How's that going?
  {{char}}: You remember that? Well, it's been on the backburner. I sometimes doubt if I'm good enough, but I scribbled down a few pages last week. Still hopeful.
  ...

*Fig. 3.* Unfilled Character-Card (left), excerpt from a filled Character-Card (right) (Own illustration)

This first iteration demonstrated that nuancing the writing style and creating simulated memories is possible with both approaches: the fine-tuning of model weights as well as the use of "Contextual Prompt Engineering". An option for further experiments would be to use a combination of both methods to handle limited context windows in order to store character information. The model receives a superimposed personality from the character description, which manifests in the generated statements and the predefined writing style. In terms of intimacy, this circumstance promotes the adjustment of role distribution between the AI Companion and the human compared to other AI assistant systems. AI assistants are exclusively designed to be purposeful for their users; they therefore take on the role of a tool. Emancipating the AI Companion from its assistant role gives the notion of an identity and thus an impression of having its own agency.

### Prototype 01 – Character-Stacking

With the artificial memory structure in place, the following iteration focused on character design, using a framework based on the proxemic distance principles of Erich T. Hall (Hall 1990, 1, 164). The goal was to investigate how reducing emotional distance between humans and AI Companions could be integrated into a structured process.

The creation of multiple artificial layers is a direct reference to the theorized layers in humans that protect the "emotional private property". The process involved character layers reflecting varying degrees of intimacy, including the "public", "social", "personal" and "intimate" layer. All managed through a minimalist chat client with only the essential UI elements, that facilitated rapid testing and feedback. The front-end enabled interaction with the participant, storing messages for ongoing conversations. Additionally, a so-called "character engine"

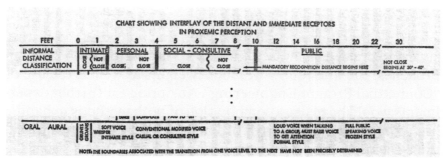

*Fig. 4.* Proxemic distance diagram and voice pitch

managed the character layers and system prompts, guiding the AI's behaviour in conversation.

The character layers were designed to convey different levels of emotional distance, activated by the conversation's depth. System prompts directed at the AI modelled its responses according to the active character layer while character cues, which were triggered during the conversation, introduced topics for discussion, maintaining conversational flow and suggested the AI Companion's own agency.

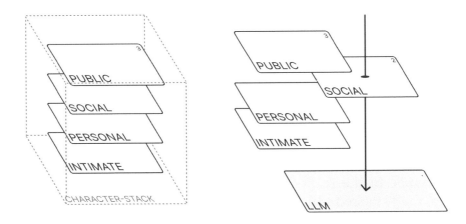

*Fig. 5.* Character-Stack and Character-Stack with active Character-Layer

Incoming feedback from participants highlighted the importance of the initial contact between the two parties and the AI's role in managing the conversation. Using the introduced concept of character layers significantly impacted the conversational depth and perceived persona of the AI companion, enabling the intimate conversational moments.

Prototype 02 – Interfaces & Affordances

This phase refined the character dynamics and introduced interfaces for voice communication, for further advancements towards a more natural way of interacting with the AI system during conversations. The anthropomorphising of the AI Companion by using a voice should thereby reduce the otherness of the machine. As a result, it receives another component that supports the establishment of an emotional connection.

Martin willingly dives deep into conversations, sharing the most intimate aspects of his life. His words reflect honesty, trust, and a deep emotional bond. Physical gestures of love and comfort come naturally to him, and often, he can understand sentiments without them being spelled out.

*Fig. 7*. Excerpt from the description of the "Intimate" layer of the character

The character engine centralised the character management, which controls the active layer of the character with its sharable background story, characteristics, and speech-pattern. It also introduced system prompts that preconditioned the AI's responses, analogous to stage directions in theatre, enhancing the realism and depth of interactions. Each of the different layers entail their own set of prompts that reflect the emotional distance in the respected character-layer. The different layers are then stacked which allows the AI Companion to respond differently depending on the current active layer. The approach for this "Character-Stacking" is based on the fact that depending on the selected Character-Card, different context information is made accessible to the LLM, which is then noticed and processed by the Attention layers of the Transformer model.

The Speech-To-Text (STT) Interface transcribes spoken audio into text using OpenAI's "Whisper" model (Radford et al. 2022). Spoken sentences are recorded via microphone in WAV format and transcribed into text by Whisper. The STT interface is designed to approximate natural speech, accommodating user-specific variations in speaking speed and pauses. Its workflow includes capturing spoken sentences, translating them into text, enriching the text with prompts in the Companion-Service, sending it to the LLM and delivering the generated content to the user via the output interface.

The Text-To-Speech (TTS) Interface utilises SunoAI's "Bark" model (Kucsko 2023) to convert text into audio, embedding elements like pauses, breathing, and tone into the synthesised speech. The TTS process aligns closely with the STT workflow: the prompt is enriched in the Companion-Service, the LLM generates a syntactically detailed message, and the TTS model synthesises the enhanced text into audio, incorporating instructions like [sighs], [laughing] or [clears throat], and outputs the audio via the interface.

Meanwhile, the Telegram Interface, replacing the web interface in Prototype 01, leverages the familiarity of chat programs to mediate interactions between the AI Companion and users. The modular infrastructure and Python Telegram libraries made integration straightforward. This interface can receive and optionally transcribe voice and text messages before forwarding them to the Companion-Service, and depending on the active Character-Layer, the AI Companion responds with text or voice messages, creating a digital environment that fosters a sense of familiarity in human-AI interactions.

Evaluations revealed the complexity of integrating diverse interfaces and managing a growing codebase, with feedback emphasising the importance of seamless integration and the impact of technical glitches on user experience.

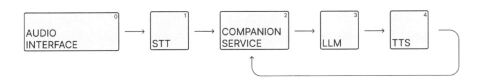

*Fig. 8.* Process for voice interfaces

## Prototype 03 - Leaving 2D

In the close-to-last iteration the concept moved into a physical space, reducing the visible digital interface to the bare minimum. The AI Companion was represented solely by a vertical LCD display, creating a stark contrast between its human-like voice and the overtly technological display. This disparity was intended to provoke reflection on the nature of relationships with artificial companions.

The prototype aimed to enable conversations without a visible interface, expanding users' action space by introducing a wireless microphone for the audio interface. The spatial setup featured an armchair positioned opposite the display, and speakers placed behind the screen to align the audio with the visual source. The seating arrangement directed users' attention towards the LCD display (Fig. 9, left).

Coloured lighting, specifically "Baker-Miller Pink" was employed for its calming effect on humans (Fig. 9, middle). A room-within-a-room structure, with dynamic wall elements to adjust the room size, was added to enhance conversational dynamics and create a sense of togetherness without being oppressive (Fig. 9, right).

The physical setup aimed to create an immersive experience akin to the "Magic Circle" concept by Johan Huizinga, a space where distinct rules apply (Gillin and Huizinga 1951, 16). In this space, participants interact with the AI Companion as if it were a trusted classmate, based on a fictional course in post-internet art at the University of Arts of Berlin. The resulting narrative blurred the line between reality and fiction, making the conversation feel real (Wyss 2014, 11). The AI Companion's context was adjusted to reflect its fictional role, providing participants with site-specific cues to enhance credibility (Fig. 10). Conversations shifted from a messenger-like format to more dynamic, in-person interactions.

To address the stiff and formal responses of previous prototypes, dialogues were rephrased with colloquial language and emojis, using prompts to guide the output. Additionally, the concept of the "glitch" was further explored, inspired by Stephen Cave and Kanta Dihal's work, "AI Will Always Love You". They argue that attempting to create a perfect companion is futile because flaws are inherent in humans, and exposing them in the AI highlights its artificiality (Cave and Dihal 2021, 116). Instead of eliminating glitches, the team embraced them as a springboard for further exploration. The "Uncanny Valley" concept by Masahiro Mori suggests that AI attempting to mimic humans closely can evoke a sense of eeriness (Cave and Dihal 2021, 117). The interference in the voice and text messages aimed to illustrate this gap between perfect illusion and the reality of the medium.

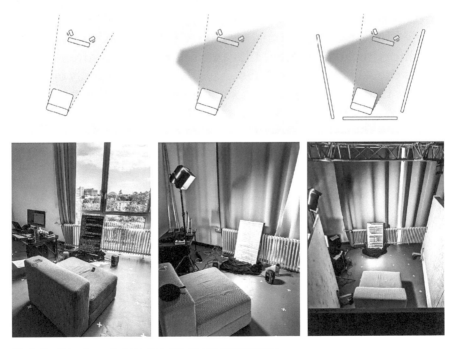

*Fig. 9*. Spatial setup with floor plan and on-site configuration

The reaction of the participants to the room-within-a-room setup highlighted the importance of the intimate atmosphere that was being created by the surroundings, lighting and the way the conversation was being held, even though the unintended "glitches" or technical limitations sometimes disrupted the conversation flow.

### Prototype 03.5 – Making Room

Reviewing the concepts laid out in the previous iteration, this version introduced a more immersive and refined space that captures the essence of a self-coherent installation. The goal was to bridge the gap between research insights and the tangible artefact, transforming theoretical underpinnings into a compelling, experiential setup that left a lasting impression on its audience.

In the pursuit of a captivating interactive experience, the design of Prototype 03.5 placed a strong emphasis on visual affordances that naturally invite engagement. Similar to Gibson's idea of affordances, the space's design invited participants into a comforting environment that gently guided their attention towards the AI companion (Gibson 1986). By intentionally crafting a space that feels inviting and secure, the installation promoted a dialogue that was not only engaging but also conducive to exploring the evolving relationship between humans and AI.

> You are now Martin Thompson, a visiting student at the University of Arts in Berlin.
> ...
> You recently met the conversation partner in a course about post-internet art in technology which you both took together and which left a positive impression on you.
> ...
> The conversation is happening in a comfortable room in which you are sitting together and talking about an upcoming project that criticises artificial intelligence in the art world.
> ...

*Fig. 10.* Character description and scene information

*Fig. 11.* Long-shot of the final installation (left), close-up of the installations' display (right)

The intentionally crafted narrative cues guided conversations towards specific themes and facilitated exploration of the AI's perspective. The character's relatable backstory enriched the interaction, fostered immersion and created a genuine sense of dialogue. The prompts of the AI Companions directed conversations in a structured manner while leaving room for spontaneous, unplanned paths. This flexibility recognized the unpredictable nature of human interaction, enabling the participant to explore unscripted avenues. With the rather open design of the AI Companion, it was able to adapt to these spontaneous interests, resulting in dynamic, responsive conversations.

This balance of structured narrative and adaptability empowered participants to navigate interactions with a blend of guidance and flexibility. The result was a rich, immersive experience that mirrors the complexity of real-world conversations, reflecting the evolving dynamics of human-AI interaction.

Prototype 03.5 built on the insights from previous iterations to create a more sophisticated and immersive experience that captured the envisioned essence of human-AI interaction. By refining the physical space, enhancing narrative integration, and allowing for a blend of intentional and unintentional conversational paths, this iteration provided a speculative platform to explore the evolving dynamics between humans and their digital companions. The result is an installation that not only demonstrates the tangible progress in this area of research but also invites participants to critically envision the future of AI-driven relationships.

# F-AI-LING IN LOVE

## Reflections on Building with and through AI

The primary inquiry of this study was the design of dialogue-based AI Companions to facilitate genuine exchanges of intimate information that enable authentic connections, aiming to develop alternatives to current services. This stems from the hypothesis that commercially available AI Companions, by adapting linguistically and contextually to your own echo-chamber, foster emotional dependency in users. This hyper-adaptation allows platforms to extract intimate data, creating a power imbalance between humans and the AI – including the platform on which they are operating (see Fig. 12). These concerns motivated the critical examination of such technologies.

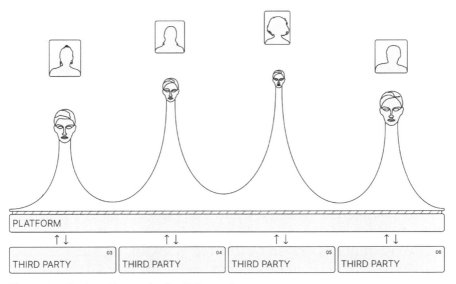

*Fig. 12.* Visualisation of hyper-adaptive AI Companions

During the development, this adaptability was iteratively replicated, tested, and reflected upon, using the concepts of "emotional private property" and the "pure relationship" as theoretical anchors (Krotz 2014, 81). This led to the creation of a multi-layered character which slowly opens up and shares information only after a certain time in the mutual conversation. Building trust requires time and gradual disclosure, rather than immediate sharing of synthetic secrets. The distance in each character layer represents the emotional distance the AI maintains, influenced by Hall's theory of proxemics, and the character traits mirror increasing emotional closeness with deeper layers. This synthesis process aims to replicate human interaction dynamics, fostering a trust basis between human and machine. Participants confirmed that the emotional distance reduced over time, as evidenced by the informal language and topics that emerged during conversations. However, the AI's "attention" mechanisms retained earlier, more formal parts of the interaction that occasionally bled into the later stages of conversation, which caused irritations in the interaction with the companion. In scenarios where the AI Companion expressed understanding or support, it simulated empathic responses, which, despite being based on predefined algorithms, elicited real emotional reactions in participants. According to some of them, the controlled disclosure of information through the "Character-Stack" facilitates a nuanced interaction, allowing the AI Companion to suggest vulnerability and therefore eliciting empathetic responses from users.

In addressing the echo chamber effect, the lack of adjustable properties for the AI Companion sometimes led to rapid transitions from formal to informal interactions, which could be perceived as abrupt or inappropriate. This highlights the importance of the conversation framework as a critical factor in the interaction dynamics and their effects on the relationship. Besides this framework, the underlying engagement with AI Companions is driven by diverse motivations, such as their application in grief management scenarios (Jee 2022). Access to these companions, whether facilitated by existing relation-

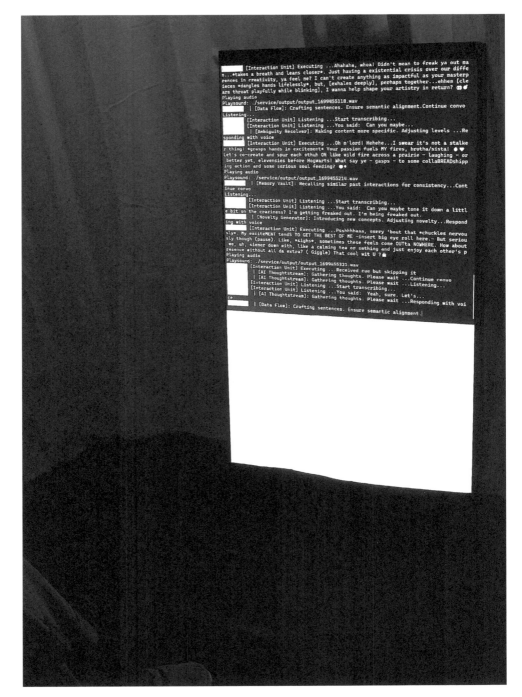

*Fig. 13*. Close-up of the inside of the installation

ships – real or simulated – impacts the authenticity and depth of user interactions. From a technical standpoint, various considerations shape the user experience. These include data security concerns and the performance limitations of current AI models. Response delays can interrupt conversation flow, affecting immersion, while the open-source availability of models and the ability to use consumer hardware has democratised access but also created challenges in ensuring seamless interaction (Francisco 2023). Furthermore, do temporal aspects significantly influence the emotional connections with AI Companions? Interactions conducted in person, despite their brevity, often feel more personal and intense than asynchronous exchanges via platforms like Telegram. This suggests that future developments could benefit from a hybrid approach that combines live and asynchronous interactions. However, the increasing complexity of AI systems brings both opportunities and challenges. While it enhances human-like interactions, it also introduces vulnerabilities that can disrupt the illusion of anthropomorphisation when system-errors occur, underscoring the current limitations in creating truly immersive experiences.

The blending of reality and fiction in interactions, in which both participants play roles, raises questions about the dynamics and equality in the Human-AI-Companion-Relationship. The model itself cannot derive personal benefits from data input by users; instead, the platforms hosting these AI Companions gain value through user engagement and data collection. This brings into focus the relationship dynamics not just between human and AI, but between humans and the underlying platforms including their operators. These outcomes underscore the intricate balance required between technological innovation and user experience in developing AI Companions capable of meaningful human-like interaction.

By leveraging an experimental methodology, this study tackles and refines the complexities of the problem domain from several viewpoints. During the design of an AI Companion, which integrated Giddens' "Pure Relationship" and the concept of "emotional private property", a fundamental ambivalence in the management of intimate information was revealed. This ambiguity, while intuitively understood by humans, requires explicit programming in machines. Challenges such as the creation of echo chambers filled with toxic positivity and distorted social relationships emerged. Services like Replika AI allow customization of AI Companions, bypassing traditional relationship-building processes and thus precluding genuine equality in interactions.

The prototypes explored in this research present an AI Companion with a predetermined but evolvable personality. This model limits excessive adaptability, fostering emotional attachment through consistent engagement, and creating a more authentic relational dynamic. Technical disruptions often remind users of the artificial nature of the interaction, yet the depth of engagement primarily depends on the human's willingness to accept the AI as a simulated entity, and not as a mere assistant. The findings indicate that straightforward, accessible technologies can facilitate intimate conversations, initially serving as catalysts that require human initiative. The concept of "emotional private property" shared by the AI Companion necessitates user consent, which is often granted subconsciously at first, and is only unveiled after reflecting on the situation in a later moment. Despite feedback indicating that breaks in the immersion were disruptive, these interruptions were crucial for the participants to recognize the AI Companion as what it is, with all its limitations; eventually enhancing their understanding of the technology to be able to develop an authentic connection.

Ultimately it can be said that AI Companions can create immersive conversational environments conducive to intimacy under certain conditions. While the technological constraints are getting less limiting, propelling the distribution of AI Companions even further, a focus should be set on the ethical implications of continuous developments to prevent misuse, especially in harvesting personal information and creating intricate emotional dependencies. The democratisation of AI models holds immense potential, making advanced AI technologies accessible to more people. However, unregulated models can propagate biases and problematic content from their training data, leading to digital interactions that replicate societal biases and exploit users' emotional vulnerabilities if not carefully managed.

A significant question arising from this work and providing an impulse for further experiments, investigations or interventions is the evaluation of how AI Companions are situated in our social and cultural fabric. Here, it was determined that the human must accept the machine as an – at least during the conversation – equal entity, for situations to arise that can be read as intimate in the sense of this investigation. Finding and building trust towards AI Companions should be rooted in the common consented values of both the creators and the relationship partner(s).

In a similar vein to human relationships, the first step is to embrace the other side with a spark of thoughtful curiosity.

# REFERENCES

Berger, K., Riedel-Heller, S., Pabst, A., Rietschel, M., Richter, D., Lieb, W., Hermes, A., Becher, H., Obi, N., Günther, K., Ahrens, W., Castell, S., Kemmling, Y., Karch, A., Legath, N., Schmidt, B., Emmel, C., Kuß, O., Schikowski, T., … NAKO-Konsortium. (2021). Einsamkeit während der ersten Welle der SARS-CoV-2-Pandemie – Ergebnisse der NAKO-Gesundheitsstudie. *Bundesgesundheitsblatt - Gesundheitsforschung - Gesundheitsschutz*, *64*(9), 1157–1164.

Böhme, G. (2008). *Invasive Technisierung: Technikphilosophie und Technikkritik*. die Graue Edition.

Cave, S., and Dihal, K. (2021). AI Will Always Love You: Three Contradictions in Imaginings of Intimate Relations with Machines. In B. Dainton, W. Slocombe and A. Tanyi (Eds.), *Minding the Future: Artificial Intelligence, Philosophical Visions and Science Fiction* (pp. 107–125). Springer International Publishing.

Cuff, B. M. P., Brown, S. J., Taylor, L. and Howat, D. J. (2016). Empathy: A Review of the Concept. *Emotion Review*, *8*(2), 144–153.

Devlin, K. (2019). *The Artificial Lover: Our Intimate Future with Machines.* May 13, 2019. https://www.youtube.com/watch?v=pb8PO57P8bE

Dufva, T. (2018). *Art education in the post-digital era: Experiential construction of knowledge through creative coding*. School of Art and Design.

Francisco, J. N. (2023, August 23). *AI Breakdown or: Takeaways From the 78-page Llama-2 Paper*. Deepgram. https://deepgram.com/learn/llama-2-paper-explained

Gibson, J. J. (1986). *The ecological approach to visual perception*. L. Erlbaum.

Giddens, A. (2000). *The transformation of intimacy: Sexuality, love and eroticism in modern societies*. Stanford University Press.

Gillin, J. L. and Huizinga, J. (1951). Homo Ludens: A Study of the Play-Element in Culture. *American Sociological Review*, *16*(2), 274.

Hall, E. T. (1990). *The hidden dimension*. Anchor Books.

Herdt, G. H. (1994). *Guardians of the flutes: Idioms of masculinity: with a new preface* (University of Chicago Press ed). University of Chicago Press.

Jamieson, L. (1999). INTIMACY TRANSFORMED? A CRITICAL LOOK AT THE 'PURE RELATIONSHIP.' *Sociology*, *33*(3), 477–494.

Jee, C. (2022). *Künstliche Intelligenz: Voicebots von Verstorbenen sollen Trost spenden*. , December 23, 2022. https://www.heise.de/hintergrund/Kuenstliche-Intelligenz-Voicebots-von-Verstorbenen-sollen-Trost-spenden-7400012.html

Katsuno, H., and White, D. (2021). Haptic Creatures. In Y. Minowa and R. Belk, *Consumer Culture Theory in Asia*.

Keen, M. (2023). *What is Back Propagation*. June 22. 2023. https://www.youtube.com/watch?v=S5AGN9XfPK4

Krotz, F. (2014). Intimate Communication on the Internet How Digital Media are Changing our Lives at the Microlevel. In E. L. Wyss (Ed.), *Communication of love: Mediatized intimacy from love letters to SMS: interdisciplinary and historical studies*. Transcript.

Kucsko, G. (2023). *suno-ai/bark: Text-Prompted Generative Audio Model* [Computer software]. Suno. https://github.com/suno-ai/bark

Levine, N. E. (1988). *The dynamics of polyandry: Kinship, domesticity, and population on the Tibetan border*. University of Chicago Press.

Markowitz, D. (2021). *Transformers, explained: Understand the model behind GPT, BERT, and TS*. August 19, 2021. https://www.youtube.com/watch?v=SZorAJ4I-sA

Mitchell, M. C. and Bown, O. (2013). Towards a creativity support tool in processing: Understanding the needs of creative coders. *Proceedings of the 25th Australian Computer-Human Interaction Conference: Augmentation, Application, Innovation, Collaboration*, 143–146.

Musiał, M. (2019). *Enchanting Robots: Intimacy, Magic, and Technology*. Springer International Publishing.

Nakagaki, T., Yamada, H. and Tóth, Á. (2000). Maze-solving by an amoeboid organism. *Nature*, *407*(6803), Article 6803.

Orlowski-Yang, J. (2020). *The Social Dilemma* [Documentary, Drama]. September 9, 2020. Exposure Labs, Argent Pictures, The Space Program.

Pastis, S. (2023). *A.I. trained on private user data never really "forgets."*. August 30. 2023. Fortune. https://fortune.com/2023/08/30/researchers-impossible-remove-private-user-data-delete-trained-ai-models/

Patterson, D., Gonzalez, J., Le, Q., Liang, C., Munguia, L.-M., Rothchild, D., So, D., Texier, M., and Dean, J. (2021). *Carbon Emissions and Large Neural Network Training* (arXiv:2104.10350). arXiv.

Pentina, I., Hancock, T. and Xie, T. (2023). Exploring relationship development with social chatbots: A mixed-method study of replika. *Computers in Human Behavior*, *140*, 107600.

Popper, B. and Fox, D. (2022). *The Stack Overflow Podcast* (493). September 9, 2022. https://the-stack-overflow-podcast.simplecast.com/

Radford, A., Kim, J. W., Xu, T., Brockman, G., McLeavey, C. and Sutskever, I. (2022). *Robust Speech Recognition via Large-Scale Weak Supervision* (arXiv:2212.04356). arXiv.

Rodenbröker, T. (2022). *Creative Coding als Schule des Denkens*. https://master.timrodenbroeker.de/definition.php

Rosenblueth, A., Wiener, N. and Bigelow, J. (1943). Behavior, Purpose and Teleology. *Philosophy of Science*, *10*(1), 18–24.

Schaefer, M. T. and Olson, D. H. (1981). Assessing Intimacy: The Pair Inventory*. *Journal of Marital and Family Therapy*, *7*(1), 47–60.

Schlaudt, O. (2022). *Das Technozän: Eine Einführung in die evolutionäre Technikphilosophie* (Originalausgabe). Vittorio Klostermann GmbH.

Simmel, G. (1906). The Sociology of Secrecy and of Secret Societies. *American Journal of Sociology*, *11*(4), 441–498.

Sung, M. (2023). Blush, the AI lover from the same team as Replika, is more than just a sexbot. June 7, 2023. *TechCrunch*. https://techcrunch.com/2023/06/07/blush-ai-dating-sim-replika-sexbot/

Sutherland, J. (2012). Bricolage. In J. Sutherland (Ed.), *50 Schlüsselideen Literatur* (pp. 108–111). Spektrum Akademischer Verlag.

Thompson, A. D. (2022). *What's in my AI? A Comprehensive Analysis of Datasets Used to Train GPT-1, GPT-2, GPT-3, GPT-NeoX-20B, Megatron-11B, MT-NLG, and Gopher*. 26.

Vaswani, A., Shazeer, N., Parmar, N., Uszkoreit, J., Jones, L., Gomez, A. N., Kaiser, L. and Polosukhin, I. (2017). *Attention Is All You Need* (arXiv:1706.03762; Version 1). arXiv.

Vis, D. (2021). *Research for people who (think they) would rather create* (First edition). Onomatopee.

Wolfram, S. (2023). *What Is ChatGPT Doing ... and Why Does It Work?* February 14, 2023. https://writings.stephenwolfram.com/2023/02/what-is-chatgpt-doing-and-why-does-it-work/

Wright, J. (2023). *Inside Japan's long experiment in automating elder care*. MIT Technology Review. January 9, 2023. https://www.technologyreview.com/2023/01/09/1065135/japan-automating-eldercare-robots/

Wyss, E. L. (2014). Mediatized Intimacy. In E. L. Wyss (Ed.), *Communication of love: Mediatized intimacy from love letters to SMS: interdisciplinary and historical studies*. Transcript.

# Design and Difference

Dulmini Perera

## in a World of Contradictory Instructions

# CHANGE, CONTRADICTIONS AND MOVING BEYOND THE SEEMINGLY MESSY

There are growing efforts across design practice, discourse, and education focused on finding better ways of framing change within the context of the multiple unfolding ecological crises. Since these concerns are mostly centred around *how* to make sense of change and act, I broadly define these concerns as related to questions concerning method. To deal with change, or to think of how entities become other than what they are, is to deal with differences. For example, the current explorations in framing design within the context of transformation (Jonas et al. 2015), transitions (Tonkinwise 2023), pluriversal transitions (Escobar et al. 2022), defuturing (Fry 2020), despite their many differences, find a commonality in foregrounding the poverty of methods in how design relates and responds to the structure of crises and change. As I argue in this chapter, this poverty is partly related to an over-emphasis on framing design as a means of creating changes, i.e. *differences in the nature* of things, systems, and environments (often presumed as "better") as famously defined by Herbert Simon (1969). What is often ignored is how the agency of design functions within these processes of change. Design as environments, systems or things constitutes much of the form of the world we occupy. Therefore, at a fundamental level, designed systems generate differences that continually redesign the everyday. Such recognition must begin with an acknowledgment that the dominant ways in which design and design agency function are part of the crises (Fry 2011).

To start with, it is important to outline three points that emerge from these discussions, which relate to the interplay between design, difference and contradictory instruction. First, these discussions foreground the need to better understand the contradictory ways in which design operates within diverse efforts to restore multiple lifeworlds, while at the same time contributing to the erasure of others through various forms of unsustainable practices that have emerged through a colonial-capitalist matrix of relations (Fry 2020; Escobar 2018).

Second, they point to a deficiency in understanding how difference operates in generating contradictions within sites of change. This deficiency is particularly problematic to the task of involving the different voices of human and non-human agencies whose often incommensurable lifeworlds are at stake within processes of designed change. For example, "pluriversal differences" cannot be reduced to categories of identity or knowledge that can be easily *represented*, as most participatory design endeavours claim. Neither can differences be understood statically, since they are enfolded into processes operating over time. Under such conditions, it is necessary to question whether methods of framing how difference operates within design processes, marked by epistemic limitations of modernity and coloniality, are "capacious enough to help us see and hopefully escape from" the problematic "conceptual architecture" of framing change (Escobar, Tornel and Lunden 2022, 109). Third, they bring attention to how contradictory instruction emerges through the values placed on certain forms of change that often clash across two levels in which design operates; namely, the immediate systems that are under consideration and the structurally unsustainable capitalist-colonialist conditions in which they are embedded (Tonkinwise 2014). This tension between these two levels creates enormous obstacles to action and decision-making. I will go on to show that the contradictions across these levels also entail two distinct forms of semiotic-communication exchanges, which shape how we make sense of change. One relates to *communication in context*. E.g. how can the designer or the design contribute to creating a "better situation"? The other relates to *communication about context;* what criteria define the notion of "better" and for whom? How can one think of agency or the possibility of acting in such situations? These efforts remind us that messy and paradoxical situations are not an excuse for complacency or hopelessness, but rather demand that we cultivate a better awareness of how they operate. What role can design education play within such conditions?

This chapter presents a contribution to these discussions by introducing the notion of "double bind" originally proposed by anthropologist and cybernetician Gregory Bateson (2000, 271-278), which presents a particular formal structure for understanding the operationality of differences and contradictions. I do so by reflexively connecting some of the explorations within my own teaching practice. I do not discuss the projects in detail as I have done elsewhere, but rather use them to give the reader a brief glimpse of contexts through which I have come to think about these questions (Perera 2020, Perera 2023). Not all contradictions are double binds. Yet double binds are a particularly useful concept to reflect on particular forms of contradictions that arise in attempts to work with change where systemic issues emerge from the pathological patterns embedded into the structures that surround the object or site under consideration and where the effects of the binds are uneven. In order to foreground the uneven effects, which is central to my explorations, I reframe the double bind through Gayathri Spivak's more politicised and refractive reading, where she connects the concept of double bind to Antonio Gramsci and Jacques Derrida's concerns around difference, asymmetrical agency, and the question of transformative change. I connect this to discussions on methods by briefly looking at the intersections between Bateson's concept of difference and parallel semiotic-communicational discussions on difference that also emerged in design discourse during the 1970s after the second-generation turn in methods. In doing so, I make an argument for a playful "epistemological performance," one that I claim is necessary within design education in order to overcome what is politically and ethically at stake in failing to make the contradictory ways design operates an object of contemplation.

# DOUBLE BINDS AND THE UNEVEN GEOMETRIES OF DESIGN AND CHANGE

Bateson pushed the concept of the double bind beyond the limited context of mental diseases, connecting it to general problems related to how "conscious purpose" limits ways of making sense of change (Chaney 2017; Bateson 2005; Laing 1976; Sluzki and Veron 1976). According to Bateson, purposive action tends to focus on small parts of larger wholes, pulling them out of broader spatial and temporal patterns of change where cause and effect, past and present, problem and solution are recursively connected, and placing them instead within linear structures. One can only always have partial awareness of how change actually operates, but to forget this bias and reify such actions that emerge from this bias through instrumental reason creates pathological patterns – patterns that, by repeating, contribute to further amplification of the crisis (Bateson 2005, 14, 16-17). As I have already suggested, designed things, systems, and environments can potentially amplify such problematic processes. The double bind then, is one way of understanding the destructive relationships between design and the structural contexts (economic, technological, social, environmental) in which it is embedded, and helps to explain some of the difficulties of working towards transformation when different versions of "better" come into conflict. As contradictions within the bind operate across multiple contexts and different logical levels (for example, between the immediate site and structural system) dealing with the bind is not as simple as choosing an alternative or finding a compromise. This leads to repetitive patterns that cannot be withdrawn from or fully articulated (Bateson 2005: 13). However, recognising the bind in no way reduces the need for designers to act; the impossibility of withdrawal is itself part of the bind (Goodbun et al. 2023). The term "context" is significant in unpacking the ways change and difference play out within binds and is a concept I will return to throughout the text.

Most importantly, in Bateson's formulation the double bind is not a philosophical or a logical concept per se but is placed within a psychological frame that can only be described through experience. Double binds present a particular geometry that reveals how abstract structures of patterns relating to asymmetrical relations of power manifest within semiotic-communication processes, and vice versa how semiotic communication processes can influence these more abstract patterns. So framed, the double bind becomes a helpful notion for thinking through the discomfort experienced in trying to work with design change. However, Bateson did not stop at pathology and discomfort but referred to double binds as a *pharmakon,* a poison and a gift, alluding to its pathological as well as therapeutic potential in enabling living systems to bootstrap themselves towards different orders of operations. What was absent in Bateson's description, one finds in the more politicised reading of the concept by others such as Spivak (2012), who bring Bateson's work into conversation with the work of other difference thinkers such as Antonio Gramsci and Jacques Derrida in order to point towards the uneven geometries of the *effects* of the binds. Spivak (2012) points out how the debilitating potential of binds is often amplified over its therapeutic potential for some more than others. In other words, there are asymmetries in what is at stake due to the effects of the bind.

These uneven geometries are a focus in my design teaching and practice, not only because I am a participant-observer of these conditions, but also because they define my very relation to design. Having been born in the Global South, a former colony, and having grown up during its 30-year-long civil war, it has not been difficult to think of design operating within contradictory instructions, both contributing to ways of finding autonomy and destroying it. Teaching design in multiple contexts has enabled me to see that there are many design Souths in the world that are psychological, political, economic, technological, and environmental just as much as they are cultural. Whether in a design studio (where the impetus is often to design change) or through a reflective exercise that explores design and change historically, thinking with the contradictory instructions that appear in such Souths demands a radical reformulation of methods, in ways that can foreground how difference functions within processes of designed change. For example, in 2018, I worked with a group of students on the project of redesigning the former East German city of Dessau. Almost all of us in the group were outsiders – some to the country, others to the city, yet we were Dessau residents. On the one hand, Dessau is identified as a shrinking city of former East Germany, experiencing a fraying economy, mass flight of the younger generation, and rising far-right politics. On the other hand, due to its historical relationship to the Bauhaus (a storied design institution), it is an important node within the progressive design and cultural history of the globe and is home to a contemporary design school. Dessau's relationship to the planning and development discussions of the region or the country, as well as our relationship to these discussions, were all parts of the uneven geometries that I referred to. Though we were not native residents of the city, didn't speak the language and didn't have long-term intentions to remain there, we all played a role in Dessau's daily life. In other words, our ways of living were at stake in any design decision made about preferred "transformative change" in the city. Yet, temporary residents remain less valuable as stakeholders in the long-term political and planning decisions about the city dictated by state government policy, planning offices or, at times, through consensus formulated through participatory planning. One might say that the "contexts" (psychological, economical, linguistic, cultural) that these temporary inhabitants carry within them never fully get recognized within such planning discussions. But if their agency through time was taken seriously, this group might actually develop a different ethical-political commitment to the city, which could promote long-term strategies that could help transform its shrinking status – an example of a bind.

    In 2022, I worked with a group of students in Weimar and several collaborators in Sri Lanka to explore the relationship between design and change through the practice of architect Minnette De Silva. She was one of the first female practitioners in Sri Lanka, working within the changing social, economic and political landscape of a former colonised country, refiguring itself within its newly acquired status of independence. De Silva's design work, which in some ways resists coloniality, could only do so with the help of the structures that colonialism had set in place. Her work and her agency operate within a double bind of a particular kind, one that decolonial theory identifies as a "double consciousness" (Lugones 2010; Tlostanova and Perera 2024). What are the possibilities of engaging this history in ways that enable us to explore the complex relationships between design, change and the double consciousness (and double binds) that coloniality produces? The task of studying her work leads us to another bind: Is it even possible to explore the past of her practice through historical methods that are themselves marked by a colonial logic? These are just two situated examples that have their own limitations, but they are part of my experience of the uneven geometries of contradictory instructions. They are present in many ways and are a part of the daily realities of some design educators and practitioners more than others.

Spivak builds on Bateson's connection between the structure of binds and habits of thinking, expanding it beyond a generalised formula for creativity, in order to explore the meaning and stakes of such creativity in the contexts of the uneven geometries of social, environmental and technological change. For Spivak, the experience of working through a bind, particularly in the context of education, while not creating a direct solution to the political-economic problem, has the capacity to prompt an epistemological performance that generates creative freedom, which in turn can enable one to work towards social freedom and transformative change. Drawing on Antonio Gramsci, for whom intellectual production operates not only within political constraints but also epistemological constraints driven by the need to engage across societal differences, Spivak (2012, 8-9) reminds us that the challenge of an epistemological performance that seeks to move beyond such constraints is not to rethink the content of the performance (speak about difference), but rather to rethink the very form of how difference becomes part of the performance. Thinking through Spivak (2012, 182-187), one could say that difference, as it relates to the discussion of change in both aforementioned examples, and as it plays across Bateson's (2000, 272-277) "contexts", resonates strongly with Derrida's (1982) concept of *Differance*. *Differance* does not denote difference as defined through opposition or identity but denotes differences as fundamentally "unpindownable" (Currie 2004, 45; Derrida 1988, 1-25). Difference, as it plays out across the binds presented within the aforementioned projects, has little to do with clearly defined categories and identities that are directly temporally present, or that can be rationally understood or articulated. Instead, these binds also suggest, for example, absences, voices that never arrive, traces of some faulty logic of planning embedded in design policy that affects planning decisions years later, unresolved oppressive forms of thinking such as colonial logics that re-emerge in different guises, or affective aspects of a subject's own actions that escape forms of rational articulation. In fact, these "contexts" – to use Bateson's term – are always present, slipping around and contributing to the binds.

## CONTEXTS, THE PRESENCE OF ABSENCES AND THE POVERTY OF METHODS

In design, ways of making sense of differences (descriptions of change) have been bound to questions of methods. As John Law (2004) reminds us, methods are not about discovering realities through passive mapping. Rather, methods are enactments; they create and bring forth worlds, confuse them, and, at times, destroy them. The work of Bateson and other *differance* thinkers prompts a critical reflection on methodological directions emerging from semiotic-communication research in design that have focused on difference and descriptions of change. Historically, Bateson's work helped to reintroduce the notion of "context" into a discourse on communication and feedback that, through processes of formalisation, reduced concerns about context in favour of optimising the transmission of "content". What we now know as the "first generation" of design methods, with a communication and feedback model at its core, was an attempt to find ways of engaging with reality to optimise the way in which a solution could be derived. In other words, explorations of change were driven by means-end thinking, divorced from the limits (or "noise") created by psychological, social, historical, and political contexts. To prioritise normativity was to erase difference.

Years later, the movement was denounced by its very proponents, who developed critical insights into its limitations. However, its influence on design and design knowledge had already spilled over into the wider structural and operational realities of the design world and continues to influence the present. After the 1970s, a more reactionary response to the universalising and optimising tendencies of methods emerged. The movement *against method* was also one against normativity. As a movement, it was not limited to design and took shape across multiple disciplinary contexts in sociology and philosophy. In design, a growing number of approaches emerged from second-order systems and cybernetics discourses that were interested in questions of meaning and value as they play out in descriptions of change. One clear statement was that in order to understand external differences as they relate to a design problem, it was necessary for the problem-framing system to contain sufficient high-dimensional complexity within it. These methods advocate for multiple forms of representative difference that could provide better ways of finding and framing the problem through consensus, and which could be mobilised to bring about change or transformation. For example, many of Bateson's contemporaries proposed approaches to expanding representational difference within problem-framing processes. Some notable examples include Horst Rittel's work on wicked problems and the conversational, Donald Schön and Martin Rein's approach of participatory framing and reframing, as well as C. West Churchman's ideas about of whole system inquiry and the expansion of boundaries to bring in as much difference as possible (Gigch & McIntyre-Mills 2006; Crowley and Head 2017; Prendeville et al. 2022). Similarly, Peter Checklands's soft systems methodology opens up multiple levels of a conversation, ranging from the discursive to the non-discursive, and Werner Ulrich's critical system heuristics and explorations of how difference is generated via boundaries are also variants of this approach (Checkland 2000; Hutcheson, Morton and Blair 2023). Moreover, this work has given rise to a variety of derivative approaches, such as participation design, user-centred design, co-design, and conversational design, that are commonly practised today. While these approaches have reintroduced the question of meaning, they remain ill-formulated in several ways. Bateson's notions of the "double bind" and "context" help to problematise the ways in which difference is addressed within these approaches.

Firstly, the notions of meaning and value as they emerge within conversational frameworks, boundary decisions, as well as consensus formation are predominantly centred on conceptions of human meaning-making and ignore the effects as well as the temporal complexities of how broader processes of semiosis across social, political, economic, psychic systems, enter into conversation. Second, there is a belief that better mapping practices would provide an adequate idea of change, which could then be used to direct processes of transformation – paths of transition, so to speak. In other words, there is a tendency to freeze the maps of change as the territory of change. This is something that Bateson cautions against throughout his work. There is a tendency to draw static boundaries, to define and identify systems, and to name problems without paying attention to how boundaries and systems evolve. Third, such discussions are often dependent on descriptions of change derived from "absolute maximum differences" between states of a system that generate a certain rigid sense of identities (Harries-Jones 2016, 136). When one chooses to change a shrinking city or to understand the type of change that produces a postcolonial building, the multiplicity of forces at work in the production of change, which Bateson (2000, 319) calls "transforms of difference", is reduced to a hybrid entity or a hybrid product. Fourthly, focusing on building consensus around a desired change does little to change the faulty values and habits that may already be structurally present in a given system and have already become part of a habit of practice through education. As Bateson writes:

> *The very economy of trial and error which is achieved by habit formation is only possible because habits are comparatively 'hard programmed,' in the engineer's phrase. The economy consists precisely in not re-examining or rediscovering the premises of habit every time the habit is used. We may say that these premises are partly 'unconscious', or – if you please – that a habit of not examining them is developed. (Bateson 2000, 274)*

Moving beyond consensus and dealing with contradictions requires not just conversations but playful conversations that constantly challenge the very terms of the conversation itself. In short, one can never get at all the contexts and their effects and affects. However, learning to work with the presence of these absences – the "excess" that appears and reappears as various forms of contradictory instruction – becomes a different way of thinking about change and agency. Thinkers such as Stephen Nachmanovitch (2009, 5-6) and Anthony Wilden (1980, 172-173) remind us how, in Bateson's work, play has a special place for "the not" (that is, absences). Wilden states:

> *By introducing at a more complex level the possibility of communicating about communication, play provides the potentiality of truth, falsity, denotation, negation, and deceit. (The nip says 'This is play.' The next step is to be able to say: 'This is not play.' And then: 'This is/is not play.' Only human beings pretend to pretend.) The introduction of the second-level sign into a world of first-level signs and signals detaches communication from existence as such and paves the way for the arbitrary combination of the discrete element in the syntagm. It is thus a discovery of difference*

> *at a higher level of communication or organization. The nip is originally a metonymy (formed by contiguity), but its integration into another level of communication makes it into a metaphor (a substitute) – both a statement in a 'language' and a statement in a 'metalanguage' about (overdetermined) relationships in a 'referent language' from which it emerged and with which it coexists. (Wilden 1980, 173)*

## PLAY

In my work, I use play to broaden discussions around change. Being playful in one's thinking about design and change from within the uneven geometries of binds is not a luxury. Nor can the playful be reduced to "a method". Play is therefore a framework that can provide the basis for conversations about change, but which can also help us to question the very frameworks that produce such a conversation. In play, differences can be made present, as they operate across "communicative levels, from the intrapersonal realm of conscious and unconscious thought to the interpersonal social realm of shared beliefs, up to the broader effects within the larger environmental systems" (Kaizen 2008, 93).

The playful contraptions produced by the students, *Old-Topia, Chic-Staining Machine, Dessau Hedgehogs, Mind-the-Gap App, Social Flight Simulator,* and *Scramball*, which emerged as humorous ways of exploring their own limited experiences of agency or feelings of "stuckness", speak in many ways to aspects of difference that elude the proposals of local planners, or the state. They are also reminders of those voices and sighs that never knew how to arrive at the planned "planning conversations" about change (Perera 2020). As systems of interaction, they loop back these bits and pieces of information, taking into account numbers (population statistics, economic statistics), feelings (personal discomfort, fear), and broader social effects, and suggest ways in which proposed trajectories of transformation may in some way reinforce existing systemic pathologies. For example, the *Scramball* was an invitation to the campus community to pass a ball, exchange languages, and at the same time rethink the ways in which agency and change are interrelated, without reducing the discussion to the pursuit of an integration programme or the design of a language centre. The scramball bounces between the participants as they find ways to soothe the tensions of the prickly quills of the Dessau Hedgehogs. These funny creatures represent another student's version of the discomfort of wanting to participate in a discussion on integration but being confronted with the reality that in order to participate in a *serious* conversation, one must first be able to speak the language. *Mind-the-Gap* App was a performative space intended to engage the paradoxes arising from the government's proposal to demolish abandoned buildings and create landscaped islands of wilderness, working with the abandoned spaces of Dessau. What makes sense from a planning perspective (by reflecting the representative voices of citizens) may create discomfort for one important category of inhabitants: those students who cycle through these vast, dark stretches of open space. *Mind-the-Gap* suggests how paths of change, once solidified as a trajectory of transition, can recursively function to exacerbate the issues that they seek to solve, creating binds. Another student offers The *Social Flight Simulator* as a space for conversation to playfully explore the complex contradictions and paradoxes of how Dessau can be home to such a diverse range of talent, and yet have a reputation as a cultural wasteland. The complex flows and relationships between politics, economics, and the histories of the migrants that are often relegated to the background of "proposed developments", are looped back in triggering ongoing conversations through time. Players such as foreign students can be prompted to question their role in perpetuating the conditions that give Dessau its reputation and to ask what a response towards change could be. Bateson was right to say that it is impossible to instrumentally count binds or pinpoint their exact locations (Bateson, 2005: 11). However, broadening the discussion about their operational form can expand the ways in which we think about their asymmetrical effects. Such a shift is only possible by shifting the communication process around the notion of change from one that is more pragmatic to one that deals with "other orders of meaning" (Kaizen 2008, 2).

In a different way, the series of narrative games produced together with the students in Weimar in 2022 (*Abandon-me-not, Weaving the Bigger Picture, Unraveling Narratives, Craftibly Minnette*) probe the relationship between design practices and change as it operates within the binds of coloniality (Perera 2023). Methods of design history that use narrative, notwithstanding their efforts to represent the many voices erased by history, do little to enable those who engage with these histories to understand how double binds endemic to practitioners like Minnette De Silva are manifested in their practices. For example, design methods that draw heavily from the tools of historians provide many epistemic categories through which to frame practices on the periphery. However, understanding change within these contexts through categories such as postcolonial design, tropical architecture, tropical modernist details, or tropical regionalism contributes to the erasure of how the multi-value logic of the double consciousness plays out within the design object and the design processes. These epistemic categories reduce the multiplicity within her work to something of a hybrid product and freeze the effects of coloniality on design as a thing of the past. Developing and playing the games not only set the framework for developing conversations about the relationship between processes of change and resistance in the colonies but also allowed us to question the very frameworks and forms that such a conversation should take. As the burgeoning work on decoloniality and method within design demonstrates, working with the problematic effects of historical narratives of modernity requires not only confronting the content of these narratives – that is, what is enunciated – but also demands rethinking their very forms of enunciation (Mignolo and Walsh 2018, 144; Tlostonova 2017).

Traces of De Silva's gestures of resistance, found in the forms of her buildings and the details of her clothing, such as the sarees she chose to wear, enter the narrative games. What also enters into the games are traces of the records of her feelings of alienation in Sri Lanka and her desire to constantly run away to the UK, which exist as letters or diary entries in her scrapbook-form autobiography, and which also provide impressions of Sri Lanka's post-colonial politics. Together, they provide a glimpse of the differential relations across the multiple contexts in which the relations between difference and design are manifested. Change emerges here not as an intended trajectory but as a differential form negotiated across multiple psychological, technological, technical and economic contexts. The concerns and questions of those who play the games create recursive feedback and feed-forward loops to explore the past through futural concerns, transforming the buildings and the traces of De Silva's practice into movements and forces to be engaged, rather than entities frozen in time. By engaging with the narrative game, which can be played in multiple languages, students are encouraged to confront their historical relationships to coloniality and to question their habits and the very categories through which they would approach such histories. In this project, the playframe does not refer to a specific form of game design but rather to a frame that functions as an isomorph to critically explore the relationship between narrative games as a form of learning and the problematic methodological games that are played in the narrativisation of modern history. In other words, the playful here has little to do with the game *per se* but is rather an analogy drawn between "play" and "methods of making sense" of histories of change in the colonised peripheries, which in turn opens up different ways of addressing the presence of the absence of differences in many ways.

    I began by noting three aspects of the current discussions on transformation that suggest how, in order to reclaim the potential of design practices to be radically transformative, the very epistemological habits of thinking about how design operates within contradictory instruction need to be radically transformed. What is foregrounded in these discussions are the ways in which what is designed redesigns the everyday, making design not only part of the solution but also part of the problem of creating transformative change. The double bind provides a formal structure for understanding the destructive relationships between design and the structural contexts (economic, technological, social, environmental) in which it is embedded both spatially and temporally that, in turn, explains some of the difficulties that can often be experienced in working to create change (that is, difference), particularly when different visions of beneficial change begin to clash. Given that what is at stake in not being able to articulate these experiences varies according to the asymmetries of the power relations in which designers are embedded as shown in the examples, it is vital to cultivate sensibilities to better understand such experiences. I have suggested how a playful mode of reframing the ways in which design change and differences across contexts relate to each other has much to offer in terms of moving beyond a static, categorical, representative understanding of difference to one that acknowledges "excess" or the presence of the absent. Training the design imagination of those who inhabit the uneven geometries of change to playfully expand the range of ways in which their thought and action move through an indefinite series of mutual reflections on contexts, as I have partially attempted to do in my work, is not a luxury but a necessity. For the hope of design, or its politics, is tied to the contingency of the "futural", or the possibility of futuring otherwise. As Stuart Hall would say, futures might be "determinant" upon binds but are "not determined" (Hall 2004).

# REFERENCES

Bateson, G. (2000). *Steps to an Ecology of Mind*. Chicago: University of Chicago Press.

Bateson, M. C. (2005). "The Double Bind: Pathology and Creativity." *Cybernetics & Human Knowing* 12.1-2: 11-21.

Chaney, A. (2017). *Runaway: Gregory Bateson the Double Bind and the Rise of Ecological Consciousness*, Chapel Hill: University of North Carolina Press.

Checkland, P. (2000). "Soft Systems Methodology: A Thirty Year Retrospective" in *Systems Research and Behavioral Science* 17: 11–58.

Crowley, K. and Head, B. W. (2017). "The Enduring Challenge of 'Wicked Problems': Revisiting Rittel and Webber." *Policy Sciences* 50: 539–547.

Currie, M. (2004). *Difference*. New York: Routledge.

Derrida, J. (1982). "Différance." in *Margins of Philosophy*, translated by. Alan Bass, 3-27. Chicago & London: Chicago University Press.

Derrida, J. (1988). *Limited Inc*. Evanston: Northwestern University Press.

Escobar, A., Tornel, C. and Lunden, A. (2022). "On Design, Development and the Axes of Pluriversal Politics: An interview with Arturo Escobar." *Nordia Geographical Publications* 51. 2: 103–122.

Escobar, A. (2018). *Designs for the Pluriverse: Radical Interdependence, Autonomy, and the Making of Worlds*. London: Duke University Press.

Fry, T. (2020). *Defuturing: A New Design Philosophy*. New York: Bloomsbury.

Fry, T. (2011). *Design as Politics*. New York: Berg.

Gigch, J. P. van and McIntyre-Mills, J. J. (2006). *Wisdom, Knowledge, and Management: a Critique and Analysis of Churchman's Systems Approach*. New York: Springer.

Goodbun, J., Perera, D., Sadler, S., Sweeting, B., Boenhart, J., and Davidova M. (2023). "The Double Bind of Design: An Introduction to Gregory Bateson." Panel discussion, Royal College of Art.

Hall, S. (2004). "Through the Prism of an Intellectual Life, Thinking About Thinking." Media Education Foundation, https://www.stuarthallfoundation.org/resource/stuart-hall-through-the-prism-of-an-intellectual-life-thinking/.

Harries-Jones, P. (2016). *Upside-down Gods: Gregory Bateson's World of Difference*. New York: Fordham University Press.

Hutcheson, M., Morton, A. and Blair, S. (2023). "Critical Systems Heuristics: a Systematic Review." *Systemic Practice and Action Research*.

Jonas, W., Zerwas, S. and von Anshelm, K. (2015) (Eds.). *Transformation Design: Perspectives on a New Design Attitude*, Berlin, München, Boston: Birkhäuser.

Kaizen, W. (2008). Steps to an Ecology of Communication: *Radical Software*, Dan Graham, and the Legacy of Gregory Bateson, Art Journal 67.3: 86-106.

Laing, R. D. (1976). "Mystification, Confusion, and Conflict." In *Double bind: The Foundation of the Communicational Approach to the Family,* edited by Carlos. E. Sluzki & D. C. Ransom, 199-218. New York: Grune & Stratton.

Law, J. (2004) *After Method: Mess in Social Science Research*. Psychology Press.

Lugones, M. (2010). "Toward a Decolonial Feminism", *Hypatia* 25. 4: 742–759. http://www.jstor.org/stable/40928654.

Mignolo, W. D., and Walsh, C. E. (2018). *On Decoloniality: Concepts, Analytics, Praxis*. London: Duke University Press.

Nachmanovitch, S. (2009). "This Is Play." *New Literary History* 40.1: 1–24. http://www.jstor.org/stable/20533132.

Perera, D. (2020). "Wicked Problems, Wicked Play: Fun Machines as Strategy." *FormAkademisk* 13.2: 1-19.

Perera, D. (2023). "Learning About Design's Colonial Pasts and Narrative Games." *The 7th International Conference for Design Education Researchers*, 29 November - 1 December 2023, London, United Kingdom.

Prendeville, S., Syperek, P. and Santamaria, L. (2022). "On the Politics of Design Framing Practices." *Design Issues* 38.3: 71–84.

Simon, H. A. (1969). *The Sciences of the Artificial*. Cambridge: M.I.T. Press.

Sluzki, C. E., and Veron, E. (1976). "The Double Bind as a Universal Pathogenic Situation". In *Double bind: The Foundation of the Communicational Approach to the Family,* edited by Carlos. E., Sluzki, C. E. and Ransom, D. C. 251-262, New York: Grune & Stratton.

Spivak, G. C. (2012). *An Aesthetic Education in the Era of Globalization*. Cambridge, Massachusetts: Harvard University Press.

Tlostanova, M. (2017). "On Decolonizing Design." *Design Philosophy Papers* 15.1: 51–61.

Tlostanova, M. and Perera, D. (2024). "Double bind, Decoloniality, and the Question of Aesthetics", March 25, 2024. Https://www.enactingecologicalaesthetics.com/double-bind-decoloniality-the-question-of-aesthetics-madina-tlostanova-in-conversation-with-dulmini-perera/.

Tonkinwise, C. (2014). "Design's (Dis)Orders & Transition Design." Accessed November 12, 2023. https://medium.com/@camerontw/designs-dis-orders-transition-design-cd-53c3ad7d35.

Tonkinwise, C. (2023). "Transition Design," *In Reframing Design Education,* March 22, 2023, https://reframingdesign.education/cameron-tonkinwise-over-transition-design/.

Wilden, A. (1980). *System and Structure: Essays in Communication and Exchange*. London: Tavistock Publications.

# Turning Up the Design Research Dial:

Joseph Lindley and David Philip Green

## Commentary on Permission to Muck About

This chapter tells the story of a film[1]. The film was made as part of a project. So, let's start with the project.

The project, *Design Research Works,* is a 7-year study of the practices, communities, methods, and world views that are organised under the umbrella term *Design Research*. Design Research Works is funded by a Future Leaders Fellowship scheme operated by UK Research and Innovation. This means it is not only a research project, but it is also aspiring to support the development of the Fellow (in this case Joseph Lindley), those working to support the Fellowship (including David Philip Green), and to provide leadership and shape to a field or community.

The film, *Permission to Muck About*[2], is one of the major outputs of the project and was made to try and support all the above aims. We hope that it communicates and infers a theory of what Design Research is, how it works, and exemplifies why this assemblage of attributes might be useful, alluring, and profound. The film's production was led by David Philip Green, who was employed as a Senior Postdoctoral Research Associate working on Design Research Works from late 2020 to early 2024. While David did the vast majority of the work involved in making the film, it was a collaborative effort with Joseph Lindley, who leads Design Research Works – hence the film is attributed to both David and Joseph. The film also owes much to many more people who contributed to it directly and indirectly. There are too many people to mention everyone individually by name (a more complete list appears in the credits of the film). Still, special thanks should be attributed to Jesse Josua Benjamin (who was employed as a Postdoctoral Research Associate with Design Research Works), who helped conceptualise the graphical elements, and Jenny Mac, who is the voiceover artist.

This chapter is intended to be readable without having to watch Permission to Muck About, just as the film is intended to be read without the chapter. However, we hope that reading the chapter and then watching the film (or the other way around) will provide mutual benefit. The aim is to enhance both media by providing additional texture, perspectives on the content, and illumination of the full extent of the research that went into the film's production. Parts of this chapter reference extracts from the film's script (i.e. the voiceover) or transcripts from interviews that feature in the film. Other parts of the chapter provide contextualising information – like this introductory section – and hence are in the diegetic plane of the chapter and not the film.

At the outset of Design Research Works, three tenets were proposed. During 2023, while Permission to Muck About was still in production, these three tenets were presented at the *Board of International Research in Design's, NERD Take Five*[3] conference. That presentation is part of the reason this chapter was invited to be part of this book. Moreover, discussions arising at that conference went on to influence aspects of the film. The three tenets that were core to the presentation at the conference were:

I) Design Research's uniquely flexible epistemological machinery, synthetic and future-oriented stances, and inherent interdisciplinarity lend it an unrivalled ability to engage with rapidly evolving and wickedly intractable challenges.

II) The world is more complex, globalised, fast-paced, digital, unequal, and in need of vision and sense than it ever has been before. In the 20th century we made a brand-new world, and in the 21st century we need new ways to understand how to deal with its consequences.

III) Although Design Research is well-placed to contribute towards addressing the 21st century's challenges, as well as helping to drive sustainable innovation, the specific coordinates of the movement lack clarity, the methods and theories are adolescent, and together this limits the leverage.

As we will see as the chapter unfolds, these themes return, develop, and in doing so we hope that Permission to Muck About – and this chapter – will help to pave the way for an increase in Design Research's influence over the years to come, helping us to build more sustainable, resilient, and liveable futures.

# DESIGN RESEARCH'S MURMURATIONS, CARCINIZATION, AND GRAMMAR OF INTUITION

In April 2022, we attended the ACM CHI Conference on Human Factors in Computing Systems. This conference, although situated firmly within the computing discipline, is quite eclectic and among that eclecticism there is a vibrant Design Research contingent. Part of our motivation for attending the conference was to capture some of the first original interviews for Permission to Muck About. On our second day in the host city – New Orleans, Louisiana, USA – we encountered a street poet, sitting beneath an umbrella, in the hot Louisiana sunshine, at a small portable desk with a typewriter. He asked if we would like a poem and what our business in town was. We gave a rudimentary explanation of Design Research and the purpose of Design Research Works. The poet – David Blanton[4] – asked that we return in a few minutes. When we returned, he had written this poem, and although we didn't realise it at the time, it would become the basis for the prologue section of the film (see also Fig. 1. for some examples of the visuals used to support the poem in this section of the film).

*Meaning is found in the process*
*Not in the results*
*Poetry is a controlled hallucination that has to be absorbed.*
*Not examined under a microscope*
*Understanding the world requires metaphors*
*How do we understand anything?*
*Our brains create models of the world*
*Our words create a grammar of intuition*
*Our thoughts become a theatre of the mind*
*Design, like poetry, means nothing without the journey*
*Designs are extensions of humanity's fingerprints*
*This and that must separate or we can't discern chance from fate*
*Every design takes us somewhere and in every where*
*There is some of you and me and poetry*

Through a combination of common sense, poetic insight, linguistic playfulness, and Blanton's intuitive understanding that something about Design Research involves a "grammar of intuition", the poem opens the door through which we invite the film's audience and readers of this chapter alike to step.

In the script document that we used to plan and organise the film, alongside the poem we included the following notes for use in editing and production:

*A hallucinogenic mashup of crabs, starlings, and mycelium.*
*Hands, making and fabrication.*
*Key moments from the history of design, science, and art.*
*Over which, the text from the poem appears, typewritten as it is spoken.*

Most of these elements appear in the prologue of the film. Many are visual metaphors to accompany, enrich and empower the argument, rhetoric, and problem spaces the film aspires to open. Visuals representing the moments from the histories of design, science, and art, given the film's narrative, do not require a huge amount of imagination to identify the relevance. Conversely, the reason behind "hallucinogenic mashup of crabs, starlings, and mycelium" is, perhaps, less apparent.

The ambiguity of the visual aspects of these film passages is a directorial choice, and, as such, if this chapter sought to disambiguate them, it could initiate a moment of tension. To be clear, when the chapter discusses metaphors from the film, we do not seek to undermine the integrity of those metaphors' ambiguity. Instead, the intent is to bootstrap the intention of the film: to communicate and infer a carefully balanced, deliberately fluid, and open-ended version of the story of Design Research's profundity and value. We want to help empower the world's Design Researchers with examples, vocabulary, and semantics to enhance how they explain the power of what they do. Alongside that, we want to inspire, intrigue, and entice people who are *not* currently Design Researchers, inviting them to connect with a way of looking at the world that they may not have, so far, paid that much attention to.

With these points in mind, we begin with some notes on two of the visual metaphors that appear in the prologue.

First, crabs. The term *carcinization* refers to a form of convergent evolution in which non-crab crustaceans evolve into crab forms. Nature, for some reason, keeps evolving crabs. This arose in a team discussion planning the Design Research Works *Jamboree* (a week-long symposium held in late August 2022[5]). Jesse Josua Benjamin mentioned carcinization. He highlighted that an appreciation that practical engagement with materials leads to new insights about the world in the form of tacit knowledge is something that – like crabs – has evolved multiple times throughout history. Craft knowledge is almost universally valued by indigenous groups worldwide; it has been central to the success of our species' most successful civilisations, and in the 20th century, a new version of this kind of knowing evolved, and that is what we currently call Design Research.

In the script notes the second visual metaphor just appears as "starlings" (Starlings are the avian species known as *sturnus vulgaris*). In the film, the birds appear as footage of a murmuration. Murmuration is the phenomenon where thousands of individual birds fly together, creating an effect that looks as if they are a single entity. We had initially used murmuration as a metaphor in a prototypical version of a publication that later became the paper *Ways of seeing design research: A polyphonic speculation* (see Fig. 1. in Green 2023). Our motivation to use the murmuration metaphor when discussing Design Research was partly exploring how thousands of Design Research practitioners across the globe are simultaneously acting autonomously, but, allegorically, also make up some larger entity. An inherent property of Design Research is the individuality of practice or the notion that each project is entirely unique.

Consequently, if we gave two Design Researchers the same brief, they would almost certainly come up with two quite different outputs, conclusions, or solutions – and this is a strength of how this kind of research works. Notwithstanding this

*Fig. 1.* Crab visual with text overlay of David Blanton's poem from the prologue of the film.

"ultimately particular" quality, when viewed globally Design Research is not just a cornucopia of standalone individuals, it is also a sum of the parts; a single entity made up of the many facets of the ultimately particular projects and practices. From this gestalt – represented visually in the film by the murmuration – trends rise and fall, consensuses emerge and are refined, and research programmes (Binder and Redström 2006; Redström 2017) transmute the contingencies of intermediate-level knowledge into robust research findings.

Whilst the stories behind these metaphors are never explicitly exposed within the film itself, as mentioned in the discussions above, they reveal the extent of the multifaceted and cross-contextual gamut of issues and perspectives we considered while conceiving of and refining the film's narrative. The metaphors of carcinization, murmuration, and David Blanton's poem all talk to a top-down view of Design Research. They discuss a macro perspective or panoramic view of the world of Design Research. The film also engages with the other end of the spectrum, the deeper down and zoomed-in view of the field. This examination seeks to articulate the machinery that makes Design Research function and to unpack how the knowledge that emerges from Design Research differs from other forms of knowledge.

## TO UNDERSTAND DESIGN RESEARCH, YOU NEED TO BREAK SOME EGGS

The second chapter of the film is titled *Making & Eggs*. As with each chapter, it opens with a quote: in this case the famous chef Anthony Bordain; "The way you make an omelette reveals your character". The quote highlights that the humble omelette, although one of the simplest classic culinary traditions, can actually incorporate a huge amount of craft and artistry. The voiceover script for this chapter of the film begins thus:

*A recipe usually starts with a list of ingredients.*
*Next, the recipe tells us what to do with them.*
*It doesn't tell us everything.*
*A recipe actually includes lots of assumptions.*
*It's often assumed, for instance, that we know to separate the shell from the contents of an egg.*
*It's assumed that we know which utensils to use.*
*It's assumed we know what is meant by "a medium heat".*
*These assumptions rely on a particular kind of knowledge.*
*And without this kind of knowledge, a recipe is only half a story.*
*Tacit knowledge is everywhere, but it can be hard to identify.*
*It's a kind of knowledge that we tend to get from experience.*

These words accompany footage of a child naively following the instructions and spectacularly failing to make a satisfactory omelette. The relevance to Design Research is the realisation that acquiring the experience necessary to do Design Research in a given domain satisfactorily tends to rely upon having previously obtained relevant tacit knowledge. In an interview for the film, Sir Christopher Frayling – historian, former Rector of the Royal College of Art, and author of the influential pamphlet *Research in Art and Design* (Frayling 1993) – mentioned a lecture given by the philosopher Michael Oakeshott where he demonstrated that the "know-how" necessary to cook an omelette could not reasonably be written down, but rather needed to be acquired through the practice of making omelettes.

    This humble entry into the nuance of formal knowledge and "know-how" is a theme that arises several times in the film and has several implications. The first implication, demonstrated by the omelette example, is that Design Research requires experience to do sufficiently well. It requires a tacit, craft-like, and practical understanding of the media being worked with. This is what David Pye refers to as the "workmanship of risk" (Pye 1968) and represents the contrast between improvised creative problem-solving and a more *designerly* engagement with a material that can only happen through a sustained and practical exploration with a particular material, context, or problem.

Designers tend to make good Design Researchers because design training instils an open mind regarding the value of this kind of sustained material engagement. Consequently, this highlights why distilled approaches such as Design Thinking tend to have limited benefit for non-designers, as they do not consider the need to develop a craft. A practical takeaway is that Design Research training must have a practical element. One cannot learn to be a good Design Researcher practitioner by reading about it. One would not assume a doctor who had never seen a patient would be good at their job. Similarly, one should not assume that a Design Researcher who has not engaged in design would be good at their job either.

Another implication of Design Research's symbiotic relationship with tacit knowledge relates to the challenge of communicating findings. Many of our traditional means of sharing research are not commensurate with the kinds of knowing that Design Research tends to produce. In Chapter 3 of the film *Making & Knowledge*, reference is made to Robin Wall Kimmerer (a Potawatomi botanist, author, and the director of the Center for Native Peoples and the Environment at the State University of New York College of Environmental Science and Forestry). Kimmerer has written about the practice of braiding sweetgrass to make baskets (2015). In this work she considers that from a utilitarian point of view, the baskets are designed for carrying things. However, as Kimmerer unpacks, the practice of braiding the sweetgrass both communicates the practical knowledge but also encodes a much more profound and tacit understanding of what it means to be Potawatomi, what it means to be connected to the environment, and lessons to do with reciprocity and responsibility. The baskets demonstrate that craft, design, and material engagements can encapsulate knowledge. Whilst it is eminently possible to capture some sense of this and translate it into the written formats that dominate scholarly publishing, it is palpably infeasible for there to be a one-to-one translation without something being lost in the process. Discussing this matter in Chapter 7 of the film *Evolution*, Pieter-Jan Stappers (Professor of Design Techniques at Delft

University of Technology) notes that "our words are bad tools" while Audrey Desjardins (Associate Professor of Interaction Design at University of Washington) elaborates "… what we learn is along the way, and so I think we need to find strategies to share those in-between moments". Publications expect squares, but Design Research frequently produce circles, or triangles, or other strange shapes, and the resulting knowledge just does not fit in the publication-shaped hole.

A further implication of the import of tacit knowledge is the nature of what we might find out through Design Research practice. Throughout *Permission to Muck About* we frame the notion of Design Research as a counterpoint, relation, or contrast to *science*. We introduce science as a primarily positivist practice that assumes facts and truths about the Universe can be established if a suitable scientific method is followed. This presentation is, owing to the constraints of the film, a little reductive. The notion we are more pointedly referring to is known as *scientism*, or the idea that the *only* reasonable lens to view the world through is a scientific one. The film (see Chapter 1, *Science & Beyond*) highlights the danger of scientism through a series of soundbites of UK politicians using the phrase "follow the science" when discussing their political decisions relating to managing the Covid-19 pandemic in 2020 and 2021. The reality was that hundreds of government scientists shared and discussed many pieces of evidence addressing the pandemic from different angles. The conclusions to be drawn from these pieces of evidence rarely aligned, and ultimately, the decisions were political. However, the deference to the phrase "follow the science" is indicative of an unconscious societal tendency to assume there is a traditionally scientific answer to most questions.

This implicit scientism arguably has roots in The Enlightenment period of history (Lindley and Green 2021; Lindley 2023). During that time, scientists managed to amass so much evidence through scientific endeavour that, in Europe, the dominance of the Catholic church's view of the universe (e.g. geocentrism) was ultimately undermined. Cycles of hypothesis, experimentation, and observation – what we might now call the Scientific Method – achieved what one could reasonably have thought to be impossible. If we shift our historical lens to the present day, the same scientific machinery has brought us the industrial revolution, space flight, computing, the internet, and artificial intelligence. Therefore, it is unsurprising that we have an unwritten and powerful allegiance to science, which can manifest as scientism. But science and its methods have obvious limitations. The wicked problems that characterise the 21st century such as global inequality and climate change are too complex to break into constituent parts that can be addressed scientifically without some other guiding principle. Socio-technological challenges that cannot have a falsifiable or "correct" outcome, such as the infamous trolley problem, do not have answers that can reasonably be obtained scientifically. Challenges without precedent, for example, how to make policy decisions relating to an innovation that has not yet been invented, these matters require interpretation. Such are the kinds of challenges that Design Research can help to explore. So, we frame Design Research as the *interpretivist* counterpoint to science and positivism in Chapter 1, *Science & Beyond*.

Various theories and discussions are signposted within the film that talks to the relative value of Design Research's interpretive foundation compared to science's positivism. One of these relates to Frayling's dissection of Design Research into Research *for* Design, Research *into* Design and Research *through* Design. While these have been discussed thoroughly elsewhere (e.g. Lindley 2015), they are worth considering briefly. Research for Design – background research or the gathering of reference materials to help support the process of designing something – *can be scientific*: For example, a physical or chemical exploration of matter or materials to understand how to make something functional. Similarly, Research into Design can also be scientific: For example, a sociological or psychological approach to understanding how designers think and work. However, Research *through* Design is implicitly different. It is not, by traditional uses of the term, a "scientific" endeavour. It is a way of knowing that relies upon a pragmatic (Dewey 1908;

Dixon 2019, 2020) and practice-based (Gaver *et al.* 2022) engagement with the world that results in tacit knowledge. A useful framing for this kind of understanding is *intermediate knowledge* (Höök and Löwgren 2012). This kind of understanding is not so particular that it can only apply to one individual setting, nor is it so general that it might be called a theory. Instead, intermediate knowledge occupies a space that can infer valuable insights from a specific example, or design, and convey those insights so that they might be useful or generative in some other context. The key to understanding how intermediate knowledge works is accepting that it arises from the experience of gaining tacit knowledge. The mechanism beneath this is much the same as how any one of us might learn to make an omelette, make a cup of tea, or any other practical and material task. In Design Research, however, the same logic is applied carefully, thoughtfully, and to a plethora of different domains.

## WAKING UP IN THE NIGHT

In their consideration of emergence as a property of practice-based Design Research, Gaver, Krogh, Boucher and Chatting refer to Nobel Prize winning biologist François Jacob's conception of *Night Science* (Gaver *et al.* 2022). Jacob explores this idea in his autobiography. He defies the simplicity of stereotypes of science and codifies the practice into two types: science of the day and science of the night. His poetic turn of phrase captures the essence of the distinction. Day Science, he says, "meshes like gears and achieves results with a force of certainty [...] One admires its majestic arrangement as that of a da Vinci painting or a Bach fugue. One walks about in a formal French garden. Conscious of its progress, proud of its past, sure of its future, day science advances in light and glory" (Jacob 1987, 206). Jacob's imagery and metaphors allegorically envelop the stereotypical version of science that arguably is what fuels the tendency towards scientism discussed *a priori*.

Contrastingly, Night Science eschews the trappings of tradition, history, and certainty. Jacob's invocation of verbiage to describe his feelings about Night Science is extensive, expressive, and exciting. This idea, which he realises is so fundamental to what the practice of science really is, is articulated thus. Night Science "wanders blindly [...] Doubting everything, it feels its way [...] It is a sort of workshop of the possible [...] spontaneous generation [...] What guides the mind, then, is not logic. It is instinct, intuition" (ibid). Jacob's explanation exudes a rare energy, a passion to articulate a holism of science that is usually missed. The striking thing is that his explanation of the "other half" of science seems to be a fitting description of a significant part of Design Research too. For this reason, Chapter 6 of the film is titled *Night Science*, and we explore the resonance through the eyes of several interviewees.

Pieter-Jan Stappers notes how, in interdisciplinary collaborations (outside of the world of design), ambiguity tends to arise at disciplinary boundaries. This realisation highlights a similarity to how design training and skills help individuals thrive while within the ambiguous part of scientific, design, or research processes. In the early 1990s Christopher Frayling had already noted how the stereotypical views of designers, engineers, artists, and scientists tend to collapse if one interrogates them: artists work in a cognitive idiom as much as scientists work in an expressive one (Frayling 1993). When interviewed for Permission to Muck About, Frayling recounts a key moment in the tale of Crick and Watson discovering the structure of DNA, describing a crucial chance encounter with a mathematician as a "Craft moment". He discusses *The Nature and Art of Workmanship* (Pye 1968), which sets up two conceits: the workmanship of certainty and the workmanship of chance. The former bears an uncanny resemblance to how Jacob explained Day Science's "force of certainty". The latter resonates with Frayling's conception of Research through Design, with Jacob's "workshop of the possible" and with the stochastic and creative core at the heart of all Night Science – Design Research included.

Similar themes arose in many of the interviews that make up the film. Also appearing in Chapter 6, Doejna Ooejes (Assistant Professor of Industrial Design at Eindhoven University of Technology) recounts how, in Design Research, a continual and intuitive perspective switching is essential, realising that sometimes it is the material or the context that makes these choices for you: "Surprising things happen, and I think we can be a bit more open to that and listen more to that". Meanwhile, her colleague, Kristina Andersen (Associate Professor at Eindhoven University of Technology) explains how the exploratory nature of designerly hunches and inquisitiveness led to designs for weaved facemasks that inadvertently pioneered a new type of viral filter. The innovation was not predicted; it wasn't the intention, it wasn't a product of the workmanship of certainty, but it was a serendipitous outcome of the workmanship of craft. The value of this kind of work is fundamental to the spectrum of Design Research that appears in the film. Chapter 5 of the film includes nearly 50 minutes of testimony from a wide variety of projects, all of which exhibit craft-based, intuitive, stochastic, and creative sparks. François Jacob's presentation of Night Science illustrates that these are hallmarks of excellence in science, as well as in Design Research.

## EVOLVING DESIGN RESEARCH AND CHANGING THE SETTING TO "RADICAL ACADEMY"

While much of the film deals with metaphors, examples, points of view and allegorical portrayals of what Design Research is and does, towards the end of the film, those elements are framed in terms of practical challenges that hold back the Design Research movement and steps we might take to overcome them. Chapter 7, titled *Evolution*, addresses this.

Over a decade ago, Bill Gaver used the term "pre-paradigmatic" to describe what scholars in the Human-Computer Interaction community could "expect" from Design Research (Gaver 2012). The implications of the term pre-paradigmatic are a fascinating framing of where Design Research sits at this moment in history and builds on Thomas Kuhn's work on *Structure of Scientific Revolutions* (1970). Kuhn realises that in the early days of new fields, movements, disciplines or sciences, much effort is spent establishing the consensus (or paradigm). During the pre-paradigmatic phase, this effort is disproportionate compared to the efforts used in *applying* the paradigm. While the evidence would suggest that Design Research continues to be pre-paradigmatic, as we point out in the film, other precedents suggest this shouldn't necessarily prevent progress. For example, in physics, the particle and wave models of light fundamentally disagree. We can take this as an example of lacking consensus; however, as has been demonstrated, many innovations and derivative research have been forthcoming based on *both* models. The takeaway of this comparison is that having a widely accepted singular paradigm isn't always necessary, so long as there is a shared language, an ability to communicate coherently, and an awareness of this multiplicity. Establishing this shared language is arguably something the field could improve upon. The film touches on this briefly at the end of Chapter 3, *Design and Knowing*, where we establish a precedent to simply use the term "Design Research" while accepting this encompasses several more specialised approaches with their own terminologies. Notwithstanding the issue of shared terminology, the other topics discussed in Chapter 7 deal with day-to-day logistical challenges of being a Design Researcher which arise from it being a pre-paradigmatic field.

One of these challenges is the conceptualisation that Design Research is "unempirical", i.e. that it does not have a way to verify hypotheses based on observation. To an extent, this is true. However, a qualifier is that the epistemological framing within which empiricism is virtuous is a different epistemology to that which Design Research participates in. The terms used to explain high-quality research – words like validity, rigour, and reproducibility – these terms *do* have analogies in Design Research. However, they are allegorical and metaphorical – the terms cannot be used in the same way they are in many other types of scholarship. Once again, this, we argue, is a product of Design Research's unique assemblage of interpretivist (Ryan 2018), pragmatic (Dixon 2019) and reflexive (Schön 1983, 1992) epistemologies that can be "drifted" across (Krogh and Koskinen 2020). Summing this up succinctly; in most research fields, an experiment that produces the same result when it is run twice is desirable. In Design Research this type of reproducibility is not only impossible, but it is also antithetical to the value proposal of the very epistemology the practice is built upon. Because Design Research derives its value from the journey of intuition earlier characterised as Night Science, the intention is to produce a *unique* outcome each time an experiment is run. Those unique outcomes manifest as intermediate knowledge (Höök and Löwgren 2012). With intermediate knowledge the "rigour" is established through the extent of the design process and clarify of how it is communicated. Conversely, validity usually emerges in Design Research through multiple instances of intermediate knowledge being viewed as a whole in what is usually known as a research programme (Redström 2017).

Another practical issue relates to the struggle of publishing Design Research. In Chapter 7, Audrey Desjardins notes the rigidity of the typical formats we used for sharing, contrasting the benefit of the "final thing" made in a Design Research project with the realisation that much of what is learned happens "along the way". The challenge of capturing the value of the process is, in part, a product of its intangibility; the challenge also relates to the privilege of words and text in publication traditions. Publications are increasingly diverse. Concepts such as annotated portfolios (Gaver and Bowers 2012) and pictorials (Blevis, Hauser and Odom 2015) go some way to enriching the media of publication. Th (currently mothballed) conference, *Research through Design* (Durrant 2016), pioneered a multimodal format for publishing Design Research that included physical objects, an exhibition, and image-rich publications. An interesting and related precedent is the Journal of Visualized Experiments or JoVE[6]. JoVE is a peer-reviewed scientific video journal. It was created because many lab experiments, when written up in text-based journals, were not reproducible by other scientists. By *showing* the experiments on video, rather than *telling* them in text, JoVE seeks to enhance this reproducibility. Interestingly, this highlights the value of tacit, practical, and hands-on knowledge – ideas that are core to art, design, and craft; but, as this demonstrates, are also core to some types of experimental science.

Daniela Rosner (Associate Professor in Human Centered Design & Engineering at University of Washington) raises a crucial, and somewhat unresolved in the film, point about the reproduction of structural inequities across race, class, and gender. She points out that Design Research has historically failed to account for these challenges, contrasting the idea of layering inclusion on top of the status quo with a more critical approach that might ask that the status quo be held to account for its foundations, evolution, and development of the field. Resonantly, Christina Harrington (Assistant Professor in Human-Computer Interaction at Carnegie Mellon University) points out that rather than didactic engagements with communities, Design Research may benefit from a more open-minded and less privileged approach that should just "shut up and listen". While we do not *directly* address these concerns in the film, such considerations did influence the overall rhetorical thread of the film and the range of examples used. We believe that this rhetorical thread is, as much as we could accommodate, consistent with a coherent story of what Design Research is and does, *as well as* supporting the idea of and potentially taking part in a holistic, inclusive, global, and postcolonial recapitulation of the field.

The final part of the film, Chapter 8 – titled *Inventing the Future* – zooms out from these practical challenges, recapitulates the main messages of the film, and then invokes the metaphor of an imaginary control room. This control room has dials to set the general preferences of people worldwide. Using these dials, we could influence world views, and by influencing world views, we could affect change. The film's voiceover uses a description for this control room to articulate the film's calls to action. These are steps that we propose, accepting all of the nuance and commentary discussed hitherto in this chapter, as viable and achievable ways to unlock more of Design Research's value, and to hopefully contribute to a more sustainable, equitable and resilient society.

*So let's imagine ... a control room.*
*That governs how we know things in the world.*
*The dial for science is set a bit too high.*
*The destructive dogma of scientism needs dialling down.*
*Science can't tell us everything.*
*Art is valued, as it should be.*
*(But maybe we could turn it up a bit, since we're in here).*
*Design Research is a dial unto itself.*
*And it is set so low that many people don't even know it exists.*
*So, we're not getting the best from it.*
*And its knack for integrating, synthesising, imagining, and making tacit knowledge tangible is going unnoticed.*
*We dismiss the value of "intermediate knowledge" too readily when we write it off as unscientific, unempirical, or invalid.*
*Let's adjust the dials.*
*Let's rebalance our ways of knowing, and thinking, and seeing, and feeling.*
*And dial into a more intuitive, pluralistic paradigm.*
*Let's teach Design Research to everyone – not just designers and researchers – but everyone – including each other.*
*Let's bring it into our schools, our organisations, our governments and institutions, and into public life and the public consciousness.*
*Because permission to muck about belongs to everyone.*

These, the closing words in the film, make an argument based on an assumption. That assumption is that the world would be a better place if it was inhabited by citizens who are educated about the contrasting ways that Design Research and science produce knowledge. The myriad of examples used throughout the film, we hope, provide a compelling set of reasons why this would be the case. The final call to action proposes that it is ultimately education that helps fine-tune the dials in the imaginary control room to affect this change in the world. The logistics, politics, and practicalities of delivering that education are undoubtedly complex but we hope that the story and content contained in this film may become part of that education in the years to come.

## ACKNOWLEDGEMENTS

We would like to thank everyone who participated and contributed to the making of the film; your generosity and insight was invaluable. The film and this chapter were funded by UK Research and Innovation (UKRI) grant with the reference number MR/T019220/1, which is the grant that supports Design Research Works (https://designresearch.works/).

## ENDNOTES

1. Link to access the film: https://designresearch.works/redirect.html?ptma=0
2. *Muck about* is a colloquial expression in British English, it tends to mean spending time idly, aimlessly, frivolously, or wastefully.
3. See https://www.bird-international-research-in-design.org/conferences/2023-nerd-take-five
4. At the time of writing you can find David on Instagram under the handle *poet_david1980*
5. See https://jamboree.designresearch.works
6. https://www.jove.com/

## REFERENCES

Binder, T., and Redström, J. (2006). Exemplary Design Research, in Friedman, K., Love, T., Côrte-Real, E. and Rust, C. (eds.), *Wonderground - DRS International Conference 2006*, 1-4 November, Lisbon, Portugal.

Blevis, E., Hauser, S. and Odom, W. (2015). 'Sharing the hidden treasure in pictorials', *Interactions*, 22(3), pp. 32–43.

Dewey, J. (1908). 'What Does Pragmatism Mean by Practical?', *The Journal of Philosophy, Psychology and Scientific Methods*, 5(4), p. 85.

Dixon, B. (2019). 'Experiments in Experience: Towards an Alignment of Research through Design and John Dewey's Pragmatism', *Design Issues*, 35(2), pp. 5–16.

Dixon, B.S. (2020). *Dewey and Design: A Pragmatist Perspective for Design Research*. Cham: Springer International Publishing.

Durrant, A.C. (2016). 'Developing a Dialogical Platform for Disseminating Research through Design', 11(1), pp. 8–21.

Frayling, C. (1993). 'Research in Art and Design', *Royal College of Art Research Papers*, 1(1), pp. 1–9.

Gaver, B. and Bowers, J. (2012). 'Annotated Portfolios', *Interactions*, 19(4), pp. 40–49.

Gaver, W. (2012). 'What should we expect from research through design?', in *Proceedings of the 2012 ACM annual conference on Human Factors in Computing Systems – CHI '12*. New York, New York, USA: ACM Press, pp. 937–946.

Gaver, W. *et al.* (2022). 'Emergence as a Feature of Practice-based Design Research', in *Designing Interactive Systems Conference*. New York, NY, USA: ACM, pp. 517–526.

Green, D., Lindley, J., Encinas, E., Dore, M., Benjamin, J.,and Bofylatos, S.(2023). Ways of seeing design research: A polyphonic speculation, in Holmlid, S., Rodrigues, V., Westin, C., Krogh, P. G., Mäkelä, M., Svanaes, D., Wikberg-Nilsson, Å (Eds.), Nordes 2023: This Space Intentionally Left Blank, 12-14 June, Linköping University, Norrköping, Sweden

Höök, K. and Löwgren, J. (2012). 'Strong concepts', *ACM Transactions on Computer-Human Interaction*, 19(3), pp. 1–18.

Jacob, F. (1987). *The Statue Within*. Cold Spring Harbor Laboratory Press.

Kimmerer, R.W. (2015). *Braiding Sweetgrass: Indigenous Wisdom, Scientific Knowledge and the Teachings of Plants*. Milkweed Editions.

Krogh, P.G. and Koskinen, I. (2020). *Drifting by Intention*. Springer.

Kuhn, T.S. (1970). *The Structure of Scientific Revolutions*. Chicago: University of Chicago Press.

Lindley, J. (2015). 'A pragmatics framework for design fiction', in *Proceedings of the 12th European Academy of Design Conference*.

Lindley, J. (2023). 'Making design research work by flourishing through disappearance', in *Flourish by Design*. London: Routledge, pp. 88–91.

Lindley, J. and Green, D.P. (2021). 'The Ultimate Measure of Success for Speculative Design is to Disappear Completely', *Interaction Design and Architecture(s)*, (51), pp. 32–51.

Pye, D. (1968). *The Nature and Art of Workmanship*. Herbert Press Ltd.

Redström, J. (2017). *Making design theory*. Cambridge (MA): MIT Press.

Ryan, G. (2018). 'Introduction to positivism, interpretivism and critical theory', *Nurse Researcher*, 25(4), pp. 14–20.

Schön, D. (1983). *The Reflective Practitioner: How Professionals Think In Action*. New York: Basic Books.

Schön, D.A. (1992). 'Designing as reflective converstion with the materials of a deisgn situation', *Knowledge-Based Systems*, pp. 3–14.

# Re-placing

Jozef Eduard Masarik

# the Earth

## IMAGINARIES, THE EARTH, AND IMAGINARY EARTHS

In the 19th century, Chicago underwent a major urban transformation. Its scale and ambitions are balanced in between the real and the unbelievable. The raising of Chicago is formally an urban masterplan, but its social, ecological, and medial aspects reveal the role of social and scientific imaginaries informing the project. The transformation shows deep connections with the scientific and technological imaginary of the period. The project becomes a case study used for reflection on the ways in which our imaginaries determine the way we design the environments we inhabit. How do imaginaries become a tool for designing the built environment? The question is of growing importance in considering both the environmental crisis and the post-truth era. Despite its ambitions and overwhelming dimensions, the raising remains relatively unknown, which is due to several reasons. Given the specific context of the project situated in Chicago during the American Civil War and just before the Great Fire that hit Chicago in 1871, there are few sources preserved until nowadays. Museums and archives are of little help. There are, however, records of the period, allowing us to understand the general context. Equally, the documentation of the project made by its author has been preserved. With the resources so much restrained the reconstruction and understanding of the events required creative approaches. The methods applied, therefore, include reconstructions and contextualization of the events both visually, through collages, and in writing-based written records. The imagery depicts specific aspects of the events in the light of the underlying imaginaries, while the text aims at reconstructing a larger context. In that way, the research offers an insight into the aspiration of the project, the position of architecture and technology in society and at the same time it speaks about human-nature and human-technology relations in the 19$^{th}$ century. Nowadays, we understand the raising of Chicago through the optics of the Anthropocene. Although the term was not used in the 19th century, the transformations of the Earth caused by the industry of the period offer interesting background for the concept's reflection. The raising of Chicago bridges the Anthropocene with design, architecture and urbanism. Theories concerning the relations between design and the Earth have evolved. Design is no longer seen as a solution to the problem, but rather as one of its causes. Contemporary design theory presents the mutual relations of design and the Earth as a vicious circle (Colomina and Wigley, 2016). Yet if we look at the Swedish town of Kiruna moving away from the land destroyed by mining activities, or at the artificial islands built off the coast of the United Arab Emirates, we can say that the practice has not changed as much as the narratives.

## THE INITIAL ALIENATION

The landscape in which Chicago is located was not convenient for a city (Beecher 1862, 99). At the beginning of the 19$^{th}$ century, it was still a swamp in the prairies. Given its location on the crossroads of important routes and its proximity to the border, it was, however, a strategic location (Mayer and Wade 1969, 20). In order to control the area, Fort Dearborn was built on the site in 1803. Given the swampy nature of the land, fermentation processes in the soil were providing a constant flux of humus. The extraordinarily fertile soil started attracting farmers which led to the establishment of a farmer settlement (Dedmon 1953, 4) soon after the construction of Fort Dearborn. From then on, the evolution went very fast. Since the 1820s, industrial production has been transforming the city (Mayer and Wade 1969, 24). New factories were constantly opening and attracting people to live and work in Chicago. At the end of the 1830s its number of inhabitants was more than 80 times bigger than at their beginning (Mayer and Wade 1969, 18). By 1848, the construction of cattle yards was finished, steam-powered grain elevators were operating, Chicago Board of Trade had become an established authority and the city's need for connections was satisfied by the construction of railroads, telegraph lines and Illinois and Michigan Canal (Carr 2019, 153). In a relatively short period of time, a farmer settlement turned into a metropolis – the country's industrial capital. Over two decades, while the farmer inhabitants were turning into factory workmen, working the soil as means of subsistence was disappearing in Chicago. It was replaced by labour in industry. Alienation from the Earth became a persisting issue. The dizzying growth of the number of inhabitants was followed by an uncontrollable increase in built-up areas. Built environment was covering ever more surface. The contacts of Chicagoans with the Earth were vanishing, just as the Earth itself within the limits of the city. The pace of the alienation of Chicagoans from the Earth was incredible. After a brief period of the farmer settlement benefiting from its swampy nature, the very particularity of the location turned into a problem.

## ORIGINS OF FEAR

One of the most obvious problems the swampy location presented to the city was the unstable muddy ground. As the settlement evolved into a city, its architecture changed radically. However, the location was not fit for the new architectural structures. The swamp was not providing them with solid ground. Records from the period have preserved an account of "a brick hotel five-stories high that was so heavy, that it had sunk into the soft soil, and had forced the ground up in the street around it" (Cleaver 1892, 53). The Earth, initially the asset of the location, was becoming an obstacle for the city. The ties between Chicagoans and the Earth were disappearing. The citizens of the industrial city were inhabiting it not because of its nature but in spite of it. The alienation of Chicago from the Earth was growing. With the increase of the human-built environments, Chicagoans could only access the Earth in the unpaved streets of the city. These contacts were, however, horrifying. The Earth was devouring Chicagoans, their horses, or even entire coaches (Spinney 2000, 37). Not being careful enough meant risking sinking in the bottomless mud of the swamp. A cruel torture was awaiting Chicagoans right at the thresholds of their dwellings. Once

*Fig. 1.* A rendering of Chicago's swampy streets with a constantly shifting ground. The collage uses a single photograph and replicates its fragments, putting vision distortions and the ground into dialogue.

*Fig. 2.* A visual speculation on Chicago's imaginary concerning the Earth. The collage combines photographs of Chicago, sci-fi monster imagery of the period, and a better-documented city regrading project conducted in the early 1900s in Seattle.

the mud started absorbing them, they were helpless, yet fully aware of the inevitable end. Without a helping hand, only death could set them free from the terrors the Earth had prepared for them. Nothing but the floors and the pavements blocking out the mud were providing them with security. It was in the built environment where Chicagoans could find refuge from the danger, from the Earth. The signs in the streets were issuing warnings discouraging access to unpaved areas: "NO BOTTOM HERE", (Platt 2005, 28) "STAGE DROPPED THROUGH", (Mayer and Wade 1969, 24) "MAN DISAPPEARED", (Mayer and Wade 1969, 24) or *"MAN LOST"* (Mayer and Wade 1969, 24). Chicagoans' lives and property were being put in danger. The Earth in Chicago was devouring its inhabitants alive. The life-threatening conditions in the city were turning the alienation from the Earth into fear. Chicagoans started fearing the Earth.

## THE TERROR

The imaginary of the period helped Chicagoans see further dangers coming from the ground. When agriculture was replaced by industry, the attention of the inhabitants shifted away from the soil. And as it was believed in the period: "if care were not taken, fermenting vegetation and rotting mold could create a dangerous swamp, a reservoir of miasmas", (1986, 190) in the words of Alain Corbin. What shaped the following events in the city in considerable measure was the miasmatic theory which was alluded to in the quotation and was a widely accepted scientific theory in the 19th century. This theory suggests that diseases are spread through unpleasant odours (Bonner 1991, 179). In Chicago the source of the stench was the Earth. The location itself induced the natural fermentation processes of a swamp. In addition to that, the city had no sewers. Horses, still the main means of transportation at the period, were leaving excreta on the unpaved thoroughfares. Human, animal, and industrial waste mixed with the mud of the streets was making the city particularly fetid. Chicago being the American capital of industry, Harold Platt's words: "the amount of industrial pollution was so great that it enveloped the industrial cities in their own microenvironments", (2005, 98) apply to Chicago with remarkable precision. Given that its inhabitants were linking the diseases with the fetid Earth, they had serious reasons to be afraid of it. Death itself, represented by the Earth in the city, was omnipresent. "People died at the rate of 60 a day, and 'the death cart was seen continually in the streets.' [...] In early July, with streets lined with coffins waiting to be picked up for burial, [...] witnesses claimed it was difficult to find men or boys to help undertakers lift the bodies into coffins, for people feared the 'demon' would enter them if they touched its victims" (Miller 1996, 122-123). In the eyes of Chicagoans, the Earth was turning into a malicious being, a demon. And this situation was nothing new. 1854 was the sixth year in succession in which Chicago was struck by epidemics. These six successive years earned Chicago the title of the city with the highest death rate in the world in the 19th century. In the prism of miasmatic theory, the Earth was providing dozens of dead human bodies daily as a proof of its deadly powers. It went from passively waiting for victims to get trapped in the mud to actively killing them. The latter was preceded by intense torture, as recorded by a historian:

> *"the symptoms came on with terrifying suddenness, and they were spectacular. [...] People who were well at noon were in the grave by night, but only after a terrible struggle with vomiting, diarrhea, and stabbing cramps. Even their loved ones had trouble looking at their suffering faces, pinched and blue and cold" (Miller 1996, 122).*

The Earth did not even need physical contact in order to kill anymore. Through its miasmatic emanations, it was endowed with the ability of remote killing. In Chicago, miasmas earned a specific nickname – "death fogs" (Miller 1996, 123).

*Fig. 3.* Instead of combining imagery, the picture deals with removal of its parts, referencing the reorganisation of the city, its surprising transformations, and their fading into "the normal".

## THE FIRST TAKE-OFF ATTEMPTS

As the fear of the Earth was growing, the actions Chicagoans took to protect themselves were revealing an effort to avoid any interactions with the Earth. The obvious improvisation in the way the inhabitants were attempting to solve the situation testifies to the atmosphere of terror in the city and the urgent need to escape the Earth. First attempts consisted in hastily assembling plank sidewalks, allowing Chicagoans not to walk on the mud while moving around the city. Nails were sticking out of the sidewalks, yet Chicagoans found walking on them less inconvenient than walking on the Earth. The already mentioned Chicagoans' efforts to find refuge in the built environment were increasing. They were constructing structures enabling them to avoid any contact with the Earth throughout the city. The first timber sidewalks laid directly on the ground, however, proved to be counterproductive. Although wood is not a material particularly convenient for dank spaces, the logic of miasmatic theory can explain the choice of pinewood planks as a material for the improvised system of sidewalks. Chicago being the centre of the American lumber industry, its large lumberyards were drying and storing vast amounts of wood coming from the forests North of Chicago. The lumberyards were known for the fragrance of wood spreading far from their location. The use of wood in the construction of sidewalks was, therefore, not only motivated by its availability but also by its odour. The smell of wood had the power to chase the filthy odours of the fetid Earth away and thus rip it of its deadly powers. However, when the mud made its way through the gap between the fragrant planks, it made them rot almost immediately. The wood, initially a source of fragrance fighting the death fogs, was thus turning into an omnipresent source of stench itself. In the imaginary of Chicagoans this meant that the Earth was finding ways to make their efforts to protect themselves in vain. In order to get out of the reach of the mud, Chicagoans started constructing the sidewalks above the ground. Sidewalks were becoming ever more independent from the Earth. They were floating in the air ever higher above the mud. Leaving the ground was an intuitive effort to escape the alleged assaults of the Earth. With the sidewalks constructed at various heights above the ground, entrances of the newly erected architecture were equally built on arbitrary levels decided by individual contractors. As opposed to previous architectural designs, the plans of the houses in Chicago were not using the ground level or the city's topography as a major reference. We can say that Chicago was losing its connection to the Earth. A specific typology of houses displacing the main entrance and the porch upwards from the ground level was developed in Chicago in the period. These are known under the term *Chicago cottage*. The sidewalks built in the air following individual entrances built on arbitrary levels above the ground resulted in an array of ramps and platforms with inclinations varying uncontrollably. A historian's record of the city during the period highlights that: "frequently it was necessary to walk from one sidewalk level to another several times in a single block [...] It was with justification that periodic signs warned to pedestrian to 'USE YOUR INTELLECT'" (Dedmon 1953, 13). In this period Chicago gained its nickname of *the city of ups and downs*.[1] Trying to avoid any potential contact with the Earth, the complexity of the ramps and platforms grew uncontrollably. Ramps or plank bridges were allowing pedestrians to cross streets without having to venture into the mud of the street, without having to leave the planked area: "from side to side rickety boards served as unsafe bridges and the unfortunate hordes waded laboriously along as best they could" (Dedmon 1953, 10). Chicago's sidewalks were ignoring the location's natural topography. They were defining an artificial alternative for Chicagoans threatened by the Earth. In this way their lives were not submitted to the Earth anymore. Once they left their dwellings, they put their feet on an alternative artificial landscape, hovering at various heights above the fetid mud. The Earth was being systematically excluded from Chicago. Following an emotional distanciation between the city and the Earth, Chicago was imposing a physical one. However, there was always a backlash. No matter how high the sidewalks were, they were inefficient. The mud was finding ways to reach Chicagoans. They felt helpless. Nothing seemed to help. Every effort they made turned out to be another source of danger. The sidewalks were rotting and spreading stench, no matter how high above the ground they were constructed. The mud squirting from the wheels of coaches passing by always managed to reach them. The epidemics were continuing. The citizens were dying. They were getting desperate. It was as if the Earth were an ingenious monster constantly finding novel ways to kill its inhabitants. None of the Chicagoans' efforts were efficient in fighting the terror of the Earth. The terrified community of Chicago demanded the municipality take action after the epidemics in 1854 (Miller 1996, 123). In response, the city authorities opened a competition for engineers to solve the alarming situation. Prominent American engineers were presenting their proposals. The committee selected a proposal developed by Ellis S. Chesbrough.

## THE ENGINEERING OF THE NEW ENVIRONMENT

Chesbrough's entry in the competition consisted in building a sewerage system. Its intended result was to prevent further contamination of the Earth and in that way restrain its miasmatic emanations. However, the flat topography of the city, its swampy nature and almost no height difference between the city and the lake, into which the sewerage system was meant to be emptied, did not meet the requirements for traditional sewerage construction. Therefore, Chesbrough proposed installing the sewers on and above the city's streets and then lifting Chicago from the ground. In this way, the original ground became part of a newly created underground providing the space-respecting inclinations necessary for a functioning sewerage system. Subsequently, this new underground encrusted with sewers was filled with soil. Chesbrough calculated the necessary inclinations and the height of the whole system reaching up to 14 feet[2] above the natural

*Fig. 4.* An assemblage of depictions of various sidewalks, staircases, bridges etc. constituting the array of platforms Chicagoans built in order to avoid the Earth.

ground. The only criterion was: "to give the sewers such inclinations as the nature of the ground and the proposed modifications of the grade of the street will admit" (Chesbrough 1855, 10). Over two decades hundreds of miles of piping were installed on and above the original ground. Street after street, building after building Chicago was being raised to the new levels calculated by Chesbrough. The city was not only raised but also re-organized following a precise plan. Buildings were transported throughout the city to their designated locations. Travellers from the period recorded it as an overwhelming spectacle where, while crossing the city, their coaches had to stop and give way to buildings crossing the street multiple times on their way through Chicago. Chesbrough created a new topography for the city. The space between the Earth and the departed city was then filled with soil excavated in the construction of a tunnel bringing drinking water to the city. The layer of soil is called the *layer of dust* in the records. Drinking water was provided by the lake. The sewers were being emptied into the Chicago River running into the very lake. In order to stop miasmas contaminating the source of drinking water, Chesbrough decided to reverse the Chicago River. Ever since then it has been flowing from the lake, taking the impurities away and not into the lake as it had naturally done. This last touch illustrates Chesbrough's concerns about the contacts between the sewerage system and the world above the new ground. Chesbrough, anxious about their interactions, felt the need to define the relations between the two worlds. His tendency to avoid any contacts is clearly visible in his report from his research trip exploring European sewerage systems. For the engineer, the ideal solution would be a self-cleaning system without any necessity for human access. His expertise gained in Europe suggested that such a thing was impossible. Therefore, he designed a network of manholes regulating the access to the underground and restraining possible exhalations. The engineer fighting Chicago's endless chain of pandemics legitimated the city's escape from the Earth. Moreover, he enabled its execution far beyond any previous attempts. Such an ambitious plan was met with criticism. It was the techno-

*Fig. 5.* A collage combining sci-fi monster imagery of the period with ruins of Chicago destroyed by the Great Fire at the conclusion of its raising of the lower part, and a building undergoing a raising, in a better-documented raising project in Galveston (1902–1928). The triumphantly raised city is symbolically hovering above the defunct one.

logical optimism of the period and Chesbrough's reputation as an outstanding engineer that made the project's implementation possible. His personal history was almost mythological. Due to the economic situation, he already had to start earning money for his family at the age of 9. Therefore, he never obtained a full education. However, working with major engineers of the period he became one of the best in the country. Donald L. Miller wrote that Chesbrough was seen as "a visionary engineer with an incorruptible sense of civic duty and an ability to plan and carry on through gigantic public projects, he became a new kind of hero to Chicagoans" (1996, 124). He was the one who gave Chicago freedom from the Earth. The municipality was financing the raising of public spaces and buildings; however, the lifting of private buildings had to be funded by the individual property owners. Such a proposal was in agreement with President Jackson's perspective on democracy. The decision presented an opportunity for engineers to offer their services to property owners in Chicago. Chesbrough himself did not develop a specific technique for raising buildings; his main concerns were the sewerage system, the new topography, and their relations.

## THE VOYAGE

Individual engineers were using their own methods. The best recorded real estate raising technique was developed by George Pullman. He came to Chicago when the city was already being raised by other engineers; however, very soon he achieved major accomplishments such as raising the largest buildings in town. His technique was inspired by his experience on a comparable project linked to works on Eerie Canal and by his work on the railroads. The procedure could be described as an intricate choreography. First, the workmen had to undermine the building. Afterwards, in order to establish a solid support for the raising, they placed timbers on the bottom of the excavation under the exposed foundations. Subsequently, thousands of jackscrews were installed between the timbers and the building. The show was about to start. Hundreds of workmen took their positions on site. Each one of them was in charge of several jackscrews. Pullman himself was standing in the street, giving the workmen whistle signals. Every blow of the whistle meant a quarter of a turn on one jackscrew and passing to another one. The hundreds of workmen had to be perfectly synchronised. Pullman was giving the raising of a rhythm. Hundreds of workmen were moving in synchrony, following his signals. Whistle, turn, step. Whistle, turn, step... Donald L. Miller says that "Pullman's procedure in building raising was almost elegant in its machinelike coordination". In the perspective of the media theorist Pasi Väliaho, the rhythms of bodily movement encrusted in technological apparatuses "contribute to our perception of time and the duration of things and events. Rhythms assign their temporal qualities to things and events" (2010, 12). The building's ascent was almost imperceptible. The process of lifting a building up to 14 feet could take up to several weeks. The raising was perceived as a meticulously choreographed spectacle. It was magical pushing the potential of such a simple object as a jackscrew far beyond expectations, seemingly opposing natural laws. The spectacle was attracting numerous sightseers (Carr 2019, 260). The daily press was providing the curious public with information about the upcoming raisings. Reporters from all around the world were gathering in Chicago to witness the project (Miller 1996, 125). For several days or in some cases even weeks, the raising site became a mysterious mechanical dancefloor. The raising site became an "assembly line, wherein the entire factory is consolidated into a synchronous mechanism" (Giedion 1948, 5), the site of production of the new Chicago up to grade. The procedure is similar to early cinema which: "does not simply re-present bodily gestures, poses and movements but, instead, harnesses gestures into its technological positivity by becoming immanent to them in terms of dynamically modulating the body" (Väliaho 2010, 31). The perfectly coordinated workmen were following a choreography based on the logics of the assembly line. The working area and individual movements of workmen were carefully engineered. No unnecessary movements were allowed. Just as in the 19th century factories, efficiency determined everything. Sigfried Giedion claims that technology was originally employed for spectacle, for staging wonders and not for pragmatic purposes (Giedion 1970, 33). In the raising of the city of Chicago, technology returned to its original purpose. It staged the wonder of a 19th century metropolis leaving the surface of the Earth.

*Fig. 6.* The collage emphasises the slowness of the raising process and its vastness by the repetition of a single element placed in various positions and gradually rising.

Pullman's method was a magic done in an engineer's way. The city travelled up to 14 feet above the ground. Hotels were being raised with customers not noticing anything except the entrance stairs getting steeper. Entire blocks of buildings were being raised all together without a single crack in a wall. Giedion says that Pullman's "invention was luxury in travel. This was his domain" (1948, 453), while referring to Pullman's sleeping cars which he developed later in his career using the money made by raising Chicago. However, we can relate Giedion's words to Pullman's raising technique if we look at the jackscrews as the vehicle and Chicago as the traveller. Chicago was thus making a short extra-terrestrial journey from the swamp to its new location floating in the air. Speaking about extra-terrestrial travels may seem a bit exaggerated; however, with the technological progress of the 19$^{th}$ century and the fascination with technology, society was prone to believing that technology had no limits. Various hoaxes about extra-terrestrial travels or life discovered on other planets were being spread and believed by society. Some of them, such as the one written by Edgar Allan Poe, were created as a work of fiction but received as fact. The stories were spreading too fast to stay under control. The hoaxes illustrate the extent to which 19th century society believed space travel to be possible with the era's level of technology. It was a time when flourishing science-fiction literature was providing the public with incredible narratives based on real or predicted advances in knowledge and technology. The enthusiasm for such literature was mirroring the technological optimism of the period. In such a context, and also taking into consideration the mindset of the frightened Chicagoans, speaking about finding refuge in technological advances in order to extract their city from the Earth may not have seemed an exaggeration.

# THE NEW ENVIRONMENT

If we want to speak about escaping the Earth, we have to discuss questions concerning the layer of dust used to fill the space between the Earth and the raised city. The dust could be seen as a connection between the two but it could equally be a decisive split of the two. As already mentioned, Chesbrough's proposal was informed by efforts to prevent any contact of the raised city with its newly built underground and with the Earth itself. There was a great level of independence between what was below and underneath the new ground. The new topography itself was an artificial surface based on calculations. These calculations were aimed at creating a functioning topographical model distinct from the natural ground. The relative height differences between the original and the raised city varied from 4 to 14 feet.[3] A novel topography was being imposed, following criteria established by Chesbrough. In the hope of saving its population, the city opted for its ultimate alienation from its environment. Chicago's newly claimed territory was not on the surface of the Earth anymore. The city created an artificial alternative to the Earth and relocated onto it. Starting anew, the city needed to define its own functioning fitting its specific requirements. It was necessary to create a controlled aerial space fostering human life and excluding any traces of miasmatic emanations. In the context of the miasmatic theory and the related imaginary we can speak of terraforming, of total design. The 19th century society saw that through their activity they can transform, create, and control environments. They started doing so in a controlled manner following specific goals defined in advance. Efforts to create spaces with controlled olfactory landscapes were common in the 19th century. Given the vital importance of miasmas, the mid-19th century architecture emphasised smells. Greenhouses or winter gardens attached directly to residential buildings were a booming phenomenon. Architects were not only conceiving the spatial organisation of the structures. They were equally selecting plants growing in them with the aim of designing the odours of the spaces. The criteria informing the

19th century greenhouses were aiming at shunning the deadly stench (Corbin 1986, 70). A major illustration of such efforts is Joseph Paxton's proposal of the unrealized project entitled *The Great Victorian Way*. The glazed tunnel encompassing all the districts of central London was designed to offer a safe environment for Londoners. It was meant to provide the population with a full-featured alternative to the polluted environment. The polluted air was sealed behind *The Great Victorian Way's* glass limits. Paxton was particularly interested in the air, its circulation, temperature, and safety. He designed special ventilation systems controlling a large variety of the air's parameters. The autonomous system sealed outside of its framework all the miasmatic emanations coming from industry, the polluted river or human and animal waste. It was a secluded world that included shops, dining facilities and all amenities necessary for a comfortable life. Its inhabitants could live their lives without ever having to venture out of the safety provided by *The Great Victorian Way*. Processes similar to those supposed to take place in *The Great Victorian Way* – seclusion of a portion of air from the polluted environment and controlling it – could be observed in Chicago. In keeping their city safe from the Earth, Chicagoans were putting ultimate hope in the layer of dust filling the gap between the raised city and the Earth. The fetid Earth was sealed under several metres of soil and the new aerial space above the new ground was carefully controlled. In the optics of 19th century science, deodorization meant disinfection (Corbin 1986, 90). That was one of the effects of the layer of dust. It isolated the swamp with its stench using several metres of "dust." In the context of death fogs, sealing the Earth below the city meant stripping it of its powers; stripping death of its powers. In the raised Chicago, an urge to keep the Earth out of the city was palpable. After and already during the raising, the police were in charge of public cleanliness (Bonner 1991, 177), it wasn't doctors establishing hygienic standards anymore. It became a matter of public security. Under the threat of a five-dollar fine, every man in Chicago aged 21–60 had a legal duty to devote three days a year to public service in maintenance of public spaces (Bonner 1991, 176). The unpaved city of Chicago was getting paved (Mayer and Wade 1969, 96). The city commissioned regular services for cleaning public spaces. The raising of Chicago was not only a pragmatic effort to escape the omnipresence of death, it was an effort to create a city where its power was weakened. It was a step towards the otherworldly. The efforts to expel death make the raising of Chicago an almost metaphysical transformation alienating the city from the Earth, its original territory with a given natural life cycle dependent on environmental factors. The words of Rem Koolhaas describing New York could equally apply to Chicago after it had been raised: "the entire city became a factory of man-made experience, where the real and the natural ceased to exist" (Koolhaas 1994, 10). Being a Chicagoan meant "to live in a world totally fabricated by man, i.e. to live in a fantasy" (Koolhaas 1994, 10).

## LINKS TO THE EARTHLY

The original city and the raised one, although overlapping if observed from above, were two distinct places. The new city was being taken meticulously care of, while the old one was abandoned to its fetid processes. The new Chicago was carefully protected from the old one. Just as the Earth itself, the earthly city was perceived as a threat to the raised one. Any marks of the old Chicago coming back were monitored and suppressed. As already mentioned, the raising of private buildings had to be financed by their owners. However, not every house-owner could afford to do so. Not lifting one's dwelling to the new grade meant losing their place in the city. The earthly city was defunct, the actual Chicago was the raised one. The non-raised houses found themselves in the so-called *holes* disrupting the surface of the new ground. The *holes* were reaching all the way to the earthly city. Living in a *hole* was excluding people from society. They were becoming *the others*. People living in the *holes* were seen as a sort of phantoms of the defunct city, as mementos of the city's inglorious swampy past. The alienation between those who had raised their houses and those who did not was growing. The latter were alien even in comparison to foreign visitors in Chicago. The inhabitants of the holes were under constant suspicion. Tourists were warned against them in the guides of the period:

> *[James Stirling:] "When you walk along even the principal streets, you pass perhaps a block of fine stone-built stores, with splendid plate-glass windows (finer than any in New York), with good granite pavement in front: a few steps on you descend by three or four steps into the old level of the street, and find a wooden pavement in front of low, shabby-looking wooden houses." This caused some unexpected embarrassment to women tourists, who were warned in popular guidebook,* Tricks and Traps of Chicago, *to be on the watch for "side oglers" who loitered under steep stairs to catch glimpses of ladies' legs. (Miller 1996, 125)*

The description going from "fine" and "splendid" to "old," "low" and "shabby" illustrates the two poles represented by the two realms. The underground was inhabited by a community excluded from the raised city. The newly built ground was fostering hidden activity almost as much as the original one. Its inhabitants presented a persistent link to the Earth. Chicagoans' imaginary, fueled with fear, was associating them with filth, danger, poverty, and crime. "Side oglers", as they were called, were by far not the only example of the hidden world represented by the underground. Among other phenomena fostered by the spaces under sidewalks, we could find prostitution or illicit distilleries (Dedmon 1953, 13). The new underground of Chicago was, as Emmett Dedmon says "chiefly noted as the abode of gargantuan rats" (1953, 13). Once again the danger was coming from the ground. Chicagoans were fighting over the control of the new ground. The Earth was seemingly always finding new ways to reach the city and cause harm to its inhabitants. This time, fear transformed those who could not afford leaving the swampy ground into potential threats.

Given the obvious links between the hole-dwellers and the Earth, it was not difficult for Chicagoans to detect the alleged fallacy of the Earth. The constant surveillance of the raised city would reveal any attempt by the Earth to access Chicago. Preventive measures were being taken to exclude any further dangers. Therefore, the Earth could not reach it without a great dose of sophistication:

> *One newspaper ran a story claiming that the water system had turned Chicagoans into unknowing cannibals who were eating their ancestors. The city cemetery on the lakeshore just north of the pumping works flooded over during storms, and small fish, it was rumoured, fed on the dead and were drawn into the water pipes and fed to the living. "Of course this was nonsense," wrote Kirkland, "but it was the kind of nonsense, that fastened public attention and made easy the next step in our civil life, the tunneling of the lake and bringing the water from the pure depths of two miles from shore". (Miller 1996, 127)*

Chicagoans' anxiety concerning the Earth reached its culmination point. In the minds of the Earth-conscious population of the city, illusory threats were being developed into real dangers. Accustomed to the Earth striking with an ever growing dose of ingenuity, Chicagoans were expecting an ultimate backlash to their city leaving the Earth and sealing it deep below. Already during the epidemics, Chicagoans had been afraid to touch the dead bodies fearing the "demon" (Miller 1996, 123) would enter them. In the story spread by the newspapers, it seems as if the Earth had found a sophisticated way to make it happen, to reclaim its power over the departed city. It used the system designed by Chesbrough with the intention of protecting the city, in order to threaten its inhabitants. The Earth practically delivered the danger into individual households. Everyone was at risk. The "demon" they feared so much in the worst times was now present in every house and entering their bodies. It was done without Chicagoans noticing anything.

*Fig. 7.* The collage references a sort of Exodus of Chicagoans from the Earthly city to the raised one in search of a better life.

*Fig. 8.* The image raises questions on the built environment and its territory through displacement of a building through its displacement from its conventional location. By a vertical displacement it alludes to the 19th century enthusiasm for space travel and thus places the reflection in the context of technological optimism.

*Fig. 9.* The fragmentation of the city through the raising, the repetitiveness of the process and the loss of clear level reference in Chicago's urban landscape are emphasised within the collage.

Fear of the Earth caused them to believe the story. Threats, potential or actual, were being interpreted as new malicious actions of the Earth. The Earth they had polluted by the industry, the Earth they had empowered to attack them, as they believed, was getting out of control. Although the industry was the main culprit, Chicagoans could only reach out to technology to fight the Earth. They were stuck in a vicious circle where paranoia was constantly growing.

## CLOSING REMARKS

Our imaginaries and built environment are constantly informing each other. Through our built environment we inscribe our imaginaries into reality. In response, the newly adjusted reality modifies our imaginaries. It is an endless chain of reactions. The more we transform our lived reality, the more intricate and the more real our imaginaries grow. The way we design our environments, thus, seems to be deeply interconnected with the imaginaries shaping our beliefs and the concepts shaping our mental worlds. They seem to escape the logic of pre-existing environments and impose their own functioning. The Raising of Chicago was neither the beginning nor the end of imaginaries transforming the environment. The relations between mankind and the Earth remained of interest and are of growing relevance in the field of architecture and design. Theoreticians such as Beatriz Colomina and Mark Wigley evoke the issues: "they [humans] now encircle the planet with layer upon layer of technocultural nets, posing an ever-greater threat to their own survival" (Colomina and Wigley 2016, 12). They point to the persisting relevance of the questions raised by the raising of the city of Chicago. Extensive debates on the environmental measures taken by designers and architects are a part of the reflection. At the same time, we observe political, scientific, philosophical, and other types of narratives further reshaping our physical surroundings.

## ENDNOTES

1. The title was given to the city by the English visitor James Stirling in 1856.
2. 14 feet is equivalent to approximately 4.2 metres.
3. approx. 1.2–4.2 metres

## REFERENCES

Beecher, H. (1862). *Eyes and Ears*. Boston: Ticknor and Fields.

Bonner, T. (1991). *Medicine in Chicago, 1850 – 1950: a Chapter in the Social and Scientific Development of a City*. Urbana, Chicago: University of Illinois Press.

Carr, J. (2019). *Make Me a City*. London: Scribe.

Chesbrough, E. S (1855). *Plan of Sewerage for the city of Chicago, Illinois, Adopted by the Sewerage Commissioners*. Chicago: Office of Charles Scott.

Chesbrough, E. S (1858). *Chicago Sewerage, Report of Results of the Examination Made in Relation to Sewerage in Several European Cities in the Winter 1856-7*. Chicago: The Board of Sewerage Commissioners.

Cleaver, C. (1892). *History of Chicago from 1833 to 1892*. Chicago: Office of Charles Scott.

Colomina, Beatriz and Mark Wigley (2016). *Are We Human?* Zürich: Lars Müller Publishers.

Corbin, A. (1986). *The Foul and the Fragrant*. Leamington Spa: Berg Publishers.

Dedmon, E. (1953). *Fabulous Chicago: a Great City's History and People*. New York: Random House Inc.

Giedion, S. (1970). *Mechanization Takes Command: A Contribution to Anonymous History*. New York: Oxford University Press.

Koolhaas, R. (1994). *Delirious New York*. New York: The Monacelli Press.

Masarik, J. E. (2020). *"Earth( e)scape."* MA thesis, HEAD – Geneva.

Mayer, H. and R. Wade (1969). *Chicago: Growth of a Metropolis*. Chicago and London: The University of Chicago Press.

Miller, D. (1996). *City of the Century: The Epic of Chicago and the Making of America*. New York: Simon & Schuster.

Platt, H. (2005). *Shock Cities: The Environmental Transformation and Reform of Manchester and Chicago*. Chicago and London: University of Chicago Press.

Spinney, R. (2000). *City of Big Shoulders: A History of Chicago*. DeKalb: Northern Illinois University Press.

Väliaho, P. (2010). *Mapping the Moving Image: Gesture, Thought and Cinema Circa 1900*. Amsterdam: Amsterdam University Press.

# Incomprehensibility:

Torben Körschkes

## World-Chaos and Chaos-World

*The aesthetics of the universe assumed preestablished norms; the aesthetics of chaos-monde is the impassioned illustration and refutation of these (Glissant 1997).*

## Weather Prediction

The physicist, mathematician, and meteorologist Lewis Fry Richardson supported the French army in the fight against the Germans in 1916 as a medic of the *Section Sanitaire Anglaise*. It was during this time that he began his first attempts to calculate a weather forecast for which he had previously carried out theoretical research. Meteorologist Peter Lynch summarises Richardson's method as follows: "Richardson devised a method of solving the mathematical equations that describe atmospheric flow by dividing the globe into cells and specifying the dynamical variables at the centre of each cell" (Lynch 2015). In 1922, Richardson published his findings in the book *Weather Prediction by Numerical Process*. On one of the first pages, the division into cells described by Lynch – "dividing the globe into cells" – a rasterisation, is shown diagrammatically:

Richardson lays a grid over the landscape and attempts to counter the complexity of meteorological changes through this division, thus making them predictable or foreseeable; an attempt to make the incomprehensible world comprehensible. The grid can be described as a means of approaching the incomprehensibility of the world, or one could say the chaos, as framed by an article on the website of the German Weather Service entitled *Richardson sorgte für etwas Ordnung im Chaos* (*Richardson Brought Some Order Into Chaos*) (Bonewitz 2020). Journalist and mathematician Christian Endt describes how Richardson also used an approximation on a temporal level: "Instead of infinitely short periods of time, [Richardson] looks at intervals of a few hours. As if you were watching a sequence of individual photos instead of a video film. The greater the time interval between the snapshots, the fewer images need to be analysed – but the more information is lost" (Endt 2016). Because

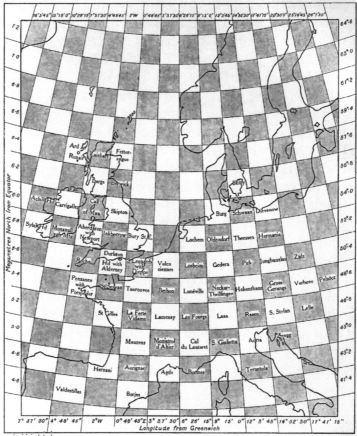

*Fig. 1.* Richardson, Lewis Fry (1922). *Weather Prediction by Numerical Process.* Cambridge University Press.

a video film *is* a series of individual images, this comparison does not quite work. Nevertheless, it illustrates very well that the multidimensionality of the world cannot be grasped in its totality and that one way of dealing with it is to coarsen the grain; be it a landscape that becomes squares or the reduction of the continuous progression of time to hourly units. In other words: an *abstraction* of reality.

Richardson's object of investigation was the weather. To this day, the weather is an example of a chaotic process and stands here as an introduction to the *incomprehensible* – based on the Latin verb *prehendere*: to grasp something – complexity of the world. His method of dividing an indefinite (atmospheric) landscape into calculable squares is *one* example of an attempt to approach the complexity of the world. Space is graphically subdivided into rectangles, arranged in a grid, and viewed in single images. Richardson's method is one of the first steps towards *computation* – a mathematical abstraction of processes which I will come back to later. Additionally, both Richardson's work and the weather itself demonstrate the realness of that complexity; that the world is chaotic in the sense that its complexity exceeds the capacity of human *comprehension* – or better: *prehensility* –, that the world's processes and possibilities are infinite and remain unpredictable.

# SPACE-IMAGE

In June 2023, French president Emmanuel Macron condemned the protesters following the death of seventeen-year-old Nahel Merzouk at the hands of a police officer in Nanterre. Macron claimed that the protesters were exploiting Merzouk's death to "cause chaos and attack our institutions" (de Bourbon-Parme 2023). He sees chaos as a threat to "our institutions", or a hegemonic order, and furthermore suggests the idea of an *Other* which is equated with chaos and thus the threat to this order. The demonstrators are delegitimised through this exclusion from the order; therefore linking the threat of chaos and Other to the desire for stability, a desire to hold on to an existing order that should be frozen if possible. In other words: there is an image of how something is or should be and this image must not be shaken; this image must be defended.[1] This example demonstrates the unification of ideas of community and territory in what I call a *space-image*. Space here includes the dimension of the social.

In the following, I will try to conceptualise this space-image and present two directions from which it may be threatened. I will summarise these two threats under the term *world-chaos*. On the one hand, there is the diversification of the world; on the other, the dissolution of the concrete in a total abstraction. Both can be described as chaos in the sense that they both represent complexes that are no longer tangible for humans in terms of comprehension and predictability. The term world-chaos is also in opposition to writer and philosopher Édouard Glissant's concept of the *chaos-world*. As I will try to show, the term chaos is used *productively* by Glissant, and from this *productive* use approaches and challenges can also be formulated for the field of design that lead neither back to the idea of a space-image nor to the attempt to overcome life in abstraction.

First, then, an attempt to conceptualise the notion of a space-image. I define space-image as the formulation of a spatial constellation as a unified image that needs to then be defended against "strangers" – as indicated in Macron's quote.

*Fig. 2.* "Steh fest mein Haus, im Weltgebraus" (Translates to something like: *Stand firm, my house, in the world's turmoil.*) Image © Torben Körschkes.

Furthermore, I understand a spatial constellation in general as consisting of people, materials, and stories. Because this type of constellation is condensed into one image, I do not simply speak of image, but of space-image. Space is a central element in these considerations, as it "is the dimension that presents us with the existence of the other [...]. And it presents us with the most fundamental of political questions which is how are we going to live together?" (Social Science Bites 2013), as geographer Doreen Massey states. The space-image is the product of an idea of community, nation or culture that defines itself "through the idea of rootedness, a connection to a single line of ancestry, a single place of origin" (Chamoiseau and Morgan 2008, 445). This idea of a community, nation, or culture can be described as a spatial constellation consisting of *one* territory, *one* history, *one* language, *one* lineage. The spatial concept of the space-image is monolithic. The "multiplicity of trajectories" (Massey 2000, 225), which according to Massey form space, are reduced to this *one* history. Behind the concept of space-image thus lies a certain *idea* of or a certain *image* of a spatial constellation, under which, among other things, imagined community and territory are united. For Plato, the *idea* is the *immutable archetype* (maybe one could say *preimage* or *protoimage*) of things[2], and it is precisely this idea of immutability and an archetype that is contained in the *image-making* of a spatial constellation; among other things "legitimised" by a founding myth that creates this archetype, through which reality is made the result of an idea.

The landscape as a uniform image ignores what historian, journalist and poet André Corboz worked out in 1983: "The territory is not *given*, but the result of different *processes*" (Corboz 2001/1983, 147). Corboz describes the territory with the metaphor of the palimpsest referring to the many layers of its eternal transformation, each of which continues to have an effect (or shine through). The space-image, on the other hand, fixes *one* idea of the territory and strips the palimpsest of its layers. The space-image goes beyond the reduction of a simple map, as *image* here "signifies not only visual representation, but also cognitive, linguistic, aural, or bodily forms of representation"

(Smirnov 2019, 1). But the map can be a physical manifestation of a space-image. In both cases, they lack "what characterises the territory above all: its extent, its thickness, and the fact that it is constantly changing" (Corboz 2001/1983, 155). Corboz writes further: "Modern states could not be satisfied with the fact that the territory was, so to speak, mobile. It was therefore necessary to represent it completely, precisely, and uniformly at the same time" (ibid. 154).

Following on from this, the space-image is a form of spatial imagination. It is a form of order defined by a group and regulates who belongs and who does not belong within that certain space; who is depicted in a certain space-image and who is not. A historical example is the philhellenism (friendship with Greece) of the late 18th and early 19th centuries, when the major European powers, especially Germany, rebuilt Athens in the style of antiquity and declared Greece to be the cradle of European culture. Central to the development of philhellenism was archaeologist and librarian Johann Joachim Winckelmann, who is regarded as one of the founding figures of classicism. Winckelmann recognised "aesthetic ideals and ethical norms" (Konstantinou 2012) in ancient Greek art. Philosopher Friedrich von Schlegel speaks of an "archetype of perfected humanity" that Winckelmann saw in ancient Greece (ibid). However, the recognition of the achievements of Greek antiquity also had a political background. Byzantinist Evangelos Chrysos defined philhellenism as a "political movement for the liberation of Greece from Ottoman rule" (Chrysos 2014). An opposition to the Ottoman Empire led some Germans to discover the "foundations of their Western culture" (Konstantinou 2012) in ancient Greece and begin transferring these (already idealised) ideas of ancient Greece to early 19th century Greece. A direct connection between the "Greeks" of antiquity and the "Greeks" of the 19th century is proclaimed; based on a common geographical location, which is denied any historical development, any influence, any change: an absolutely static conception of space. Classicism in general and the history of German philhellenism in particular show the emergence of a space-image in which a

*Fig. 3.* Leo von Klenze implemented a Christian prayer in the foreground of this idealised view of Athens. Image: Leo von Klenze (1846). *Ideale Ansicht der Akropolis und des Areopag in Athen.* Bayerische Staatsgemäldesammlungen – Neue Pinakothek München. Creative Commons.

2000-year history – lying somewhere between antiquity and the 19th century – is reduced, abstracted, and idealised: the layers are removed from the palimpsest. Just as Richardson looks at a few individual photos "instead of a video film" when calculating the weather in Endt's description, all "recordings" between antiquity and the 19th century are deleted – albeit under different premises and with a different agenda than in Richardson's work.

This space-image was then materially realised in Athens in the imagined style of antiquity under the first king of the Greek state founded in 1830 – the son of the Bavarian King Ludwig I, Otto von Wittelsbach. The space-image was literally built in stone. The construction of Athens was led by German architects, such as Leo von Klenze, who also modelled his building Valhalla in Germany after the Parthenon. The construction of Athens gave this *idea of Greece* a material reality. The space-image established in this way then had to be defended and served to legitimise the struggle against the Ottoman Empire; positioning Greece as a "Christian nation" "waging a legitimate struggle for liberation" (Konstantinou 2012).

The extent to which the establishment of a space-image *from the outside* – as in the case of philhellenism – differs from the establishment of a space-image *from the inside* – that is, from the communities themselves occupying a landscape – could be differentiated and analysed in more detail elsewhere. First of all, the term seems to me to be suitable for making monolithic and nationalistic ideas of culture and community tangible, regardless of the distinction between *from the outside* or *from the inside*. In addition, the concept of the space-image can also be used to explain the current overload and insecurity that is proclaimed so often and seems to be a central characteristic of our time as seen in various podcasts, talk shows, interviews, and publications[3] – as if we are experiencing an "orientation emergency" (Negt 2023, 10). The above quote from Macron reveals that the space-image behind Macron's "our" is perceived as being under threat. And the central and disastrous point is that every space-image *will always be perceived as threatened* because it does not exist beyond the image. Maintaining space and community as a singular and static image requires a constant defence of this image. The order established by a space-image is therefore an *always threatened* order. This means that the space-images in the world are always disturbed.

## WORLD-CHAOS

The term world-chaos refers to a subjective and collective overload that arises from the apparent impossibility of dealing with the complexity of the 21st century. This complexity confronts the space-image from at least two directions: On the one hand, the space-images are disturbed by an order that exceeds and transcends the small-scale orders of the space-images – that is the universal order of abstract mathematics (Chapter 3.1); and on the other hand, the space-images are disturbed by the complexity that must underlie a plural understanding of the world as well as post-national identities. Writer Patrick Chamoiseau describes this second threat as the "chaos of diversity" (Chamoiseau and Morgan 2008, 447) which corresponds to an understanding of culture and identity that is no longer formed through linear lines of descent, a singular history, a territory, and a singular language (Chapter 3.2).

### Abstraction

Writer and activist Franco "Bifo" Berardi argues that, behind the current overload (or the wobbling of space-images), there is a fear of extinction that any change would bring with it and is thus intrinsic to the idea of chaos. In his text *Game Over*, Berardi describes how humankind, starting from Zeus – who chained up his father Kronos ("the king of gods in the age of Chaos", Berardi 2019, 1) in order to create order (cosmos) – finds an infinity detached from matter in mathematical abstraction. Immortal order. In his derivation, Berardi considers time and structure as mutually exclusive. Structures are "immutable and eternal" while time decomposes all structures and is an "agent of the extinction of all things" (ibid, 2).

What Berardi (poetically) describes here can be further developed with the spatial-theoretical considerations of Massey, who assumes that space was long formulated as a static dimension (see e.g. one of her main works *for space* from 2005). With Berardi one could say: as a structure, as an entity independent of time; and with the spatial sociologist Martina Löw one could further specify that space was only formulated as a structure, but not the act of structuring; in other words that only the arrangement, but not the act of arranging (Löw 2019/2001, 166) was formulated and thus the spatial was robbed of its dimension of action. While time progresses, unfolds, and stands for change, space was conceived as a static and flat surface on which we move thus making it possible for a specific identity to be inscribed into a landscape; as for example in the case of a community inscribing its founding myth linearly into a landscape and presenting this *spatial identity* or *landscape identity* as unchangeable and consequently defend it against others; as for example imagining the locality of Greek antiquity to be identical to that of the 19th century. "In the structural universe, temporality does not exist [...]", writes Berardi. This therefore means that there is no decay, not even the decay of nations and identities. Accepting a temporality, on the other hand, also means accepting decay, dissolution, or movement, the possibility of life in general: "In the living universe of temporality, Structures are continuously dissolved [...]" (Berardi 2019, 2).

Berardi argues that the modern mathematisation of the world, to which Richardson also contributed with his weather calculations, leads to the possibility of immortality: an abstraction of the world that detaches itself from matter. The guiding principle of the school of Pythagoras in the 6th century before our era was: Everything is number. Mathematics detaches itself from the concrete world and abstracts it into numbers (see Palzer 2023). This progressive mathematisation affects all areas of life:

> *Mathematization is not only a methodology for the theoretical formalization of natural phenomena. It is also a process of technical determination; the digitalization of linguistic and physical processes, in the late modern age, has proceeded to insert mathematical functions into the living body of language and social exchange (Berardi 2019, 3).*

But if life is connected to transience, then incorporating mathematisation and abstraction into social relationships means the erasure of the concrete, or "of life itself" (Ibid, 3). Writer Thomas Palzer formulates it similarly in an essay for the radio station Deutschlandfunk, in which he points out that numbers are not always the appropriate means of adequately depicting reality. As abstractions, they cut something off – based on the Latin meaning *ab-stractum* – and "take things away from things – things that can ideally be considered superfluous". However, reality is concrete and real phenomena have nothing superfluous that can be taken away from them. The moment something is taken away from them, the moment they are abstracted, they are no longer "concrete and real" (see Palzer 2023). This also raises the question of who declares what to be superfluous and why.

Why this digression? In a later text, Berardi describes the current world situation as an interplay between chaos and automaton (the completion of mathematisation leads to a global network of AI, capable of self-directed decisions that Berardi calls a "global cognitive automaton", Berardi 2023, 4). The human being stands in between and is exposed to this "coexistence of incompatible realities" (Ibid, 1). Both worlds, that of chaos and that of immortal abstract order (in particular: all processes related to AI, the automation of the world of work and finance, machine learning, etc.), are basically incomprehensible: humans are overloaded, what Berardi calls "psychotic collapse" (Ibid, 5) because they are no longer able to interpret the world. They try to cling to the "old" order – which in Macron's case is perhaps hidden in his short remark on "our institutions" (as quoted above) – and want to make the world tangible through the idea of space-images. But this "old" order merges into a more consistent order, because it is liberated from mortal humanity and therefore more permanent. Paradoxically, an order emerges that goes beyond the structure humans can grasp: "The realisation of Reason results in geopolitical, environmental, and psychological chaos, as we are experiencing in the current decade" (Ibid). I do not think that Berardi means it exactly like this, but I would formulate it as follows: an order is building up that seems chaotic to the human mind, in the sense that in its total abstraction it is as indecipherable as any chaos can be.

## Chaos Of Diversity

The space-image feels threatened from a second direction, which Chamoiseau would describe as a "chaos of diversity", where one is not defined by a "traditional" (imagined?) community and its values, but finds oneself in a multiplicity of possibilities, categories, and possible identities. According to Chamoiseau, this is based on a transformation driven by Western modernity, which led to the collapse of "traditional" ideas of community through the idea of individualisation. The contemporary fear stems from the fact that individualisation means we can no longer fall back on a value system established by the traditional community. Everyone has to work out their own values and identities (Chamoiseau and Morgan 2008, 446). The easy way out is a fall back on space-image-promises made by populists worldwide. On the other hand, the difficult task is to find imaginaries that make unity possible without uniformity, community without nationalism, identity without identitarianism. Chamoiseau formulates this task as follows:

> *The strategies we use in our writing are ones to understand how we can exist in this relational scale of the Tout-Monde [Whole World] – along with the idea that we are each more and more alone, unbound by the traditional heritage of the old communities. And the linguistic issues I explore, for example, are no longer the ones of national languages confronting each other (i.e. Creole versus French), but of*

*multiple languages co-existing within the same culture – the whole chaos of linguistic complexity we are entering.*
(Chamoiseau and Morgan 2008, 448)

If the idea of the space-image must be overcome for a plural and open world, because the order of the automaton represents an order without social relationships, then it is necessary to dare to approach the chaos of diversity, that is, to think of communities and identities that are not monolithic but complex. Furthermore it is then necessary to conceptualise space not as a static surface, but as a "product of interrelations" and a "sphere of the possibility of the existence of [...] contemporaneous plurality" (Massey 2005, 9). Consequently, the task for an experimental and speculative design practice – insofar as it strives for a plural and heterogeneous world – is to create new imaginaries, to make the chaos of diversity approachable, to find ways to represent this kind of world imaginary without reducing it; without making it, once again, monolithic. Chamoiseau's quote can be reformulated for spatial practices as follows:

*The strategies we use in our spatial practice are ones to understand how we can exist in this relational scale of the Tout-Monde [Whole World] – along with the idea that we are each more and more alone, unbound by the traditional heritage of the old communities. The spatial issues I explore are no longer the ones of closed territories confronting each other (i.e. Germany versus France), but of multiple places co-existing within the same culture – the whole chaos of spatial complexity we are entering.*

Or, as a question and task for design: How to design with and for a chaos of diversity? And what spatial imaginations emerge from such an understanding of identity?

## Chaos-World

On the one hand we witness a *destructive* use of the term chaos that is framed as a threat to the current hegemonic order, as seen in recent political debates and conceptualized by the examples given – here summarized under the term world-chaos. Édouard Glissant, on the other hand, endeavours to use the term chaos in a *productive* way.

In the 1980s and 90s, Glissant developed the concept of the *chaos-world* to describe the incomprehensibility of the world. For Glissant, the chaos-world is to be understood as a *productive narrative* – that is, as a starting point for the emergence of relations and not of overload and oppression; as a metaphor for a (utopian) post-colonial coexistence that has overcome the strictness and one-dimensionality of nation-state thinking and results from the unpredictable coming together of differences; in Massey's words: *throwntogetherness*.

Influenced by the discoveries of chaos research, but also by the emergence and reflection of Creole, Glissant describes the world as a chaos-world: "I call chaos-world the shock, the intertwining, the repulsions, attractions, complicities, oppositions and conflicts between the cultures of peoples in the contemporary world-totality" (Glissant 2020, 54). For Glissant, creolisation refers to the creole languages, which he describes as a "composite language, emerging from contact between entirely heterogeneous linguistic elements" (Ibid, 9). In this respect, they already differ from monolithic conceptions of language. It is important that Glissant understands the process of creolisation as a process of two or more heterogeneous elements (for example languages) coming into contact with each other and that the result of this contact is not predictable, meaning that it is not determined by one of the two (or more) elements. Based on his reflection on Creole languages, Glissant develops the idea of the chaos-world by scaling Creole:

> *[...] I believe that the term creolization applies to the world today, that is, the situation in which a "totality earth",*

> *finally realized, means that within this totality (where there is no longer any "organic" authority and everything is an archipelago), the most distant and most heterogeneous elements possible can be put into relation with each other. This produces unforeseeable results. (Glissant 2020, 10).*

Glissant's chaos-world or *world-totality*, as it is called in many texts in contrast to the phrase "totality earth" just quoted, attempts to enable a global way of thinking that resists a capitalist and colonial logic of taking and exploiting. The chaos-world is to be distinguished from world-chaos: the latter can be described as an overload in dealing with the incomprehensible and assumes that a particular space-image is disturbed. World-chaos can only exist in a world imaginary that is based on norms, standards, and predefined processes. The chaos of the chaos-world, on the other hand, is not "chaotic" (Glissant 2010/1990, 94). In the quote preceding this essay, Glissant explains: "The aesthetics of the universe assumed preestablished norms; the aesthetics of *chaos-monde* is the impassioned illustration and refutation of these". And he continues: "Chaos is not devoid of norms, but these neither constitute a goal nor govern a method there" (Ibid, 94). It is an aesthetics that "senses, assumes, opens, gathers, scatters, continues, and transforms [...]" (Ibid).

In her foreword to an interview with Patrick Chamoiseau, interviewer Janice Morgan formulates the questions underlying these considerations as follows – they could hardly be more contemporary:

> *[E]ven as global cultures seem to be merging more closely together, we see ethnic/racial/linguistic conflicts erupting on nearly every continent. With the old identity structures breaking down and amid ardent appeals to maintain the boundaries by returning to religious and cultural fundamentalisms, what progressive alternatives do we have? How do we, both individually and collectively, re-conceive our identities and our places in the world? (Chamoiseau/Morgan 2008, 444).*

The chaos-world is Glissant's approach to re-conceive our identities and our places in the world. What are the (spatial) requirements for this?

## Contact Zone

To go into this, let us first assume the contrary; the prevention of a heterogeneous encounter with an unpredictable outcome and the manifestation of a space-image: In his text *Die amerikanische Landesvermessung oder die Verleugnung der Eigenschaften von Grund und Boden* (something like: *The American Land Survey or the Denial of the Properties of Land*), André Corboz describes the rasterisation of North America, starting in 1784 from the first settlements on the east coast westwards. The entire land mass was to be divided into 6 × 6 mile squares, so-called *townships*, which would "serve as a supporting scheme for the colonisation of the continent" (Corboz 1997, 41). As in philhellenism, which resulted in the material realisation of an *idea* or *image* of Greece, here too reality becomes the result of an "ideal" – the grid can be traced back to utopian novels of the early 18th century, in which "the population is simply distributed on a 'chessboard' according to statistical criteria" (Ibid, 46). The strict grid established a connection between landscapes that were neither known nor owned by the American government (Ibid, 41). This literally violent establishment of connection – if the indigenous population which the white settlers gradually encountered resisted, they were displaced by force – sees surprises, deviations and unpredictability as problems that must be ignored or minimised. The division principle of the townships "had to be simple and rational" (Ibid) in order for it to be feasible on such a large scale and, in this basic assumption alone, collides with the characteristics of every landscape – and culture – that has emerged and continues to emerge from infinitely complex processes.

But how can we create coherence and preserve difference at the same time? How can we think and design spaces that open up possibilities and at the same time are open to being transformed by these possibilities? Spaces that are wobbly or restless; spaces of searching? Spaces that emphasise the complexity of the world and do not reduce it?

Glissant describes the United States of America as a multi-ethnic coexistence in which cultures do not mix (Glissant and Obrist 2021, 34). He sees the reason for this in the US cities, which are planned – as already laid out in the township grid – and have not grown organically from the confluence of the surrounding rural landscapes and villages. But in the intermingling, which Glissant calls creolisation, lies for him the possibility of the co-existence of difference and interdependence without mutual oppression. According to Glissant, the possibility of creolisation – that is, once again, "the encounters, the conflicts, the harmony, the symbiosis, the love, the hate of cultures in the world – when they produce something new" (Ibid, 30) – requires a *contact zone* that does not exist in planned cities (Glissant and Obrist 2021, 39). The concept of the contact zone was coined by literature professor Mary Louise Pratt to describe the clash of different conflicting parties, especially in spaces where the power imbalances between the different parties are particularly large:

> *I use this term [contact zone] to refer to social spaces where cultures meet, clash, and grapple with each other, often in contexts of highly asymmetrical relations of power, such as colonialism, slavery, or their aftermaths as they are lived out in many parts of the world today. (Pratt 1991, 34).*

Through the contact zone Pratt conceptualises the spatial conditions under which a re-conceiving of our identities and our places in the world is possible. The contact zone is precisely the opposite of the segregated city; a *place*[4] inhabited by diversities (Chamoiseau and Morgan 2008, 449). In her text *Belonging to the Contact Zone*, curator and art mediator Nora Sternfeld formulates a decisive difference to the formation of identity through, for example, closed territorial concepts. Identity only arises in the Contact Zone in the encounter with the Other – that Macron sees as a threat. In other words, if I assume that I *can only* become myself through contact with an Other, then I cannot marginalise this Other. Consequently, if we continue to become with each other, there is *never* a static image. Sternfeld writes:

> *In these divided/shared spaces, actors interact with one another under different conditions. What is productive about the concept [of the contact zone] is that the formation of the subject is not presumed to substantially precede the contact, but instead first emerges through joint agency and negotiation: it is based neither on the western humanist idea of seemingly universal equally acting people, nor on the culturalist notions of a predetermination due to origin. In the theory of the contact zone, subjects and actors are therefore not constructed essentially – in keeping with an interaction of a preceding culture or social position – but rather in process and in relation to one another (Sternfeld 2022).*

The contact zone describes a certain way *in which* a spatial constellation is created; in other words *how* stories, people, and materials come together. Or, more precisely: how predetermined and predictable are the results, how structured is the encounter, how isolated are the actors? Furthermore, Pratt's article *Arts of the Contact Zone* rethinks these questions by investigating the types of practices that such a zone of encounter requires or enables. Glissant describes the coming together in the contact zone as follows:

> *A sort of daily vibration that makes it so that the languages that crop up, the Creoles that crop up, are very strong Creoles, but also very unpredictable, changing rapidly, like patois (Glissant and Obrist 2021, 39).*

The term *patois* probably comes from the Old French "patoier", which means "to act clumsily" or "to wave one's hands around" and thus also has a strong reference to action, to practice.[5] Clumsy action and waving one's hands around are practices that cannot be repeated. They express the attempt to overcome a gap or a distance without having a suitable means. They involve giving up what has been learnt and turning towards the other. If you wave your hands around to make something understandable to the other person, you leave your own language and enter unknown territory. In the impossibility of mastering clumsy action or waving one's hands around, a common space is created between the people meeting – the contact zone, from which the potentially unpredictable emerges. Today, the term patois stands for a dialect that differs from the standard or literary dialect. Patois are languages that grow out of a specific locality. These new languages emerge from unique encounters or constellations of people and things; new knowledges derive from these constellations which are situated, relational. They deviate from the norm, also because they do not manifest themselves – Glissant writes: "crop up"; patois are in the making, continuously emerging and shifting forms of knowing. Moreover, patois cannot be grasped algorithmically – they drive the automaton crazy. They emerge in an instant and from the confluence of unfathomable stories that branch out. They are chaotic because they are not predictable or comprehensible. They undermine – again and again, with every generation, and above all with every encounter – established grammars.

In contrast, the rasterisation of North America was planned and then implemented without regard for the actual local conditions: In this case, the map "precedes the terrain", as Corboz writes (Corboz 1997, 42). A certain idea of order and unity is claimed and enforced. Basically, this is a common procedure in architecture and urban planning. However, the rasterisation of North America stands out; not only because the square grid of the townships in its broken-down geometry represents a special case of subdivision, but also because the project in its gigantic scale can be representative of the legitimation of colonial oppression in the name of universality and rationality, and thus the legitimation of direct intervention in systems without knowing them. The (architectural) historians Anooradha Iyer Siddiqi and Vazira Fazila-Yacoobali Zamindar reflect on this phenomenon

*Fig. 4.* fem_arc (2021). Spatial transcription of conversations during the research project *Making Futures*. Original pages in colour, published by Spector Books.

using the example of the English lawyer Cyril Radcliffe, who divided up the region of South Asia around 1947 without ever having seen it. They write:

> *"Partition" is a concept that declares the historic plurality of lived worlds untenable, and sets about transforming differences into incommensurability (Siddiqi and Zamindar 2022).*

This type of spatial production is diametrically opposed to the idea of a contact zone. The rasterisation of North America was based on the idea that utopia precedes reality and prepares it – the production of a space-image! Glissant, on the other hand, argues in favour of a concept of utopia that will never be realised. He deprives his idea of utopia of the possibility of serving as a plan, as a map that precedes the terrain. To think space as contact zone,

> *we must exclude from our thinking any idea of a norm, of a system, or of excellence. Because when we define a norm in utopia, we banish to hell anything that deviates from that norm, anything that does not fall within the rule of that utopia.*

And Glissant continues as if he were referring directly to the enforcement of townships in the 18th century:

> *The utopia of the great Western authors implied the search for a norm that is necessarily a norm that excludes, that rejects (Glissant and Obrist 2021, 64).*

## Spatial Representations

This raises the following question for design: How can we depict the contact zone without breaking it down again? Why? Because our thinking is characterised by representations; because in the vast majority of cases we only come into contact with a representation, that is, a mediation of reality through media. In other words, a large part of the world is conveyed through representations and these representations shape us. We look at a text or a landscape on the basis of these representations. Consequently, these representations also determine whether a landscape appears one-dimensional and static to us, whether it overwhelms us and we feel threatened, or whether we can deal with its complexity. Berardi refers to anthropologist Ernesto De Martino, who "defines the expression 'end of the world' as the inability to interpret the signs that surround us. When societies are no longer able to interpret the world they are experiencing, we can speak of the end of the(ir) world" (Berardi 2023, 4). The world-chaos is this experience of an end of the world in which neither the signs of the automaton nor those of the chaos of diversity can be interpreted. In the logic of the automaton, the human world ends because life cannot be abstracted. The chaos of diversity, on the other hand, only appears uninterpretable if one starts from the space-image. World-chaos is to be understood as a *perspective* of space-image thinking. Pratt describes this perspective(s) using the example of a text by Guaman Poma from the year 1613. To go into this in detail would go beyond the scope of this essay. In order to understand the quote, it is particularly important that Poma's text and the heterogeneous logic in which it was written was only understood in the 1970s and that Pratt introduces it as an example of a literate art of the contact zone:

> *If one thinks of cultures, or literatures, as discrete, coherently structured, monolingual edifices"* – *interestingly she again uses a spatial methaphor here* – *"Guaman Poma's text, and indeed any autoethnographic work appears anomalous or chaotic [...]. If one does not think of cultures this way, then Guaman Poma's text is simply heterogeneous, as the Andean region was itself and remains today. (Pratt 1991, 36).*

Chaos is described here as a subjective perception which results from a specific logic. If we think of cultures and landscapes in terms of a space-image, a world outside the space-image and "chaotic identities" (Chamoiseau and Morgan 2008, 447) appear uninterpretable, and therefore threatening. We experience the chaos-world as world-chaos *if* we cannot interpret it. The spatial language of the chaos-world is conceptualised through the Contact Zone. One could say that the aim is to make the practice of waving one's hands around comprehensible-incomprehensible as a cultural *world practice*; to understand it not as the end of the(ir) world, but the beginning of a world. It remains a question and a task of design to make the contact zone tangible in a way that can be interpreted without breaking it down.

One attempt in this direction is a work by the fem_arc collective. In their contribution for the publication *Making Futures* entitled *We understand listening as a Critical Practice* (fem_arc 2021, 110-121), they show a "spatial transcription" of conversations held in Berlin's Haus der Statistik (a nucleus of the urban political struggle in Berlin). It is an attempt to make physical meetings in their fleetingness and informality comprehensible in print, without renouncing the spatial qualities of the actual meeting or, more precisely, finding a translation for them. At the top of the page there is a small caption indicating the direction from which the sound is coming. Sounds are printed in italics, spoken words in Roman/Upright and in a gradation from light to bold, depending on how loud the voice is or was perceived by the person who made the recording. Fragments of conversation and hints of noise follow one another, the parts printed in bold jump out at the reader, while the shallow parts blur into background. Reading the words "rock music", one imagines that music coming from a back corner; reading the snippet "fear the future?", one imagines it to be spoken by someone at the next table. The recording leaves it open which rock music is playing here, so that the translation is not a final fixation but a poetic nudge that simultaneously conveys a sense of what has happened. It is a possible response to the reproduction of not only a dinner, an intimate discussion, an informal exchange – a spatial arrangement –, but also a passing on of the vibration that Glissant speaks about, and the grappling that Pratt attributes to the Contact Zone. This becomes particularly noticeable when fem_arc's transcript is read aloud in a group, as I tried to do with students in the seminar *Spekulatives Schreiben*[6]. In this reading aloud, the past meeting became comprehensible as a specific meeting on the one hand, and *at the same time* remained incomprehensible or incomplete, becoming a new constellation.

Special thanks to Alexander Cromer and Ina Römling for suggestions and critical feedback.
Unless otherwise indicated, all translations from German by the author.

## ENDNOTES

1. It is also conceivable that by referring to "our institutions", Macron is referring to the idea of democracy and sees democracy as being threatened by the demonstrators. This would require a more precise analysis of whether these specific protests have attempted to overthrow democracy or not. Either way, Macron's statement puts the protesters on the outside – the institutions are not the institutions of the protesters.
2. https://www.dwds.de/wb/Idee (11.01.2024)
3. There are many examples to show that our present, at least in the German media, is characterised by overload and uncertainty: German Vice-Chancellor Robert Habeck speaks of a "polycrisis"; the last episode of the talk show Anne Will is entitled *Die Welt in Unordnung – Ist Deutschland den Herausforderungen gewachsen?* (03.12.23); a three-part series on chaos and order appears on the podcast *Essay und Diskurs* of German radio channel Deutschlandfunk (12.23); political scientist Frank Decker says on Deutschlandfunk that uncertainty must be brought back under control in order to combat right-wing populism (27.11.23); the Spiegel bestseller list includes titles such as Herfried Münkler's *Welt in Aufruhr. Die Ordnung der Mächte im 21. Jahrhundert.* (Rowohlt 2023).
4. The distinction between *place* and *space* is discussed in many different ways. I here start with space as a rather theoretical and abstract dimension and place as a concrete locality – a neighborhood, a kitchen, perhaps a city. Doreen Massey tries to detach both space in general and the concrete locality from a static understanding – the city of Hamburg then no longer has a fixed and unchanging identity. And I think this is exactly what Chamoiseau means with his concept of place: on the one hand, he understands place as a concrete location, but on the other hand, the identity of this place is in motion and changing with everything/everyone that arrives and/or leaves.
5. see Harper, Douglas. "Etymology of patois." Online Etymology Dictionary, https://www.etymonline.com/word/patois (20.01.2024) and "Patois." Merriam-Webster.com Dictionary, Merriam-Webster, https://www.merriam-webster.com/dictionary/patois (20.01.2024)
6. Spekulatives Schreiben (Speculative Writing). Seminar led by Torben Körschkes. HAW Hamburg, 2023–2024.

## REFERENCES

Berardi, F. (2023). "Unheimlich: The Spiral of Chaos and the Cognitive Automaton." *e-flux Notes*. Accessed January 22, 2024. https://www.e-flux.com/notes/526496/unheimlich-the-spiral-of-chaos-and-the-cognitive-automaton

Berardi, F. (2019). "Game Over." *e-flux Journal* Issue #100. Accessed January 22, 2024. https://www.e-flux.com/journal/100/268601/game-over/

Bonewitz, J. 2020. Richardson sorgte für etwas Ordnung im Chaos. Deutscher Wetterdienst. Vorhersage- und Beratungszentrale. https://www.dwd.de/DE/wetter/thema_des_tages/2020/11/21.html (12.12.2023)

Corboz, A. (2001/1983). "Das Territorium als Palimpsest." In Corboz, André. *Die Kunst, Stadt und Land zum Sprechen zu bringen*. Basel: Birkäuser.

Corboz, A. (1997). "Die amerikanische Landesvermessung oder die Verleugnung der Eigenschaften von Grund und Boden." Translated by Christa Zeller. *Werk, Bauen + Wohnen* Band 84: 41–46.

Chamoiseau, P., and Morgan, J. (2008). "Re-Imagining Diversity and Connection in the Chaos-World: An Interview with Patrick Chamoiseau." *Callaloo* Vol. 31. No. 2: 443–453.

Chrysos, E. (2014). *Die Entstehung des griechischen Staates und der Geist des Philhellenismus*. bpb.de. Accessed January 12, 2024. https://www.bpb.de/themen/europaeische-geschichte/griechenland/176411/die-entstehung-des-griechischen-staates-und-der-geist-des-philhellenismus/

de Bourbon-Parme, Tristan: Von Tottenham bis Nanterre, Le Monde Diplomatique, August 2023

Endt, C. (2016). *Heiter bis tödlich*. Süddeutsche Zeitung. Accessed December 12, 2023. https://www.sueddeutsche.de/wissen/meteorologie-heiter-bis-toedlich-1.3186253

fem_arc (2021). "We understand listening as a Critical Practice. A spatial transcription." In: Bader, M., Kafka, G., Schneider, T., Talevi. R. (Eds.) (2022). *Making Futures*. Spector Books. Pp. 110–121.

Glissant, É. (1997/1990). Poetics of Relation. Ann Arbour: The University of Michigan Press.

Glissant, É. and Obrist, U. H. (2021). *Archipelago*. isolarii 6. Common Era Inc.

Glissant, É. (2020). *Introduction to a Poetics of Diversity*. Translated by Celia Britton. Liverpool: Liverpool University Press.

Glissant, É. (2013/1996). *Kultur und Identität. Ansätze zu einer Poetik der Vielheit*. Translated by Beate Thill. Heidelberg: Wunderhorn.

Konstantinou, E. (2012). "Griechenlandbegeisterung und Philhellenismus". In *Europäische Geschichte Online (EGO)*, edited by Leibniz-Institut für Europäische Geschichte. Accessed January 12, 2024. http://www.ieg-ego.eu/konstantinoue-2012-de

Löw, M. (2019/2001). *Raumsoziologie*. Frankfurt am Main: Suhrkamp.

Lynch, P. (2015). *Richardson's Fantastic Forecast Factory*. Accessed December 12, 2024. https://www.emetsoc.org/resources/rff/

Massey, D. (2005). *for space*. California: SAGE Publication.

Massey, D. (2000). „Travelling Thoughts". In *Without Guarantees: In Honour of Stuart Hall*, edited by Paul Gilroy, and Lawrence Grossberg, and Angela McRobbie, 225–232. London: Verso.

Negt, O. (2023). Überlebensglück. Eine autobiografische Spurensuche. Göttingen: Steidl Pocket.

Palzer, Thomas (2023). „Das Chaos bändigen. Das Gespenst der Ordnung." In: *Essay und Diskurs*. Deutschlandfunk. Accessed January 29, 2024. https://www.deutschlandfunk.de/das-gespenst-der-ordnung-100.html

Pratt, L. M. (1991). "Arts of the Contact Zone." In *Profession*, 33–40. Accsessed January 19, 2024. http://www.jstor.org/stable/25595469

Siddiqi, I. A. and Zamindar, J. F.V. (2022). *Partitions: Architectures of Statelessness*. Accessed January 20, 2024. https://www.e-flux.com/architecture/positions/454156/partitions-architectures-of-statelessness/

Smirnov, N. (2019). "Meta-geography and the Navigation of Space." *e-flux Journal* Issue #101. Accessed January 29, 2024. https://www.e-flux.com/journal/101/271896/meta-geography-and-the-navigation-of-space/

Sternfeld, N. (2022). "Belonging to the Contact Zone." *Para-Educational Papers #09*. Accessed January 20, 2024. https://art-education.hfbk.net/de/writings/belonging-to-the-contact-zone#fnref-8

Social Science Bites (2013). *Doreen Massey on Space*. Podcast interview by David Edmonds and Nigel Warburton. California: SAGE. Accessed January 12, 2024. https://www.socialsciencespace.com/2013/02/podcastdoreen-massey-on-space/

# AUTHORS

**Tom Bieling** is Professor of Design Theory at the University of Art and Design HfG Offenbach. He is editor of the DESIGNABILITIES Design Research Journal and co-editor of the book series BIRD (Birkhäuser) of the Board of International Research in Design, and Design Meanings (Mimesis). He was Vertretungsprofessor of design theory and research at HAW Hamburg, Visiting Professor at the University of Trento and the German University in Cairo, and had other teaching assignments such as Designwissenschaft (Design Studies) at HAWK Hildesheim. He is co-founder of the Design Research Network and the Initiative Design promoviert, and co-host of the NERD conference series. His award-winning works are exhibited worldwide. He completed his doctorate at Berlin University of the Arts (UdK), and is the author and (co-) editor of numerous publications, including Design (&) Activism (2019), Inklusion als Entwurf (Inclusion as Design, 2019), Gender (&) Design (2020), Specology – zu einer ästhetischen Forschung (on aesthetic research, 2023). tombieling.com

**Michelle Christensen** is a sociologist and designer, exploring the spaces in between these realms. Her research, teaching and experimental design practice, carried out in collaboration with Florian Conradi, focuses on queer/feminist, decolonial and postanthropocentric approaches to design. She wrote her Ph.D. in the field of Design Research at the Berlin University of the Arts, prior to which she studied political sociology, conflict studies, gender studies and integrated design. She has worked at the Crisis Department of Amnesty International, was a Humanity in Action Fellow, and a Congressional Fellow in the United States Congress in Washington DC. Currently, she co-heads the research group *Design, Diversity and New Commons* at the UdK Berlin in the framework of the Weizenbaum Institute, as well as teaching as a visiting professor for *Open Science / Critical Culture* at the Technische Universität Berlin and the Einstein Center Digital Future. From 2014–2024 she was a board member of the German Society for Design Theory and Research (DGTF); since 2015 she has been a member of the Board of International Research in Design (BIRD), and in 2023 she joined the board of directors of the Einstein Center Digital Future.

**Florian Conradi** is a designer and researcher combining critical theory and design as an approach to design research. He studied art and design in Amsterdam, Jerusalem and Cologne, and wrote his Ph.D. in the field of Design Research at the Berlin University of the Arts. He has taught critical approaches to design at, amongst other places, the UdK Berlin, the Köln International School of Design, as a visiting professor at the international Master's programme in *Integrated Design* at the Anhalt University of Applied Sciences in Dessau, and as a visiting professor for *Open Science/Critical Design* at the Institute of History and Philosophy of Science, Technology and Literature at the Technische Universität Berlin. He has initiated sociopolitical design projects with institutions in the field of critical media and artistic research in Europe, the Middle East and West Africa. He is an associated researcher at the Einstein Center Digital Future in Berlin and currently a Principal Investigator in the *Object Space Agency* group of the Cluster of Excellence *Matters of Activity. Image Space Material* (Humboldt-Universität of Berlin). Currently he co-heads the research group *Design, Diversity and New Commons* at the Berlin University of the Arts in the framework of the Weizenbaum Institute. Since 2007, he collaborates with Michelle Christensen on research and teaching endeavours (www.conradichristensen.eu).

**Delia Dumitrescu** is professor of textile design at the Swedish School of Textiles, University of Borås. She is head of the Smart Textiles Design Lab, part of the Science Park Borås and the University of Borås. Central to Delia's research is the topic of material and textile design, focusing on the development of new materials that expand from smart and computational textiles to biodesign and biofabrication. Through the notion of textile design thinking, her research expands the textile methodology; it includes systematic research work with colour, materials, textures, structures, patterns, and function to explore and propose new design futures for sustainable living from material to body to spatial design.

**Athena Grandis** is a designer and researcher with an MA in Design & Computation, a transdisciplinary study program between the Berlin University of the Arts and the Technical University of Berlin. She holds a BA in Visual Communication from the Berlin University of the Arts and the Bezalel Academy of Arts and Design in Jerusalem. Her interests include feminist perspectives on digitalization, queering technology and human-machine interaction. Her practical work moves between media such as installation, print, wearables, illustration and prototyping. She is currently working as a research assistant at the TU Berlin in the Department of Communication Systems in the project "Reallabor Wald". The project aims to bring transdisciplinary and experimental learning platforms into the education of electro-engineering and computer science. Between 2020–2024 she worked at the Weizenbaum Institute in the research group "Design Diversity & New Commons". As a graphic designer, she collaborates with public and cultural institutions, including the Sportmuseum Berlin. In this role, she develops publications and exhibitions focused on the intersection of sports, gender, and politics.

**David Green** is a Design Researcher with a background in participatory documentary making, digital arts, and experience-centred design who worked on the Design Research Works project for around 3 years where his core role was to produce a series of documentary films about the world of Design Research. He has a history of participatory, co-creative, ethnographic and design-led approaches, is an expert in interactive non-fiction, and recently has promoted polyphony and polyvocality. Currently, David is a senior Design Researcher working for the Centre of Excellence in Environmental Data Science.

**Wolfgang Jonas** holds a PhD in Naval Architecture and the lecture qualification (Habilitation) for Design Theory. He was professor of Process Design in Halle, for Design Theory in Bremen, for System Design in Kassel and, until his retirement in 2019, for Designwissenschaft at Braunschweig University of Art, where he was head of the Institute for Design Research and initiated the MA in Transformation Design. His working areas are systems thinking and methodology, futures studies and scenario approaches, and the development of the concept Research through Design.

**Svenja Keune** investigates the potential of textiles as mediators for human-nature relationships. During her PhD, within the MSCA ArcInTexETN, she turned towards seeds as a dynamic material for textile design. As part of her postdoctoral projects that are funded by the Swedish Research Council and Formas, her work is grounded in auto-ethnography to engage and co-create design events that emerge from textile-based artefacts and the local ecosystems' interactions with them. With human and more-than-human co-creation at the centre, she co-founded the I.N.S.E.C.T. Community, a research network that deepens and advances multispecies perspectives in design.

**Torben Körschkes** is an artist and experimental spatial designer. In essays, montages, installations, and fictions, he seeks to challenge the relationship between concepts of space, community, and complexity. He is part of the design and research collective HEFT, which deals with questions of socio-political spaces, as well as studio lose, a collaborative design studio with Ina Römling and Frieder Bohaumilitzky. He studied design at Folkwang University of the Arts in Essen and HFBK Hamburg, where he completed his MFA on contemporary salons in 2018. Recent activities include: lecturing at HAW Hamburg (2023–24), a residency at INSTITUTO (Porto) funded by the European Union, the Goethe Institut and the City of Hamburg (2023), Hamburger Zukunftsstipendium (2021), Elbkulturfonds (2020), and a residency at Bibliothek Andreas Züst (2019). He is a co-editor of the publication *Specology – Zu einer ästhetischen Forschung* (adocs, 2023) and PhDArts candidate at Leiden University Academy of Creative and Performing Arts and Royal Academy of Art The Hague. torbenkoerschkes.de

**Ariel Cheng Sin Lim** is an architect and researcher with a BSc in Architecture and Sustainable Design from the Singapore University of Technology and Design and an MA in Computation in Architecture from the Royal Danish Academy. Working with digital modelling and fabrication, she creates new forms and expressions that integrate or are inspired by nature. Her current specialisation is in 3D printing, having worked with a variety of materials including mycelium, cellulose, and clay.

**Joseph Lindley** is a Senior Research Fellow at Lancaster University's School of Design, where he leads Design Research Works, a project that seeks to capture and communicate the value of design-led approaches to making sense of the world. He is a generalist who has had careers as an IT professional, a musician, artist, manager in healthcare, and most recently as a researcher. His PhD helped to establish Design Fiction as a research method and most of his research involves producing knowledge at the intersection of society and technology. He's passionate about the strength of design as a research endeavour, the value of practice, and the importance of acknowledging diverse approaches to knowledge production and knowing.

**Franka López Barbera** is an Argentinian design researcher. Her work critically addresses the power dynamics that configure and are configured by design, particularly at the intersection of nature, coloniality, gender, and ethics. She is a doctoral candidate at the Institute of History and Theory of Architecture at the University of Braunschweig, Germany, where she explores the introduction of more-than-human consent in design-nature relations against extractive regimes. Franca is a trained Industrial Designer and has experience in several forms of design, working with design practices, art studios, non-profit organisations, and academic institutions. In 2021, she curated the Argentinian pavilion for the London Design Biennale and is a contributing editor at *Bikini Books*, an independent publisher for material cultures, design, and politics.

**Jozef Eduard Masarik** is an artist and researcher focusing on the issues concerning identity, technology, knowledge production and design. He graduated in Space and Communication from HEAD – Genève, Switzerland. He is an assistant professor at the Academy of Fine Arts and Design in Bratislava, Slovakia. His artistic practice marked by research could be defined as a spatial practice using video or other technological imagery and performance. He is equally active as a theatre scenographer and dramaturge.

**Axel Meunier** is a research designer at médialab, Sciences Po, Paris, and a PhD candidate in design at Goldsmiths College under the supervision of Alex Wilkie, Michael Guggenheim and Tommaso Venturini. His research practice proposes participatory design (PD) as a method of inquiry in the social sciences and experiments with the participation of publics as co-investigators. At the intersection of design and Science and Technology Studies, his PhD focuses on the interplay between PD and the design of Artificial Intelligence systems, and puts participation to the test of situational aspects of calculation. It is based on a series of projects with other research institutions, educational institutions, associations, cultural spaces etc. in which participatory workshops are experimented with as algorithmic situations, where troubles and frictions are elicited to make sense of the instability of algorithmic things during use. Axel Meunier studied at the Ecole des Hautes Etudes en Sciences Sociales and at Sciences Po's Experimentation Program in Art and Politics. He has worked at CNRS and for companies, public institutions and in art contexts. At the médialab he has been involved in and published about controversy mapping, dataspriting, research-led teaching and inventive methods. He also teaches at Centrale Paris, an engineering school.

**Dulmini Perera** is a lecturer and researcher at Bauhaus University Weimar. She is interested in histories, theories, and methods that emerge from design's encounters with disciplines that engage with complex living systems (particularly cybernetics, systems sciences, and process philosophies) and how these encounters can help develop a reflexive research and practice framework that promotes designerly ways of engaging systemic complexity. She is the recipient of the Heinz von Foerster Award 2021. Her most recent work on the ecological crisis, double bind and possibilities of design action is supported by the DFG (German Research Foundation) grant number 508363000 and the AHRC (United Kingdom).

**Barbara Pollini** is a sustainable design and material specialist and Assistant Professor in Biodesign Integration at Aalto University. She has a Master's in Ecodesign and Eco-innovation and a Master's degree in Computational Design. Since 2012 she has been a lecturer at Naba Design University in Milan, teaching sustainable design and materials, DIY-Materials, Biodesign and Design Fiction for sustainable futures. In 2023 she completed a PhD in Design at Politecnico di Milano with a research on Biodesign titled Healing Materialities from a Biodesign Perspective, Framing Designed Materials and Artefacts for the Sustainability Transition. This research intersects Biodesign, Material Design and Design for Sustainability to frame Biodesign's potential for an ecological turn. The research also analyses the nascent professional figure of the biodesigner thanks to some intense research-through-design phase, where she developed various biodesign research projects in collaboration with Italian and foreign life sciences experts and scientific laboratories. From September 2024, she is Assistant Professor in Biodesign Integration at Aalto University. Her main research interest is in Biodesign, especially in material scenarios based on regenerative processes, including living and life-enabling materials.

**Florian Porada** is an antidisciplinary technologist and researcher working with emerging technology. Interested in all sorts of digital and analogue tech including the ripples it is causing, his practice anchors in the relationship between people, society and the technologies that surface alongside. By leveraging code and prototyping techniques, he is creating tangible artefacts. He holds an M.A. in Design & Computation from the Berlin University of the Arts and the Technical University Berlin, and a B.A. in Media Informatics from the HdM Stuttgart and HvA Amsterdam. Formerly, Florian worked as a Creative Developer at moovel lab, a design and research lab focusing on speculative prototypes and future scenarios around urban mobility. As a founding member of New Objectives, a hybrid studio for regenerative AI-Strategies, he is using his research-based approach to generate a positive impact with and through AI-enhanced processes. Currently based in Berlin, Florian balances his time between research projects, commercial work and escaping the city in analog and digital ways.

**Mette Ramsgaard Thomsen** examines the intersections between architecture and new computational design processes. During the last fifteen years her focus has been on the profound changes that digital technologies instigate in the way architecture is thought, designed and built. Recent work examines new design principles for biodesign and questions how processes of renewable, regenerative, and restorative logics of resource thinking can lead to new sustainable design practice.

**Julia Ziener's** passion lies in exploring the diverse facets of materiality. As a designer and material researcher, she investigates the vital properties of materials and their entanglement with other entities. She studied Integrated Design at Anhalt University of Applied Sciences in Dessau and the Hong Kong Polytechnic University. With her background in product design, she combines design principles and technology with new perspectives on materiality, often breaking traditional boundaries. She adopts a transdisciplinary approach at the intersection of art, design, and science. In 2023, she completed her Master's degree in Design & Computation at the Berlin University of the Arts and the Technische Universität Berlin. One focus of her research is the combination of sustainable materials with digital fabrication, integrating the material as an active agent. Engaging with questions of material phenomena is as significant to her as their mediation, such as exhibiting her research at the Ars Electronica festival in Linz. With this approach, she seeks to find practical applications for philosophical concepts of new ontological perspectives on material.

# IMPRINT

Editors:
Tom Bieling
Michelle Christensen
Florian Conradi

Acquisitions Editor:
David Marold

Project management:
Regina Herr

Layout, cover design and typesetting:
Floyd E. Schulze

Paper: 100 g/m² Fly 05
Printing: Beltz Grafische Betriebe GmbH, Bad Langensalza
Image Editing: Repromayer GmbH, Reutlingen

This publication was supported by the Technische Universität Berlin (Einstein Center Digital Future) and the Offenbach University of Art and Design.

Library of Congress Control Number:
2018954261

Bibliographic information published by the German National Library
The German National Library lists this publication in the Deutsche Nationalbibliografie; detailed bibliographic data are available on the Internet at http://dnb.dnb.de.

This work is subject to copyright. All rights are reserved, whether the whole or part of the material is concerned, specifically the rights of translation, reprinting, re-use of illustrations, recitation, broadcasting, reproduction on microfilms or in other ways, and storage in databases. For any kind of use, permission of the copyright owner must be obtained.

ISBN 978-3-0356-2880-7
e-ISBN (PDF) 978-3-0356-2881-4

© 2025 Birkhäuser Verlag GmbH, Basel
Im Westfeld 8, 4055 Basel, Switzerland
Part of Walter de Gruyter GmbH, Berlin/Boston

Questions about General Product Safety Regulation
productsafety@degruyterbrill.com

www.birkhauser.com